About Island Press

Island Press is the only nonprofit organization in the United States whose principal purpose is the publication of books on environmental issues and natural resource management. We provide solutions-oriented information to professionals, public officials, business and community leaders, and concerned citizens who are shaping responses to environmental problems.

In 2001, Island Press celebrates its seventeenth anniversary as the leading provider of timely and practical books that take a multidisciplinary approach to critical environmental concerns. Our growing list of titles reflects our commitment to bringing the best of an expanding body of literature to the environmental community throughout North America and the world.

Support for Island Press is provided by The Bullitt Foundation, The Mary Flagler Cary Charitable Trust, The Nathan Cummings Foundation, Geraldine R. Dodge Foundation, Doris Duke Charitable Foundation, The Charles Engelhard Foundation, The Ford Foundation, The George Gund Foundation, The Vira I. Heinz Endowment, The William and Flora Hewlett Foundation, W. Alton Jones Foundation, The John D. and Catherine T. MacArthur Foundation, The Andrew W. Mellon Foundation, The Charles Stewart Mott Foundation, The Curtis and Edith Munson Foundation, National Fish and Wildlife Foundation, The New-Land Foundation, Oak Foundation, The Overbrook Foundation, The David and Lucile Packard Foundation, The Pew Charitable Trusts, Rockefeller Brothers Fund, The Winslow Foundation, and other generous donors.

Wildfire

A READER

Wildfire

A READER

edited by

ALIANOR TRUE

ISLAND PRESS

Washington • Covelo • London

Library of Congress Cataloging-in-Publication Data

Wildfire : a reader / edited by Alianor True.
   p. cm.
Includes bibliographical references (p.   ).
 ISBN 1-55963-906-7 (cloth : alk. paper) —
ISBN 1-55963-907-5 (pbk. : alk. paper)
 1. Fire ecology. I. True, Alianor.
 QH545.F5 W56 2001
 577.2—dc21

                                                                        2001001893

British Library Cataloguing in Publication Data available.

Printed on recycled, acid-free paper
Designed by Joyce C. Weston
Manufactured in the United States of America
2 4 6 8 9 7 5 3 1

For John

Contents

Contents

Part III. Fire as Foe, Fire as Friend

By forces seemingly antagonistic and destructive Nature accomplishes her beneficent designs—now a flood of fire, now a flood of ice, now a flood of water; and again in the fullness of time an outburst of organic life.

— John Muir, *Mt. Shasta*

Sometimes fire is totally devastating, but sometimes it is beneficial in cleaning out diseased trees, clearing out the forest floor, aiding bacteria in decomposition, providing light and space for new forest growth.

— Ann Zwinger, *Beyond the Aspen Grove*

The train went up on the track out of sight, around one of the hills of burnt timber… There was no town, nothing but the rails and the burned over country.

— Ernest Hemingway, *The Big Two Hearted River*

Introduction:
Fire from the Sky

The storm begins with a sharp crack in the sky, electrons streaming up from the earth and down from the volatile atmosphere, meeting in a jagged line. As lumber-sized splinters from a broken ponderosa pine lie scattered outward, the chemical reaction between air, wood, and heat causes licks of flame to flicker in the pine duff. Small wisps of smoke waft up through the dry air. Twigs and needles crackle in the dry heat. Quickly, the flames spread outward, pushed north and east by the coaxing breeze. Brown pine needles in tufts of three, pine cone shavings, fir and spruce needles, and decomposing litter in the soil feed the 4-inch flames, leaving a mosaic of black patches on the forest floor. The flames gain size and speed with the late morning breeze, climbing the lower pine trunks and consuming the twigs and branches piled beneath fallen trees. The smoke rises above the canopy, a whitish gray puff wavering with the wind. On the ground, the fire has taken hold in the parched sawdust of a decomposing log, gaining strength and energy for the run it will make in a few hours, when the humidity plummets and the winds pick up. It has a life of its own now, a breathing energy. A wildfire is born.

My colleague and I stand in ash-covered boots on the North Rim of the Grand Canyon, a two-by-four of fresh pine planted so deep in the soil beside us that the two of us cannot budge it. We can only flex and bend it, and watch the pale yellow trickle of sap ooze toward the ground. We are patrolling the Imperial fire, a 7-acre wildfire that began here, with this ponderosa and the heat from a bolt of lightning that crashed from a dark monsoon sky. The fire has been controlled; a line of dirt surrounds the patchy black forest floor, and no puffs of smoke rise from the piles of limbs or the layer of duff we march through. Yellow jackets buzz around us, flies land on our helmets. A young mule deer watches us watch her, not afraid, as she paws through the ash and scrapes her flanks on the blackened standing trunks. The burn has been without active flame for three days. I bend and pick up a ponderosa pinecone, and toss it back over my shoulder onto the ash-covered soil.

Fire has been an active element of this Arizona forest for thousands of years, just as wildfires have been an influential force of nature for hundreds of millions of years, since vegetation began taking root on young continents. Life on this planet, especially in the temperate regions of North America, has evolved under the continual presence of fire. As a selective force, it has altered and impressed itself upon nearly every plant community in every bioregion in America, from the cypress swamps of South Florida to the sagebrush plains of the Great Basin to the immense tallgrass prairies that once filled the Great Plains. These ecosystems evolved under the evolutionary pressure of fire, and thus require it to maintain their health, even in a modern era where wildfires are not always a welcome reminder of the natural world.

As long as people have been in North America, there has been a record of wildfire. Fire is an essential component of many Native American tales and origin myths, and an integral part of ceremonies and rituals. As a tool for manipulating the environment, fire was skillfully used by Native Americans for centuries in every region of America. European settlers moved across the country and brought with them written language. Tales of wildfire were told countless times and were eventually written in fictional and true-life descriptions of the interactions between people and nature. In the earliest accounts of the New World, one can find references to fire, especially "Indian burning." As explorers and settlers moved west, they chronicled both wild and ignited fires in journals of their expeditions. Early writers, with their European view of fire as a destructive force that should be eradicated from wild lands, rarely grasped that fire can have positive values as well.

The attitudes toward wildfire in American literature gradually changed with the advent and evolution of the conservation movement.

Fire from the Sky

So, too, did the practice and techniques of fighting wildfires in America's great public lands. As national parks and forests were set aside as treasures and stocks of natural resources, the spread of naturally ignited wildfire was halted. Human-ignited fires were suppressed with equal vigilance. The landscape was not without fire, as it likely never will be, but the motions of fire over the landscape were controlled as much as humans could possibly constrain a wild force.

As the growing American population spread across the country, knowledge of wildfire and its suppression expanded. American writers recorded how wildfires changed the land around them, and they documented the relationship between wildfire and firefighters. Attitudes changed as scientific knowledge about wildfire increased and as fire ecology developed as a field. American writers captured conflicting ideas in their works, noting the effects of a Smokey Bear suppression policy as well as the need to control wildfire near human populations. Describing the effects of wildfire on ecosystems became an important part of the literature surrounding wildfire. More recently, wildfires have been documented by those who know the flames and smoke best, America's wildland firefighters. Firefighters are uniquely positioned to portray their intimate knowledge of the environment and fire behavior against the adrenaline-charged backdrop of a wildland fire.

Understanding fire in America begins with an understanding of fire ecology and how fire has altered plant and wildlife communities in nearly every portion of the continent. Fire history is measured in millions, not thousands, of years. While combustion and fire have almost certainly been present on this planet since its inception, wildfire has been known to affect the environment for at least the past 350 million years. In fossil charcoal records, fire can be traced back through the millennia to Carboniferous times, where ash is found in what are now coal deposits. Given the historical significance of wildfire, understanding the role of fire in today's ecosystems requires a long-term perspective.

Distinct fire environments are composed of climatic characteristics, atmospheric conditions, fuels, and human cultural activities that may change through time and from region to region. In addition, a wildfire that lasts for only days or weeks can produce effects that endure for decades and longer. Fire is episodic by nature, appearing at irregular intervals that may be influenced by external factors, like accumulation of plant debris on the forest floor or the presence of drought conditions. For these reasons, placing a wildfire into an ecological worldview involves knowledge of how fire fits into this complex working environment.

Wildfire is a natural disturbance to the environment, similar in magnitude to hurricanes, tornadoes, floods, volcanic explosions, or insect invasions. Flames sweeping through a forest or prairie disturb the established community and create new open space for plant species to colonize. How much new space is created depends on the nature of the fire itself, and external conditions, such as drought, that may be conducive to the spread of fire. Once the community has been altered, new species may colonize and prosper where before they would have had to compete for resources with the dominant species. Fire may also allow fresh new growth of dominant species, their success ensured by the nutrient-rich ash and access to sunlight and other resources.

The lack of fire can also dramatically alter a community's structure. Some plant communities require fire and are adapted to resist fires, reseed quickly after fires, or both. These fire communities include the chaparral shrublands of California, grasslands, and some coniferous forests. Without fire, dominant species may be overtaken by opportunistic species that could not survive the heat of a wildfire. An example is the thickets of white fir that sprout up around ponderosa pine stands in the absence of periodic fire. Without fire, the structure of the forest can gradually shift from an open ponderosa stand to a thick stand of white fir. When a wildfire does sweep through, the firs provide ladder fuels from the ground to the branches of the ponderosas, allowing fire to damage the mature trees. Before the thick growth of white fir, fires would have burned through the surface litter, emitting enough heat to release nutrients in the soil and create open space for the growth of shade-intolerant ponderosas. These fires would not burn hot or high enough to cause lasting damage to the mature ponderosas.

Wildfires exist in nearly every North American ecosystem, from wetland swamps of the Southeast to palm oases of the Mojave Desert, and they affect vegetation distribution within each region. Vegetation distribution is the arrangement of different plants within an ecosystem. Many external factors can affect distribution, including water, sunlight, and proximity to other plant types. Fire is the one factor that can create new spaces for growth, influence soil fertility, and increase range and dominance of species. That fire affects change did not go unnoticed by our forebears. In fact, Native Americans and peoples worldwide used fire to influence plant communities that provided needed food or other resources. In the Pacific Northwest, the Salish tribes used fire to encourage growth of bracken, camas, and nettles for food and utilitarian purposes. Frequent fires eliminated competitive plants and provided nutrient-rich soil to foster new growth. By using fire to encourage growth of particular species, this Native American group altered the previous distribution of vegetation to their advantage.

Fire is a focused agent of natural selection, applying tremendous pressure on the evolution of plant species across the continent. It can be said that fire is the most influential force in determining the history of North American forests. For a plant to survive in a fire regime, it must be adapted to the regular passage of fire through the ecosystem. The unique adaptations are multifold, and include developing a thick bark, releasing seeds soon after a fire passes, and storing nutrients underground in roots and tubers, safe from the heat of a fire. High-temperature tolerance in vegetative buds and the ability to reproduce from underground structures, like quaking aspen trees, are characteristics of plants that are exposed to frequent fires. Seed dormancy and fire-stimulated germination are common in these plant groups, especially when germination and establishment are unlikely in the absence of fire. In the case of the giant sequoia trees of California, seeds are held tight inside closed cones for up to twenty years. The hot air from a fire dries the cones, and a few days afterward, the cones open and release tiny seeds upon soil burned clean of duff and litter. This fresh earth is crucial for the success of a sequoia, for in order for the seeds to prosper, they must fall onto bared mineral soil. Only cleared post-fire ground is free of the undergrowth that competes with a young sequoia for valuable resources, such as sunlight and water.

Natural burn intervals exist in every environment that sees fire on a regular basis. A burn interval is the period of time a naturally occurring fire would burn through an ecosystem, and can vary from region to region. In Florida's wetland environments, the sawgrass between cypress stands can be expected to burn every three to five years. In the lodgepole pine forests of Yellowstone, the burn interval is much longer, from 100 to 300 years. These intervals between fires allow ecosystems to adapt and recover.

Plant communities are not the only aspects of ecosystems that are affected by wildfire. The physical environment, including air, water, and soil quality, can be affected by the impacts of fire. Airborne smoke and ash can travel hundreds of miles, leaving a swath of gray skies and smoky air across states. Any late-summer visitor to northern Nevada may see smoke from fires that burn as far away as the rugged mountains of Northern California. Smoke from fires in northern Arizona has been seen as far away as Salt Lake City. And closer to a wildfire, residents and firefighters must regularly breathe air that falls far short of clean-air requirements. On a positive note, wildfire smoke can have a detrimental effect on the fungus that causes root rot in trees, an organism that affects the health of trees across the West. Ash can affect water chemistry, upsetting the delicate pH balance that so many organisms depend on. Soil, as the nutrient base for plants, depends on the recycling effect of fire to release nutrients; this tenet is the basis for slash-and-burn agriculture techniques used worldwide. However, water often carries away ash and nutrient-rich soil before vegetation can secure the topsoil, as in the Southwest, where monsoon rains are blamed for washing away inches of crucial topsoil before new growth can claim it. For a region hit particularly hard during a wildfire season, the effects of severe soil degradation, decreased water quality, and higher particulate matter in the local atmosphere can leave a lasting mark on the local environment.

Fire can influence wildlife communities as well. The endangered Kirtland's warbler, a tiny dark-gray and yellow bird, nests in thickets of young jack pine scattered across the Michigan upcountry. The few remaining stands of native jack pine require periodic fires to spur reproduction. The pinecones stay closed on the branches until heated, and when they open, the seeds drop onto fertile ash to germinate. Kirtland's warblers only nest and raise their young in pine stands that are eight to eighteen years old. They depend on fires to produce the conditions needed for the growth of new stands. Without wildfires consuming and renewing these jack pine forests, there is a continual loss of species habitat as well as the loss of a native plant community.

Suppressing fires, as has been the human tradition of the past century, often has unforeseen consequences in environments where fire plays a large role. In the absence of fire, flammable fuels accumulate and fuel structure changes. Fire severity increases as a result, often in a way that has detrimental effects on those species that evolved in the presence of less intense fire. As forests become denser with more growth, not all trees can gain adequate access to water or sunlight. As thick stands of stunted or dead standing trees remain, insects may move in, further weakening defenses against fire. When the forest ignites, especially under drought conditions, the effect is a catastrophic fire. It may be effective in clearing out the dead and downed forest litter and collected debris, but it is also of immense size and strength and virtually impossible to extinguish, even using all the tactics of modern firefighting. These fires are often quelled only by winter snows or rain, suppressed by the same entity that started them: Nature. In ecosystems where more frequent low-intensity fires are a natural part of the community, these high-intensity fires may have a longer lasting and unhealthy impact on the environment, decreasing soil fertility and drastically changing the composition of flora and fauna.

The high-intensity fires of recent years are not only the result of management practices in America's forests for the past century. Climate change and global warming can also impact the dynamics between wildfire and flammable forests. The twentieth century has seen worldwide temperatures rise more dramatically than in the past 1,500 years. As human activities increase levels of carbon dioxide and other greenhouse gases in the earth's atmosphere, gradual rises in temperature occur across all seven continents and oceans. According to climatologists, warmer temperatures worldwide lead to more frequent heat waves. As warmer temperatures increase evaporation, more common and severe droughts are likely. Regional droughts are always a factor in severe fire seasons, as the summer of 1998 proved in Florida. Dry conditions brought the worst fires in more than fifty years, burning over 500,000 acres of forest, more than 17 times the annual average. Global warming has also been linked to more intense and frequent El Niño events. The

Wildfire

1998 event was the strongest of the century, bringing severe drought to the eastern and southern United States. El Niño also brought enough precipitation to the West that plant growth, due to the moist conditions, drastically increased, and supplied even more fuel for the fires of the following summer.

With increasing residential zones near public lands, a century of fire suppression, and the added threat of climate change due to global warming, the wildfires of the future are a frightening prospect. The summer of 2000 saw the worst fires to sweep the West since 1910, when an unseasonably dry summer fueled torching fires across the Northwest, sparking the modern practice of fire suppression and instilling fear of wildfire in the American consciousness. Any force of nature that works outside of human control and with the ability to wreak so much change to the environment naturally imparts a sense of fear and mistrust. Such is the case with wildfire, a tricky element to restore in natural ecosystems without losing control and causing harm to people and property nearby.

In the case of wildfire in America, history can illuminate the future. Recent years have showcased the results of a century-old suppression policy, as well as the added complexity of human occupation near fire zones. Add weather cycles and the increased propensity for drought in the face of global warming, and the firestorms that occur once or twice a century could become as common as hurricanes battering the Caribbean every fall. This presents a modern predicament for America's land managers and the general public. Annual property damage from wildfires approaches billions of dollars, and every recent summer has seen injured and killed firefighters on the firelines throughout the country. Wildfire may be the most important environmental issue facing our country today, as homes continue to burn, and runaway fires make headlines from coast to coast.

Tracing the role of fire ecology and the history of wildfire inevitably leads us to Native American populations, who used fire in many ways to alter the landscape and maintain the natural place of fire in the environment. There is scant written evidence recorded by Native Americans about the uses and practices of fire, but their role in developing modern firefighting methods, especially prescribed burning, is not to be overlooked. Tribes across the country used fire for hunting, communication, and clearing excess plant growth. As more European settlers populated the country, especially the South, knowledge and experience with periodic "Indian burning" grew. The tradition developed over generations into seasonal burning by backcountry settlers, who realized the value of regular fire in rejuvenating grass, reducing insect populations, clearing underbrush, and attracting game. The practice of burning southern longleaf pine forests and pastures was passed down through generations and eventually came to be known as controlled burning. By the early twentieth century, the U.S. Forest Service began to take note. With the emergence of fire ecology as a scientific discipline in the 1960s and the gradual recognition of the rightful place of fire in the environment, what was once backwoods burning had developed into a working knowledge of prescribed fire. By the close of the century, prescribed burns had become an integral part of fire management in America's public lands.

Without the initial knowledge and experience that Native American tribes imparted to settlers, the modern practice of prescribed fire might have been longer in coming. When Europeans came to America, they brought with them an intense fear and mistrust of wildfire; they viewed it as a wholly destructive force. This feeling is often portrayed in records documenting early experiences with fire between settlers and explorers and Native Americans. Only through witnessing the beneficial uses of wildfire in ecosystems were the newcomers convinced of fire's ability to enhance and enrich the natural environment.

Thus no collection of works concerning wildland fire can be complete without the inclusion of Native American voices. Finding written record of fire history in that voice, however, is a daunting task. In my search to accurately represent the perceptions of wildland fire in America, remarkably little record emerged that was derived from the Native American community. This lack of written information is due to several factors. One, most Native American tribes recorded oral histories about wildfire. European settlers and explorers recorded the written history of precolonial-era fire practices and imparted their own bias against wildfire to their writings. In addition, it is possible that most Native Americans considered fire a useful, though unremarkable, tool and did not make a concerted effort to pass knowledge of history and practice down through generations. Settlers and their descendants, who viewed fire as a dangerous and destructive event, would have had reason to record and retell their memorable experience with fire. Finally, with the considerable loss of their land and destruction of their heritage, perhaps the Native American voice of fire history did not survive to the present day. What has survived are Native American voices from the early 1900s recounting the origin myths of fire in specific tribes, and a body of modern Native American poetry where fire is an integral element. The origin myths are included in this collection to represent the role Native Americans played in determining this country's fire history and to illustrate how important fire is to Native American cultures across the country.

This collection gathers together for the first time some of the finest stories and essays ever written about wildfire in America. Each selection examines in a different way the relationship between wildfires and the American landscape, both natural and cultural. From Lewis and Clark to Native American origin myths, to modern stories of firefighting, there are works that are historically, geographically, and culturally significant. Realizing how many of America's most beloved and recognized authors have written of wildfire represents just what a timely and important event it is in so many of our lives. From Henry David Thoreau to Mark Twain, and Norman Maclean to Edward Abbey, writers across the country have depicted and recorded wildfire with depth and clarity. An ecological perspective is well represented through the words of John Muir, Aldo Leopold, and John McPhee. Stephen Pyne, a noted fire historian, offers a historical perspective on the 1910 fires that set the stage for the modern firefighting movement. Other voices include Ed Engle, Louise Wagenknecht, and Gretchen Yost. These firefighters from the front lines give us exciting accounts from a first-person perspective and relive the personal encounter with a forest fire. Such a diverse assemblage of voices is long overdue in a country that has had such an intense and lasting relationship with wildfire.

What strikes me most about this literary collection is how much, as Americans, our relationship with and attitudes toward wildfire have changed over the past 200 years. This collection is organized around shifts in thinking about wildland fire. The earliest accounts in this book

Fire from the Sky

were written at a time of discovery and exploration. Meriwether Lewis captured the bestial quality of wildfire in his journals, and with the exception of John Muir, writers of the nineteenth century continued to record fire as a destructive event in their fiction and nature writing. Not until the 1920s did thinking begin to shift in terms of the possibly beneficial role of fire in natural ecosystems. Beginning with Aldo Leopold and others, the next 50 years were times of argument and trial, as traditional theories of fire suppression conflicted with newly emerging and contrary views. In the nature writing of the time, differing opinions are offered as to the value and place of fire, of Smokey Bear, and of the role of fighting fire in ecosystems that were meant to burn. A new day in wildfire writing was born with the Yellowstone fires in 1988, which brought increased attention and focus upon wildfires. The conflagrations of that drought-scarred summer left Americans reeling and anxious to effect change with the tools of fire ecology, prescribed burning, and a shift away from complete suppression. Writing from this period reflects the new acceptance of fire in the natural world, from the perspective of naturalists and firefighters, and addresses the problems encountered from a century of fire suppression.

Even as this book is published, yet another shift in thinking about wildfire is on the horizon. The waves of wildfire that swept through Los Alamos, through suburban Colorado, across every Western state, and raged through Montana, left a lasting impression of the power and presence of fire on Americans from coast to coast. After the severe fire season of 2000, lauded as the worst in recorded American history (worse even than 1988 or 1910), new thinking about wildfire is emerging. No longer is prescribed fire sufficient to cleanse the forest of crowding deadfall and debris. Prescribed fire did not prevent the firestorms of 2000. In some cases, it even prompted them. With the complex dynamics of an increasing population in rural and forested areas, of patchy logging properties where timber stands grow thick and close, of protected forests in public lands that have been robbed of fire, the pressures on America's land managers have become heavier than ever. The cost of firefighting efforts in the season of 2000 also spawned new interest in controlling the problem. With financial costs in excess of one billion dollars, and environmental and health costs too great to quantify, the country clearly cannot continue the present efforts. What is next for America's forests and rangelands remains to be seen. Much depends on policies set by the nation's largest landholders, the U.S. Forest Service, the National Park Service, and the Bureau of Land Management. Certainly prevention, suppression, and prescribed fire will still play a role, but so will new efforts, such as the mechanical thinning of thick forests. One thing is certain, though, and that is that the new policies and wildfires will continue to be recorded by authors from all walks of life and experience. Writers will continue to capture the fury and heat of the great flames or the quiet reflection of wildflowers sprouting from ashes, so long as fires burn through forests and prairies, inspiring us, and reminding us of the eternal power of Mother Nature and her role here on Earth.

Part I

Big Country, Big Fires

We are the fire that burns the country.
—Bantu Proverb

VISIT VIRTUALLY any wild place in America, and you will uncover evidence of both ancient and modern wildfire. Hike through an open ponderosa stand in Arizona, and notice the fresh grass creeping up on blackened stumps, and mule deer browsing in the absence of brush. Scramble up a smooth scarred slope in Southern California's brush country, and notice where chapparal burned clean last year now sprouts stubbly new growth. Pass through the high plateau of Yellowstone, where hundreds of thousands of acres were cleared by the Great Fire of 1988, and rest in the rich forest of aspen and lodgepole pine trees. Two thousand miles across the country, in the Great Smoky Mountains, observe the broad stands of beech trees of similar height and girth along the Appalachian Trail, all sprouted from seeds nurtured in the fertile ash of a forest fire.

In each case, some as recent as a year ago and others as old as two centuries ago, fires have played a defining role in creating the environments we now inhabit. In the hands of people and in wild nature, fire is the force that cleans and regenerates, enhances and destroys. With great power and an almost intuitive sense, fire stimulates evolutionary adaptation among plants and animals, produces its own stormy weather in convective cloud cells, and distributes airborne ash that fertilizes terrain near and far. Across North America, the subtle shapes of wilderness and wild country lost reveal an intimate and historical relationship to fire. The patterns of forest and meadow, the distribution of vegetation, the migrations and daily movements of wildlife—all are related to the presence of fire on the land at some point in the past.

During presettlement days, the frequent wildfires streaming across the prairies had more to offer than many early American settlers realized. Fire is essential for preventing the encroachment of the trees that invade edges of open areas such as grasslands and meadows. After flames consume both woody material and grass, it is the quick sprouting and growing of grasses that leads to dominance. For the native plants that evolved under the pressures of periodic fire, seeds lying dormant often require the coaxing of fire to germinate. Regular firing of the land also allows nurturing sunlight and moisture to penetrate deep to the roots of prairie species while nutrients released from burnt material fertilize young plants as they grow.

Native Americans used their own flames along with naturally burning wildfires to expand and enrich the borders of the original North American grasslands. Stretching from the coastal plains of the Eastern seaboard to the foothills of the Appalachians, and west and north to the wide open Great Plains, fire made seasonal appearances, leaving the ground ashen and bare, releasing nutrients and setting the stage for the healthy greens of spring. Native American uses of fire varied from a means of communication—columns of smoke rising from one hilltop to another, to large area burns used to eradicate hordes of insect pests. Fire played a role in hunting by clearing underbrush and attracting game; and in agriculture by facilitating the harvest of roots and nuts, berries and beans. Both natural and anthropogenic flames altered the natural distribution of vegetation, from spacious grasslands to parklike forests clear of underbrush and full of game. These traditional ways of handling fire and introducing it into the landscape often shaped the country that settlers encountered as they moved west across America.

Early American writers realized the importance of fire; it served as a regular backdrop for many well-known stories. Writers such as Henry David Thoreau, John Muir, Washington Irving, and Mark Twain all described and commented upon fires in their books. In these early writings, humankind did not dominate wildfires as they blazed through the surrounding forests and prairies. Instead, fire was a force to be reckoned with, respected, and feared; a force that could mercilessly destroy valuable resources and property. Stephen Pyne places the fires of 1910, which darkened the skies from the Northwest clear to Chicago and New England and spurred the creation of our modern firefighting culture, into the context of recent large-scale wildfires and fire management policies. Wildfire stories from this early period are also captured in Native American literature through origin tales and myths of how fire was brought to people.

These readings span the beginning of more than 200 years of nature writing and wildfire, before the trappings of modern civilization spawned fire suppression and a daily life disconnected from the common pressures of nature. Fire was not under the human thumb, nor was it controlled in any organized manner. More than a century would pass

Introduction

before fire behavior could be quantified and the movement of fire, as a living creature over the landscape, could be predicted. These early writings chronicle the relationship between wildfire and the American landscape in what now seems a quaint and distant time, before there were hotshot crews and smokejumpers and air tankers dropping slurry from the sky. In these pages, the reader will find no mention of the regenerative forces of fire, of its fertilizing powers and integral role in nurturing the natural environment in a healthy equilibrium.

In this first section, readers will sample writings from the buffalo-dotted Great Plains to the hills surrounding Lake Tahoe to the woods of Maine. Wildfire, as reality and as myth, is seen as a curious paradox—both familiar and unknown, entertaining and terrifying. Later readings will chronicle the integration of fire into the fields of forestry and environmental science, the development of military firefighting structures, and the growing sense of the role of fire in environmental history. For now, though, let us travel back to a different time, when campfires were often the only means of providing light and warmth, and nature was a much larger, and older, presence in the human experience.

The First Fire

CHEROKEE TALE

I N T H E B E G I N N I N G T H E R E was no fire, and the world was cold, until the Thunders (Ani'-Hyun'tikwala'ski), who lived up in Galun'lati, sent their lightning and put fire into the bottom of a hollow sycamore tree which grew on an island. The animals knew it was there, because they could see the smoke coming out at the top, but they could not get to it on account of the water, so they held a council to decide what to do. This was a long time ago.

Every animal that could fly or swim was anxious to go after the fire. The Raven offered, and because he was so large and strong they thought he could surely do the work, so he was sent first. He flew high and far across the water and alighted on the sycamore tree, but while he was wondering what to do next, the heat had scorched all his feathers black, and he was frightened and came back without the fire. The little-screech owl (Wa'huhu') volunteered to go, and reached the place safely, but while he was looking down into the hollow tree a blast of hot air came up and nearly burnt out his eyes. He managed to fly home as best he could, but it was a long time before he could see well, and his eyes are red to this day. Then the Hooting Owl (U'guku') and the Horned Owl (Tskili) went, but by the time they got to the hollow tree the fire was burning so fiercely that the smoke nearly blinded them, and the ashes carried up by the wind made white rings about their eyes. They had to come home again without the fire, but with all their rubbing they were never able to get rid of the white rings.

Big Country, Big Fires

Now no more of the birds would venture, and so the little Uksu'hi snake, the black racer, said he would go through the water and bring back some fire. He swam across to the island and crawled through the grass to the tree, and went in by a small hole at the bottom. The heat and smoke were too much for him, too, and after dodging about blindly over the hot ashes until he was almost on fire himself he managed by good luck to get out again at the same hole, but his body had been scorched black, and he has ever since had the habit of darting and doubling on his track as if trying to escape from close quarters. He came back, and the great blacksnake, Gule'gi, "The Climber," offered to go for fire. He swam over to the island and climbed up the tree on the outside, as the black-snake always does, but when he put his head down into the hole the smoke choked him so that he fell into the burning stump, and before he could climb out again he was as black as the Uksu'hi.

Now they held another council, for still there was no fire, and the world was cold, but birds, snakes, and four-footed animals, all had some excuse for not going, because they were all afraid to venture near the burning sycamore, until at last Kanane'ski Amai'yehi (the Water Spider) said she would go. This is not the water spider that looks like a mosquito, but the other one, with black downy hair and red stripes on her body. She can run on top of the water or dive to the bottom, so there would be no trouble to get over to the island, but the question was, How could she bring back fire? "I'll manage that," said the Water Spider; so she spun a thread from her body and wove it into a *tusti* bowl, which she fastened on her back. Then she crossed over to the island and through the grass to where the fire was still burning. She put one little coal of fire into her bowl, and came back with it, and ever since we have had fire, and the Water Spider still keeps her tusti bowl.

How Tol'-le-loo Got the Fire for the Mountain People

A TALE OF THE NORTHERN MIWOK

THE MOUNTAIN PEOPLE lived in the Sierra near the Mokelumne River, which they called Ut'-ta Wah-kah'-loo, meaning big river. They had no fire and the world was dark. The Valley People lived on the San Joaquin Plain, which they called Ol-law'-win. Their roundhouse was not far from the spot now occupied by the city of Stockton. They had a small fire in the middle of the roundhouse and Wit'-tab-bah the Robin was its keeper.

Wek'-wek the Falcon and We'-pi-ah'-gah the Golden Eagle were Chiefs of the Valley People. Among the members of their tribe were Mol'-luk the Condor; Hoo'-a-zoo the Turkey Buzzard; Hoo-loo'-e the Dove; Te-wi'-yu the Red-shafted Flicker, who must have been very close to the fire as anyone can see from the red under his wings and tail; and Wit'-tab-bah the red-breasted Robin, who was keeper of the fire. There were also Hah-ki'-ah the Elk, Hal'-loo-zoo the Antelope, Sahk'-mum-chah the Cinnamon Bear, and others.

The Mountain People were in darkness and wanted fire but did not know where it was or how to get it. O-la'-choo the Coyote-man tried hard to find it but did not succeed. After a while Tol'-le-loo the White-footed Mouse discovered the fire and the Mountain People sent him to steal it.

Big Country, Big Fires

Tol'-le-loo took his flute (loo'-lah) of elderberry wood and went down into the valley and found the big roundhouse of Wek'-wek and We'-pi-ah'-gah and began to play. The people liked the music and asked him to come inside. So he went in and played for them. Soon all the people felt sleepy. Wit'-tab-bah the Robin was sure that Tol'-le-loo had come to steal the fire, so he spread himself over it and covered it all up in order to hide it, and it turned his breast red. But Tol'-le-loo kept on playing his flute and in a little while all the people were sound asleep; even Wit'-tab-bah could not keep awake.

Then Tol'-le-loo ran up to Wit'-tab-bah and cut a little hole in his wing and crawled through and stole the fire and put it inside his flute. When he had done this he ran out with it and climbed up to the top of the high mountain called Oo'-yum-bel'-le (Mount Diablo) and made a great fire which lighted up all the country till even the blue mountains far away in the east [the Sierra Nevada Range] could be seen. Before this all the world was dark.

When Wek'-wek awoke he saw the fire on Oo'-yum-bel'-le and knew that Tol'-le-loo had stolen it. So he ran out and followed him and after a while caught him.

Tol'-le-loo said, "Look and see if I have the fire."

Wek'-wek looked but could not find it, for it was inside the flute. Then Wek'-wek pitched Tol'-le-loo into the water and let him go.

Tol'-le-loo got out and went east into the mountains and carried the fire in his flute to the Mountain People; then he took it out of the flute and put it on the ground and covered it with leaves and pine needles and tied it up in a small bundle. O-la'-choo the Coyote smelled it and wanted to steal it. He came up and pushed it with his nose and was going to swallow it when it suddenly shot up into the sky and became the Sun.

O-la'-choo sent Le'-che-che the Hummingbird, and another bird, named Le-che-koo'-tah-mah, who also had a long bill, after it, but they could not catch it and came back without it.

The people took the fire that was left and put it into two trees, oo'-noo the buckeye and mon'-o-go the incense cedar, where it still is and where it can be had by anyone who wants it.

Excerpt from

The Journals of the Expedition under the Command of Captains Lewis and Clark

MERIWETHER LEWIS

October 29th, 1805

In the evening, the prairie took fire, either by accident or design, and burned with great fury, the whole plain being enveloped in flames: so rapid was its progress that a man and a woman were burnt to death before they could reach a place of safety, another man with his wife and child were much burnt, and several other persons narrowly escaped destruction. Among the rest a boy of the half white breed escaped unhurt in the midst of the flames; his safety was ascribed to the great medicine spirit, who had preserved him on account of his being white. But a much more natural cause was the presence of mind of his mother, who seeing no hopes of carrying off her son, threw him on the ground, and covering him with the fresh hide of a buffalo, escaped herself from the flames; as soon as the fire had passed, she returned and found him untouched, the skin having prevented the flame from reaching the grass on which he lay.

The Alarm Camp

WASHINGTON IRVING

Fire—The Wild Indians

We now came to a halt, and had to content ourselves with an indifferent encampment. It was in a grove of scrub oaks, on the borders of a deep ravine, at the bottom of which were a few scanty pools of water. We were just at the foot of a gradually sloping hill, covered with half-withered grass, that afforded meagre pasturage. In the spot where we had encamped, the grass was high and parched. The view around us was circumscribed, and much shut in by gently swelling hills.

Just as we were encamping, Tonish arrived, all glorious from his hunting match; his white horse hung all round with buffalo meat. According to his own account, he had laid low two mighty bulls. As usual, we deducted one half from his boastings; but now that he had something real to vaunt about, there was no restraining the valour of his tongue.

After having in some measure appeased his vanity by boasting of his exploit, he informed us, that he had observed the fresh track of horses, which, from various circumstances, he suspected to have been made by some roving band of Pawnees. This caused some little uneasiness. The young men who had left the line of march in pursuit of the two buffaloes had not yet rejoined us. Apprehensions were expressed that they might be waylaid and attacked. Our veteran hunter, "old Ryan," also, immediately on our halting to encamp, had gone off on foot, in company with a young disciple. "Dat old man will have his brains knocked out by de

The Alarm Camp

Pawnees yet," said Beatte; "he tink he know every ting, but he don't know Pawnees any how."

Taking his rifle, the Captain repaired on foot to reconnoitre the country from the naked summit of one of the neighbouring hills. In the mean time, the horses were hobbled and turned loose to graze in the adjacent fields, and wood was cut, and fires made, to prepare the evening's repast.

Suddenly there was an alarm of fire in the camp! The flame from one of the kindling fires had caught to the tall dry grass: a breeze was blowing; there was danger that the camp would soon be wrapped in a light blaze. "Look to the horses!" cried one; "drag away the baggage!" cried another; "take care of the rifles and powder-horns!" cried a third: all was hurry-scurry and uproar. The horses dashed wildly about; the men snatched away rifles and powder-horns; others dragged off saddles and saddle-bags: meantime, no one thought of quelling the fire, nor, indeed, knew how to quell it. Beatte, however, and his comrades, attacked it in the Indian mode, beating down the edges of the fire with blankets and horse-cloths, and endeavouring to prevent its spreading among the grass; the rangers followed their example, and in a little while the flames were happily quelled.

The fires were now properly kindled in places from whence the dry grass had been cleared away. The horses were scattered about a small valley, and on the sloping hillside, cropping the scanty herbage. Tonish was preparing a sumptuous evening's meal from his buffalo meat, promising us a rich soup and a prime piece of roast beef; but we were doomed to experience another and more serious alarm.

There was an indistinct cry from some rangers on the summit of the hill, of which we could only distinguish the words, "The horses! the horses! get in the horses!"

Immediately a clamour of voices arose: shouts, enquiries, replies, were all mingled together, so that nothing could be clearly understood, and every one drew his own inference.

"The Captain has started buffaloes," cried one, "and wants horses for the chase." Immediately a number of rangers seized their rifles, and scampered for the hilltop. "The prairie is on fire beyond the hill," cried another. "I see the smoke! the Captain means we shall drive the horses beyond the brook."

Big Country, Big Fires

By this time a ranger from the hill had reached the skirts of the camp. He was almost breathless, and could only say that the Captain had seen Indians at a distance.

"Pawnees! Pawnees!" was now the cry among our wild-headed youngsters.

"Drive the horses into the camp!" cried one. "Saddle the horses!" cried another. "Form the line!" cried a third. There was now a scene of clamour and confusion that baffles all description. The rangers were scampering about the adjacent fields in pursuit of their horses. One might be seen tugging his steed along by a halter; another, without a hat, riding bare-backed; another driving a hobbled horse before him, that made awkward leaps like a kangaroo.

The alarm increased. Word was brought from the lower end of the camp, that there was a band of Pawnees in a neighbouring valley. "They had shot old Ryan through the head, and were chasing his companion!" "No, it was not old Ryan that was killed, it was one of the hunters that had been after the two buffaloes." "There are three hundred Pawnees just behind the hill!" cried one voice. "More, more!" cried another.

Our situation, shut in among hills, prevented our seeing to any distance, and left us a prey to all these rumours. A cruel enemy was supposed to be at hand, and an immediate attack apprehended. The horses by this time were driven into the camp, and were dashing about among the fires, and trampling upon the baggage. Every one endeavoured to prepare for action: but here was the perplexity. During the late alarm of fire, the saddles, bridles, rifles, powder-horns, and other equipments, had been snatched out of their places, and thrown helter-skelter among the trees.

"Where is my saddle?" cried one. "Has anyone seen my rifle?" cried another. "Who will lend me a ball?" cried a third, who was loading his piece. "I have lost my bullet-pouch."

"For God's sake help me to girth this horse!" cried another; "he is so restive I can do nothing with him!" In his hurry he had put on the saddle the hind part before.

Some affected to swagger and talk bold; others said nothing, but went on steadily preparing their horses and weapons; and on these I felt the most reliance. Some were evidently excited and elated with the idea of an encounter with Indians, and none more so than my young Swiss

The Alarm Camp

fellow-traveller, who has a passion for wild adventure. Our man Beatte led his horses in the rear of the camp, placed his rifle against a tree, then seated himself by the fire in perfect silence.

On the other hand, little Tonish, who was busy cooking, stopped every moment form his work to play the *fanfaron,* singing, swearing, and affecting an unusual hilarity, which made me strongly suspect that there was some little fright at bottom to cause all this effervescence.

About a dozen of the rangers, as soon as they could saddle their horses, dashed off in the direction in which the Pawnees were said to have attacked the hunters. It was now determined, in case our camp should be assailed, to put our horses in the ravine in rear, where they would be out of danger from arrow or rifle ball, and to take our stand within the edge of the ravine. This would serve as a trench, and the trees and thickets with which it was bordered would be sufficient to turn aside any shaft of the enemy. The Pawnees, beside, are wary of attacking any covert of the kind; their warfare, as I have already observed, lies upon the open prairies, where, mounted upon their fleet horses, they can swoop like hawks upon their enemy, or wheel about him and discharge their arrows. Still I could not but perceive that, in case of being attacked by such a number of these well-mounted and warlike savages as were said to be at hand, we should be exposed to considerable risk, from the inexperience and want of discipline of our newly-raised rangers, and from the very courage of many of the younger ones, who seemed bent on adventure and exploit.

By this time the Captain reached the camp, and every one crowded around him for information. He informed us that he had proceeded some distance on his reconnoitring expedition, and was slowly returning towards the camp, along the brow of a naked hill, when he saw something on the edge of a parallel hill that looked like a man. He paused and watched it; but it remained so perfectly motionless that he supposed it a bush, or the top of some tree beyond the hill. He resumed his course, when it likewise began to move in a parallel direction. Another form now rose beside it, of some one who had either been lying down, or had just ascended the other side of the hill. The Captain stopped and regarded them; they likewise stopped. He then lay down upon the grass, and they began to walk. On his rising they again stopped, as if watching him. Knowing that the Indians are apt to have their spies and sentinels thus posted on the summit of naked hills, commanding extensive prospects, his doubts were increased by the suspicious movements of these men. He now put his foraging cap on the end of his rifle, and waved it in the air. They took no notice of the signal. He then walked on until he entered the edge of a wood which concealed him from their view. Stepping out of sight for a moment, he again looked forth, when he saw the two men passing swiftly forward. As the hill on which they were walking made a curve toward that on which he stood, it seemed as if they were endeavouring to head him off before he should reach the camp. Doubting whether they might not belong to some large party of Indians, either in ambush or moving along the valley beyond the hill, the Captain hasted his steps homeward, and, descrying some rangers on an eminence between him and the camp, he called out to them to pass the word to have the horses driven in, as these are, generally, the first object of Indian depredation.

Such was the origin of the alarm which had thrown the camp in commotion. Some of those who heard the Captain's narrative, had no doubt that the men on the hill were Pawnee scouts, belonging to the band that had waylaid the hunters. Distant shots were heard at intervals, which were supposed to be fired by those who had sallied out to rescue their comrades. Several more rangers, having completed their equipments, now rode forth in the direction of the firing; others looked anxious and uneasy.

"If they are as numerous as they are said to be," said one, "and as well mounted as they generally are, we shall be a bad match for them with our jaded horses."

"Well," replied the Captain, "we have a strong encampment, and can stand a siege."

"Ay, but they may set fire to the prairie at night, and burn us out of our encampment."

"We will then set up a counter-fire."

The word was now passed that a man on horseback approached the camp. "It is one of the hunters!"—"It is Clements!"—"He brings buffalo meat!" was announced by several voices as the horseman drew near.

It was, in fact, one of the rangers who had set off in the morning in pursuit of the two buffaloes. He rode into the camp with the spoils of the chase hanging round his horse, and followed by his companions, all sound and unharmed, and equally well laden. They proceeded to give an account of a grand gallop they had had after the two buffaloes, and how many shots it had cost them to bring one to the ground.

"Well, but the Pawnees—the Pawnees—where are the Pawnees?"

"What Pawnees?"

"The Pawnees that attacked you."

"No one has attacked us."

"But have you seen no Indians on your way?"

"Oh, yes; two of us got to the top of a hill to look out for the camp, and saw a fellow on an opposite hill cutting queer antics, who seemed to be an Indian."

"Pshaw! that was I," cried the Captain.

Here the bubble burst. The whole alarm had arisen from this mutual mistake of the Captain and the two rangers. As to the report of the three hundred Pawnees, and their attack on the hunters, it proved to be a wanton fabrication, of which no further notice was taken, though the author deserved to have been sought out and severely punished.

There being no longer any prospect of fighting, every one now thought of eating; and here the stomachs throughout the camp were in unison. Tonish served up to us his promised regale of buffalo soup and buffalo beef. The soup was peppered most horribly, and the roast beef proved the bull to have been one of the patriarchs of the prairies: never did I have to deal with a tougher morsel. However, it was our first repast on buffalo meat, so we ate it with a lively faith; nor would our little Frenchman allow us any rest, until he had extorted from us an acknowledgment of the excellence of his cooking, though the pepper gave us the lie in our throats.

The night closed in without the return of old Ryan and his companions. We had become accustomed, however, to the aberrations of this old cock of the woods, and no further solicitude was expressed on his account. After the fatigues and agitations of the day, the camp soon sunk into a profound sleep, excepting those on guard, who were more than usually on the alert; for the traces recently seen of Pawnees, and the certainty that we were in the midst of their hunting-grounds, excited to constant vigilance. About half-past ten o'clock, we were all startled from sleep by a new alarm. A sentinel had fired off his rifle, and run into camp, crying out that there were Indians at hand.

Every one was on his legs in an instant. Some seized their rifles; some were about to saddle their horses; some hastened to the Captain's lodge, but were ordered back to their respective fires. The sentinel was examined. He declared he had seen an Indian approach, crawling along the ground, where-upon he had fired upon him, and run into camp. The Captain gave it as his opinion that the supposed Indian was a wolf; he reprimanded the sentinel for deserting his post, and obliged him to return to it. Many seemed inclined to give him credit to the story of the sentinel; for the events of the day had predisposed them to apprehend lurking foes, and sudden assaults during the darkness of the night. For a long time they sat round their fires, with rifle in hand, carrying on low murmuring conversations, and listening for some new alarm. Nothing further, however, occurred; the voices gradually died away; the gossipers nodded, and dozed, and sunk to rest, and by degrees silence and sleep once more stole over the camp.

Selection from

The Allegash and East Branch

HENRY DAVID THOREAU

SHORTLY AFTER THIS I overtook the Indian at the edge of some burnt land, which extended three or four miles at least, beginning about three miles above Second Lake, which we were expecting to reach that night, and which is about ten miles from Telos Lake. This burnt region was still more rocky than before, but, though comparatively open, we could not yet see the lake. Not having seen my companion for some time, I climbed, with the Indian, a singular high rock on the edge of the river, forming a narrow ridge only a foot or two wide at top, in order to look for him; and, after calling many times, I at length heard him answer from a considerable distance inland, he having taken a trail which led off in search of the river again. Seeing a much higher rock, of the same character, about one third of a mile farther east, or down stream, I proceeded toward it, through the burnt land, in order to look for the lake from its summit, supposing that the Indian would keep down the stream in his canoe, and hallooing all the while that my companion might join me on the way. Before we came together I noticed where a moose, which possibly I had scared by my shouting, had apparently just run along a large rotten trunk of a pine, which made a bridge, thirty or forty feet long, over a hollow, as convenient for him as for me. The tracks were as large as those of an ox, but an ox could not have crossed there. This burnt land was an exceedingly wild and desolate region. Judging by the weeds and sprouts, it appeared to have been burnt about two years before. It was covered with charred trunks, either prostrate or standing, which crocked our clothes and hands, and we could not easily have distinguished a bear there by his color. Great shells of trees, sometimes unburnt without, or burnt on one side only, but black within, stood twenty or forty feet high. The fire had run up inside, as in a chimney, leaving the sap-wood. Sometimes we crossed a rocky ravine fifty feet wide, on a fallen trunk; and there were great fields of fire-weed *(Epilobium angustifolium)* on all sides, the most extensive that I ever saw, which presented great masses of pink. Intermixed with these were blueberry and raspberry bushes.

Having crossed a second rocky ridge like the first, when I was beginning to ascend the third, the Indian, whom I had left on the shore some fifty rods behind, beckoned to me to come to him, but I made sign that I would first ascend the highest rock before me, whence I expected to see the lake. My companion accompanied me to the top. This was formed just like the others. Being struck with the perfect parallelism of these singular rock hills, however much one might be in advance of another, I took out my compass and found that they lay northwest and southeast, the rock being on its edge, and sharp edges they were. This one, to speak from memory, was perhaps a third of a mile in length, but quite narrow, rising gradually form the northwest to the height of about eighty feet, but steep on the southeast end. The southwest side was as steep as an ordinary roof, or as we could safely climb; the northeast was an abrupt precipice from which you could jump clean to the bottom, near which the river flowed; while the level top of the ridge, on which you walked along, was only from one to three or four feet in width. For a rude illustration, take the half of a pear cut in two lengthwise, lay it on its flat side, the stem to the northwest, and then halve it vertically in the direction of its length, keeping the southwest half. Such was the general form.

There was a remarkable series of these great rock-waves revealed by the burning; breakers, as it were. No wonder that the river that found its way through them was rapid and obstructed by falls. No doubt the absence of soil on these rocks, or its dryness where there was any, caused this to be a very thorough burning. We could see the lake over the woods, two or three miles ahead, and that the river made an abrupt turn southward around the northwest end of the cliff on which we stood, or a little above us, so that we had cut off a bend, and that there was an important fall in it a short distance below us. I could see the canoe a hundred rods behind, but now on the opposite shore, and supposed that the Indian had concluded to take out and carry round some bad rapids on that side, and that that might be what he had beckoned me for; but after waiting a while I could still see nothing of him, and I observed to my companion that I wondered where he was, though I began to suspect that he had gone inland to look for the lake from some hilltop on that side, as we had done. This proved to be the case; for after I had started to return to the canoe, I heard a faint halloo, and descried him on the top of a distant rocky hill on that side. But as, after a long time had elapsed, I still saw his canoe in the same place, and he had not returned to it, and appeared in no hurry to do so, and, moreover, as I remembered that he had previously beckoned to me, I thought that there might be something more to delay him than I knew, and began to return northwest, along the ridge, toward the angle in the river. My companion, who had just been separated from us, and had even contemplated the necessity of camping alone, wishing to husband his steps, and yet to keep with us, inquired where I was going; to which I answered that I was going far enough back to communicate with the Indian, and that then I thought we had better go along the shore together, and keep him in sight.

When we reached the shore, the Indian appeared from out the woods on the opposite side, but on account of the roar of the water it was difficult to communicate with him. He kept along the shore westward to his canoe, while we stopped at the angle where the stream turned southward around the precipice. I again said to my companion, that we would keep along the shore and keep the Indian in sight. We started to do so, being close together, the Indian behind us having launched his canoe again, but just then I saw the latter, who had crossed to our side, forty or fifty rods behind, beckoning to me, and I called to my companion, who had just disappeared behind large rocks at the point of the precipice, three or four rods before me, on his way down the stream, that I was going to help the Indian a moment. I did so,—helped get the canoe over a fall, lying with my breast over a rock, and holding one end while he received it below,—and within ten or fifteen minutes at most I was back again at the point where the river turned southward, in order to catch up with my companion, while Polis glided down the river alone, parallel with me. But to my surprise, when I rounded the precipice, though the shore was bare of trees, without rocks, for a quarter of a mile at least, my companion was not to be seen. It was as if he had sunk into the earth. This was the more unaccountable to me, because I knew that his feet were, since our swamp walk, very sore, and that he wished to keep with the party; and besides this was very bad walking, climbing over or about the rocks. I hastened along, hallooing and searching for him, thinking he might be concealed behind a rock, yet doubting if he had not taken the other side of the precipice, but the Indian had gotten along still faster in his canoe, till he was arrested by the falls, about a quarter of a mile below. He then landed, and said that we could go no farther that night. The sun was setting, and on account of falls and rapids we should be obliged to leave this river and carry a good way into another farther east. The first thing then was to find my companion, for I was now very much alarmed about him, and I sent the Indian along the shore down stream, which began to be covered with unburnt wood again just below the falls, while I searched backward about the precipice which we had passed. The Indian showed some unwillingness to exert himself, complaining that he was very tired in consequence of his day's work, that it had strained him very much getting down so many rapids alone; but he went off calling somewhat like an owl. I remembered that my companion was near-sighted, and I feared that he had either fallen from the precipice, or fainted and sunk down amid the rocks beneath it. I shouted and searched above and below this precipice in the twilight till I could not see, expecting nothing less than to find his body beneath it. For half an hour I anticipated and believed only the worst. I thought what I should do the next day, if I did not find him, what I *could* do in such a wilderness, and how his relatives would feel, if I should return without him. I felt that if he were really lost away from the river there, it would be a desperate undertaking to find him; and where were they who could help you? What would it be to raise the country, where there were only two or three camps, twenty or thirty miles apart, and no road, and perhaps nobody at home? Yet we must try the harder, the less the prospect of success.

I rushed down from this precipice to the canoe in order to fire the Indian's gun, but found that my companion had the caps. I was still thinking of getting it off when the Indian returned. He had not found him, but he said that he had seen his tracks once or twice along the shore. This encouraged me very much. He objected to firing the gun saying that if my companion heard it, which was not likely, on account of the roar of the stream, it would tempt him to come toward us and he might break his neck in the dark. For the same reason we refrained from lighting a fire on the highest rock. I proposed that we should both keep down the stream to the lake, or that I should go at any rate, but the Indian said, "No use, can't do anything in the dark; come morning, then we find 'em. No harm,—he make 'em camp. No bad animals here, no gristly bears, such as in California, where he's been,—warm night,—he well off as you and I." I considered that if he was well he could do without us. He had just lived eight years in California, and had plenty of experience with wild beasts and wilder men, was peculiarly accustomed to make journeys of great length, but if he were sick or dead, he was near where we were. The darkness in the woods was by this so thick that it alone decided the question. We must camp where we were. I knew that he had his knapsack, with blankets and matches, and, if well, would fare no worse than we, except that he would have no supper nor society.

This side of the river being so encumbered with rocks, we crossed to the eastern or smoother shore, and proceeded to camp there, within two or three rods of the falls. We pitched no tent but lay on the sand, putting a few handfuls of grass and twigs under us, there being no evergreen at hand. For fuel we had some of the charred stumps. Our various bags of provisions had got quite wet in the rapids, and I arranged them about the fire to dry. The fall close by was the principal one on this stream, and it shook the earth under us. It was a cool, because dewy, night; the more so, probably, owing to the nearness of the falls. The Indian complained a good deal, and thought afterward that he got a cold there which occasioned a more serious illness. We were not much troubled by mosquitoes at any rate. I lay awake a good deal from anxiety, but, unaccountably to myself, was at length comparatively at ease respecting him. At first I had apprehended the worst, but now I had little doubt but that I should find him in the morning. From time to time I fancied that I heard his voice calling through the roar of the falls from the opposite side of the river; but it is doubtful if we could have heard him across the stream there. Sometimes I doubted whether the Indian had really seen his tracks, since he manifested an unwillingness to make much of a search, and then my anxiety returned.

It was the most wild and desolate region we had camped in , where, if anywhere, one might expect to meet with befitting inhabitants, but I heard only the squeak of a nighthawk flitting over. The moon in her first quarter, in the fore part of the night, setting over the bare rocky hills garnished with tall, charred, and hollow stumps or shells of trees, served to reveal the desolation.

Selection from

John of the Mountains

JOHN MUIR

Camp in a hollow sequoia in the midst of a burning forest on divide between Middle and East Forks of Kaweah River.

Sequoia Forest Fire

Varied beauty of fire effects: fire grazing, nibbling in the floor among old close-packed leaves; spinning into thousands of little jets—lamps of pure flame on twigs hung loosely, and taller spurts of flame; big bonfires blazing where heavy branches are smashed in heaps; old prostrate trunks glowing like red-hot bars.... Smoke and showers of white fluffy ashes from the fire boring out trunks, rills of violet fire running up the furrows swiftly, lighting huge torches flaming overhead two hundred feet, on tops of pillars dried and fractured by lightning strokes. Down below working among arches of roots and burning whole trunks hollow into huge tubes as they stand up, which you may look through as telescopes and see the stars at noon-day.... Smoke fragrant like incense ascending, browsing on fallen twigs and tiny rosebushes and Chamaebatia, flames advancing in long bent lines like a flock of sheep grazing, rushing in a roaring storm of energy like devouring lions, burning with fierce fateful roar and stormy booming; black and lurid smoke surges streaming through the trees, the columns of which look like masts of ships obscured in scud and flying clouds. Height and hollow filled with red surges, billows roaring uphill in ragged-edged flapping cataracts. Every living thing flaming.

Big Country, Big Fires

The destruction, in great conflagrations, of fine buildings on which loving art has been lavished, sad as it is, seems less deplorable than the burning of these majestic living temples, the grandest of Gothic cathedrals.

In two-leaved pine groves thousands burn at once in one continuous flame, flying like storm-clouds with terrific grandeur—an ocean of billowy flame reddening the sky at night.

Selection from

My First Summer in the Sierra

JOHN MUIR

August 11

Fine shining weather, with a ten minutes' noon thunderstorm and rain.
Rambling all day getting acquainted with the region north of the river.
Found a small lake and many charming glacier meadows embosomed in
an extensive forest of the two-leaved pine. The forest is growing on
broad, almost continuous deposits of moraine material, is remarkably
even in its growth, and the trees are much closer together than in any of
the fir or pine woods farther down the range. The evenness of the
growth would seem to indicate that the trees are all of the same age or
nearly so. This regularity has probably been in great part the result of
fire. I saw several large patches and strips of dead bleached spars, the
ground beneath them covered with a young even growth. Fire can run in
these woods, not only because the thin bark of the trees is dripping with
resin, but because the growth is close, and the comparatively rich soil
produces good crops of tall broad-leaved grasses on which fire can
travel, even when the weather is calm. Besides these fire-killed patches
there are a good many fallen uprooted trees here and there, some with
the bark and needles still on, as if they had lately been blown down in
some thunderstorm blast. Saw a large black-tailed deer, a buck with
antlers like the upturned roots of a fallen pine.

After a long ramble through the dense encumbered woods I
emerged upon a smooth meadow full of sunshine like a lake of light,

about a mile and a half long, a quarter to half a mile wide, and bounded by tall arrowy pines. The sod, like that of all the glacier meadows hereabouts, is made of silky agrostis and calamagrostis chiefly; their panicles of purple flowers and purple stems, exceedingly light and airy, seem to float above the green plush of leaves like a thin misty cloud, while the sod is brightened by several species of gentian, potentilla, ivesia, orthocarpus, and their corresponding bees and butterflies. All the glacier meadows are beautiful, but few are so perfect as this one. Compared with it the most carefully leveled, licked, snipped artificial lawns of pleasure-grounds are coarse things. I should like to live here always. It is so calm and withdrawn while open to the universe in full communion with everything good. To the north of this glorious meadow I discovered the camp of some Indian hunters. Their fire was still burning, but they had not yet returned from the chase.

From meadow to meadow, every one beautiful beyond telling, and from lake to lake through groves and belts of arrowy trees, I held my way northward toward Mount Conness, finding telling beauty everywhere, while the encompassing mountains were calling "Come." Hope I may climb them all.

Selection from

Roughing It

MARK TWAIN

L F THERE IS ANY LIFE THAT is happier than the life we led on our timber ranch for the next two or three weeks, it must be a sort of life which I have not read of in books or experienced in person. We did not see a human being but ourselves during the time, or hear any sounds but those that were made by the wind and the waves, the sighing of the pines, and now and then the far-off thunder of an avalanche. The forest about us was dense and cool, the sky above us was cloudless and brilliant with sunshine, the broad lake before us was glassy and clear, or rippled and breezy, or black and storm-tossed, according to Nature's mood; and its circling border of mountain domes, clothed with forests, scarred with land-slides, cloven by cañons and valleys, and helmeted with glittering snow, fitly framed and finished the noble picture. The view was always fascinating, bewitching, entrancing. The eye was never tired of gazing, night or day, in calm or storm; it suffered but one grief, and that was that it could not look always, but must close sometimes in sleep.

We slept in the sand close to the water's edge, between two protecting boulders, which took care of the stormy night-winds for us. We never took any paregoric to make us sleep. At the first break of dawn we were always up and running foot-races to tone down excess of physical vigor and exuberance of spirits. That is, Johnny was—but I held his hat. While smoking the pipe of peace after breakfast we watched the sentinel peaks put on the glory of the sun, and followed the conquering light as it swept down among the shadows, and set the captive crags and forests free. We watched the tinted pictures grow and brighten upon the water till every little detail of forest, precipice and pinnacle was wrought in and finished, and the miracle of the enchanter complete. Then to "business."

That is, drifting around in the boat. We were on the north shore. There, the rocks on the bottom are sometimes gray, sometimes white. This gives the marvelous transparency of the water a fuller advantage than it has elsewhere on the lake. We usually pushed out a hundred yards or so from shore, and then lay down on the thwarts, in the sun, and let the boat drift by the hour whither it would. We seldom talked. It interrupted the Sabbath stillness, and marred the dreams the luxurious rest and indolence brought. The shore all along was indented with deep, curved bays and coves, bordered by narrow sand-beaches; and where the sand ended, the steep mountain-sides rose right up aloft into space— rose up like a vast wall a little out of the perpendicular, and thickly wooded with tall pines.

So singularly clear was the water, that where it was only twenty or thirty feet deep the bottom was so perfectly distinct that the boat seemed floating in the air! Yes, where it was even *eighty* feet deep. Every little pebble was distinct, every speckled trout, every hand's-breadth of sand. Often, as we lay on our faces, a granite boulder, as large as a village church, would start out of the bottom apparently, and seem climbing up rapidly to the surface, till presently it threatened to touch our faces, and we could not resist the impulse to seize an oar and avert the danger. But the boat would float on, and the boulder descend again, and then we could see that when we had been exactly above it, it must still have been twenty or thirty feet below the surface. Down through the transparency of these great depths, the water was not *merely* transparent, but dazzlingly, brilliantly so. All objects seen through it had a bright, strong vividness, not only of outline, but of every minute detail, which they would not have had when seen simply through the same depth of atmosphere. So empty and airy did all spaces seem below us, and so strong was the sense of floating high aloft in mid-nothingness, that we called these boat-excursions "balloon voyages."

We fished a good deal, but we did not average one fish a week. We could see trout by the thousand winging about in the emptiness under us, or sleeping in shoals on the bottom, but they would not bite—they could see the line too plainly, perhaps. We frequently selected the trout we wanted, and rested the bait patiently and persistently on the end of his nose at a depth of eighty feet, but he would only shake it off with an annoyed manner, and shift his position.

We bathed occasionally, but the water was rather chilly, for all it looked so sunny. Sometimes we rowed out to the "blue water," a mile or two from shore. It was as dead blue as indigo there, because of the immense depth. By official measurement the lake in its centre is one thousand five hundred and twenty-five feet deep!

Sometimes, on lazy afternoons, we lolled on the sand in camp, and smoked pipes and read some old well-worn novels. At night, by the camp-fire, we played euchre and seven-up to strengthen the mind—and played them with cards so greasy and defaced that only a whole summer's acquaintance with them could enable the student to tell the ace of clubs from the jack of diamonds.

We never slept in our "house." It never recurred to us, for one thing; and besides, it was built to hold the ground, and that was enough. We did not wish to strain it.

By and by our provisions began to run short, and we went back to the old camp and laid in a new supply. We were gone all day, and reached home again about night-fall, pretty tired and hungry. While Johnny was carrying the main bulk of the provisions up to our "house" for future use, I took the loaf of bread, some slices of bacon, and the coffee-pot, ashore, set them down by a tree, lit a fire, and went back to the boat to get the frying-pan. While I was at this, I heard a shout from Johnny, and looking up I saw that my fire was galloping all over the premises!

Johnny was on the other side of it. He had to run through the flames to get to the lake shore, and then we stood helpless and watched the devastation.

The ground was deeply carpeted with dry pine-needles, and the fire touched them off as if they were gunpowder. It was wonderful to see with what fierce speed the tall sheet of flame traveled! My coffee-pot was gone, and everything with it. In a minute and a half the fire seized upon a dense growth of dry manzanita chapparal six or eight feet high, and then the roaring and popping and crackling was something terrific. We were driven to the boat by the intense heat, and there we remained, spell-bound.

Big Country, Big Fires

Within a half an hour all before us was a tossing, blinding tempest of flame! It went surging up adjacent ridges—surmounted them and disappeared in the cañons beyond—burst into view upon higher and farther ridges, presently—shed a grander illumination abroad, and dove again—flamed out again, directly, higher and still higher up the mountainside—threw out skirmishing parties of fire here and there, and sent them trailing their crimson spirals away among remote ramparts and ribs and gorges, till as far as the eye could reach the lofty mountain-fronts were webbed as it were with a tangled net-work of red lava streams. Away across the water the crags and domes were lit with a ruddy glare, and the firmament above was a reflected hell!

Every feature of the spectacle was repeated in the glowing mirror of the lake! Both pictures were sublime, both were beautiful; but that in the lake had a bewildering richness about it that enchanted the eye and held it with the stronger fascination.

We sat absorbed and motionless through four long hours. We never thought of supper, and never felt fatigue. But at eleven o'clock the conflagration had traveled beyond our range of vision, and then darkness stole down upon the landscape again.

Hunger asserted itself now, but there was nothing to eat. The provisions were all cooked, no doubt, but we did not go to see. We were homeless wanderers again, without any property. Our fence was gone, our house burned down; no insurance. Our pine forest was well scorched, the dead trees all burned up, and our broad acres of manzanita swept away. Our blankets were our usual sand-bed, however, and so we lay down and went to sleep. The next morning we started back to the old camp, but while out a long way from shore, so great a storm came up that we dared not try to land. So I baled out the seas we shipped, and Johnny pulled heavily through the billows till we had reached a point three or four miles beyond camp. The storm was increasing, and it became evident that it was better to take the hazard of beaching the boat than go down in a hundred fathoms of water; so we ran in, with tall white-caps following, and I sat down in the stern-sheets and pointed her head-on to the shore. The instant the bow struck, a wave came over the stern that washed crew and cargo ashore, and saved a deal of trouble. We shivered in the lee of a boulder all the rest of the day, and froze all the night through. We were so starved that we ate up the rest of the Brigade's provisions, and then set out to Carson to tell them about it and ask their forgiveness. It was accorded, upon payment of damages.

We made many trips to the lake after that, and had many a hair-breadth escape and blood-curdling adventure which will never be recorded in any history.

The Big Blowup

STEPHEN J. PYNE

I T MAY BE THE MOST OBSCURE site on the National Register of Historic Places. Rockfall and wild growth clog the entry. The West Fork of Placer Creek splashes a few feet below. It is not an easy place to find. It has the feel of some mythical grotto, a sepulchre, an oracle, the source of a sacred spring like Lourdes. The Nicholson mineshaft is, in truth, all of these, for here, on the 20th of August, 1910, flames burned through conifer stands like prairie grass and came over the ridges, as one survivor recalled, with the sound of a thousand trains rushing over a thousand steel trestles. One ranger said simply, "The mountains roared."

The trek to the site is arduous, not because it is long (it isn't), but because the primary trail, which used to trend to Striped Peak, is abandoned and overgrown, vanishing into a Northern Rockies hillside beneath rockslides, talus, roots, forbs, the slender shafts of willow and alder. A secondary path to the old mineshaft is even more obscure. You need a reason to come here, and you need a tool. You need something sharp to slash through the scrub. You need something durable to grub out steps through the loose rubble and root-clogged slopes. You need a pulaski.

What happened that astonishing summer was that American society and American nature collided with almost tectonic force. Spark, fuel, and wind merged violently and overran 2.6 million acres of dense and variously-disturbed forest from the Selways to the Canadian border. The sparks came from locomotives, settlers, hobo "floaters," backfiring crews, and lightning. The fuel lay in heaps alongside the newly hewn Milwaukee Railway over the Bitterroots, down the St. Joe valley, and across hillsides ripped by mines and logging, and untouched woods primed by drought. The Rockies had experienced a wet winter followed by a dry spring that ratcheted, day by day, into a summer drought, the worst in memory. Duff and canopies that normally wouldn't burn now could. The winds came with the passage of shallow cold fronts, rushing ahead from central Washington and the Palouse and the deserts of eastern Oregon, acting like an enormous bellows that turned valleys into furnaces and side canyons into chimneys. Southwesterly winds rose throughout the day to gale force by early evening, and then shifted to the northwest. Perhaps 75 percent of the total burn occurred during a single 36-hour period that became known as the Big Blowup.

The summer witnessed the first great firefight by the U.S. Forest Service. As the weeks wore on, the fires had alternately crept and swept, thickening during calms into smoke as dense as pea-fog, then flaring into wild rushes through the crowns. The fledgling Forest Service, barely five years old, tried to match them. It rounded up whatever men it could beg, borrow, or buy and shipped them into the backcountry. The regular army contributed another thirty-three companies. The crews established camps, cut firelines along ridgetops, and started backfires. Over and again, one refrain after another, the saga continued of fires contained, of fires escaping, of new fronts laid down. Then the Big Blowup shredded it all. Smoke billowed up in columns dense as volcanic blasts, the fire's convection sucking in air from all sides, snapping off mature larch and white pine like matchsticks, spawning firewhirls like miniature tornadoes, flinging sparks like a sandstorm. Crews dropped their saws and mattocks and fled. That day seventy-eight firefighters died. One crew on the Cabinet National Forest lost four men; one on the Pend Oreille lost two; the rest of the dead fell on the Coeur d'Alene.

The Coeur d'Alene was ground zero. In the St. Joe Mountains between Wallace and Avery, Idaho, some 1,800 firefighters and two companies of the 25th Infantry manned the lines when the Blowup struck. A crew north of Avery survived when Ranger William Rock led them to a previously burned area, except one man who panicked and shot himself, twice, rather than face the flames. A crew on Stevens Peak lit an escape fire in bear grass, then lost it when the winds veered, and one man died when he stood up and breathed the searing air. A crew at the Bullion Mine split, the larger party found its way into a side tunnel, the rest, eight in all, died in the main shaft. On Setzer Creek some twenty-eight men, four never identified even as to name, perished as they fled and fought their way uphill only to collapse in a ring of death. A gaggle of nineteen spilled off the ridge overlooking Big Creek and sought refuge in the Dittman cabin. When the roof caught fire, they ran out. The first eighteen died where they fell in a heap, along with five horses and two bears; the nineteenth, Peter Kinsley, twisted his ankle in crossing the threshold and collapsed to the ground, where he found a sheath of fresh air; two days later he crawled, still alive, out of a creek. Another group dashed to the Beauchamp cabin where they met a party of homesteaders. A white pine thundered to the ground, crushing two men immediately while trapping a third by his ankle; he died, screaming, in the flames. Another seven squirmed into a root cellar where they were roasted alive.

And then there was the crew cobbled together by Ranger Ed Pulaski. He had gone to Wallace for supplies and was returning on the morning of the 20th when the winds picked up tempo, casting flame in a broadening path. He began to meet stragglers, and then a large gang spalled off from the main ridge camp. All in all he gathered forty-five men, and with the smoke thickening in stygian darkness, turned to race down the ravine of the West Fork toward Wallace. One man lagged and died in the flames. Pulaski hustled the rest over the trail before tucking them into a mine shaft. Then he hurried downcanyon with a wet gunnysack over his head before returning and herding the group into a larger tunnel, the Nicholson mineshaft, which had a seep running through it. Pulaski tried to hold the flames out of the entry timbers and the smoke out of the mine with hatfuls of water and blankets. But by now the men were senseless. They heard nothing but the din, felt nothing but heat, saw nothing but flame and darkness, smelled only smoke and sweat. As the firestorm swirled by the entrance, someone yelled that he, at least, was getting out. At the entry, rudely silhouetted by flames, he met Ed Pulaski, pistol drawn, threatening to shoot the first man who tried to flee.

The Big Blowup

By the 1990s the American fire establishment was a wonder of the world. It could field crews and aircraft to fight fire in numbers larger than the military of some Third World nations. It also seemed to many critics, and to not a few of its own members, to have broken. In 1994 wildland fires burned 2.5 million acres of the public lands, killed thirty-four firefighters, and swallowed up $965 million off-budget; the summer of 2000 burned still more land, more intensely, and may have doubled the costs. For all this, a century of federal protection had created a crisis of forest health. Many lands suffered either too much or too little fire. They experienced deluges of wildfire and droughts of the fire famine.

The full costs of fire suppression became public knowledge, along with the understanding that firefighting alone could not contain wildfire. But perhaps controlled burning could. That naïve formulation finally ended in the spring of 2000 as the National Park Service kindled two prescribed fires under extreme conditions. One escaped Bandelier National Monument and scoured Los Alamos. The other forced the evacuation of the North Rim of the Grand Canyon. It seemed that the American fire establishment could neither adequately fight nor light fires.

Yet it is possible that the breakdown is not simply one of execution but rather the upshot of a flawed debate, a false choice between one practice or the other, that we either had to start or to suppress. But how did this dichotomy arise? Why these choices and no others? The options became polarized in the usual way, by politics, personalities, and professional pride. In this case the choices also had fire to catalyze the social chemistry. With uncanny timing, this happened as the fire crews on the Coeur d'Alene were fighting for their lives.

The idea that fire protection on the public lands meant firefighting was, in 1910, a novelty. Most of the general public was indifferent or hostile to aggressive fire control, excepting fires that immediately threatened property or lives. Rural Americans relied on fire—burned everything from ditches to fallow fields—and accepted the occasional wildfire as they did floods or tornadoes. The argument that one ought to systematically fight the flames, all of them, seemed odd, academic, and ridiculously expensive. The assumption was that wildfires would go the way of wild animals as the feral landscapes that fed them were domesticated into farms, pastures, and towns. The reservation of extensive lands for public parks and forests, however, broke that laissez-faire logic. Wildland

Big Country, Big Fires

fire would flourish because wildlands prone to fire would persist. In retrospect the choices are obvious: either convert those lands to something less combustible or do the burning yourself. And that was what critics at the time proposed: abolish the reserves or inoculate the forests by wholesale burning. Better fires of choice than fires of chance.

But in 1910 those options seemed stickier. The national forests existed to preserve the forests, not wipe them away. If federal agents logged them off, they would be no better than lumber companies or homesteaders. If they adopted wholesale burning, the lands would be no differently managed than if they had not been reserved at all. To forestry officials, however, it appeared plausible that clearing people out of the landscape, fielding patrols, and attacking the wayward flames would be enough. Several decades of "improvements"—roads, trails, telephone lines, lookout towers—would stamp fire out of the scene. This was, according to the received wisdom of European forestry, what had to be done, and what the great colonial powers were attempting in India, Algeria, Australia, and Africa. It was what Americans had to do.

Yet the critics were adamant. The doctrine of light burning, or the "Indian way," as it was called, was remarkably pervasive. Almost all categories of settlers burned, and saw no reason to cease. An occasional fire would escape and perhaps raze the occasional town, but that, regrettably, was the price of progress. Smoke in the woods was the complement to smoke from factories. Where land was not farmed but logged or grazed, the preferred means of dampening wildfire was to lightly burn over the understory as often as the fuels would allow. In California, for example, major timber owners hired gangs to prepare sites for burning by filling basal cavities with dirt or raking around snags. They burned after a couple inches of summer rain had fallen. The fires burned weakly because they had not much to burn; they scorched perhaps half the area targeted; they smoldered in windfall. That was how most people living on the frontier wanted matters, and they found intellectuals to back them up. Advocates included the poet Joaquin Miller, the novelist Stewart Edward White, the state engineer of California William Hall, and the Southern Pacific Railroad. Not every forest could burn this way, but most of those that mattered to people could. Light burning by the American Indian, after all, was what had created the forests for which everyone now lusted.

Yet foresters detested and denounced the practice. However slight its

The Big Blowup

apparent damage, they knew in every fiber of their professional being that it was evil. It sacrificed future growth to current old growth. It abraded soils, gnawed the bases of the big timber, abetted frontier habits of sloth, and promoted folk indifference to the cause of conservation. It was the lost nail that would end with a lost war. To convince the public otherwise—especially those who lived on the land—demanded decades of trench warfare.

In August 1910, the quarrel took a quantum leap when *Sunset* magazine printed a direct challenge, matching arguments point by point and suggesting that the regular army do the burning so that private landowners could protect themselves from federal malfeasance. Then, after the Big Blowup, Secretary of Interior Richard Ballinger championed the cause in a national press release. Clearly, he argued, the Forest Service had failed in its firefight; another strategy was worth pursuing. Gifford Pinchot and Chief Forester Henry Graves blasted the argument in the *New York Times*. Fighting fires in forests, Pinchot enunciated carefully, as though to idiots, was no different than fighting fires in cities. Left unsaid was the corollary: no one would burn off carpets to protect houses from roof fires.

Their polar pronouncements placed the Great Fires squarely in the political firestorm that was about to consume the administration of William Howard Taft. Gifford Pinchot had been a favorite of the Roosevelt administration—had had free access to TR, had been allowed to trespass across bureaucratic borders, and, most critically, had convinced the president to transfer the forest reserves from the fumbling General Land Office in the Interior Department to the Bureau of Forestry, which Pinchot oversaw for the Agriculture Department. That happened in 1905. Roosevelt also brought in Richard Ballinger to clean up the GLO, to bring it up to the standards of a Progressive-era bureau. Ballinger did, but posted legal guards along the agency borders and told Pinchot to steer clear. Then Taft arrived as Roosevelt's annointed successor. Like Ballinger, he insisted that Pinchot hold to his own turf, and worse, he appointed Ballinger as secretary of interior.

Pinchot found himself, in relative terms, marginalized, and he believed that Taft was similarly marginalizing the grand scheme of Rooseveltian conservation, which for him had assumed the status of a political crusade. When a murky matter involving Ballinger and Alaskan coal lands surfaced, Pinchot seized on it to force Ballinger into disrepute and eventually a resignation. No formal charges of illegality and corruption were ever filed, but Pinchot and his allies launched a campaign to discredit Ballinger in the court of public opinion. Someone had to go, Pinchot insisted, and on January 7, 1910, Taft decided that that someone was Pinchot and fired the chief forester.

The next few months, as congressional committees began their own inquiry, Pinchot, the Forest Service, and their allies sought to vindicate the patriarchal Pinchot by vilifying Ballinger. While both men insisted they were "Rooseveltian conservationists," they represented two very different versions. Pinchot stood for the new wave of technocratic, federal administration; Ballinger, an old guard, sensitive to local politics and western ambitions. These differences had practical consequences. They mattered, for example, in how each person responded to the problem of fire. For both, the Great Fires became a test of larger philosophies. One had to choose between them. One had either to suppress fires or to start them.

He came to shortly after midnight. No one else in the tunnel stirred, and at the entrance he found the body of Ed Pulaski crumpled in a heap. He crawled out into the dark and began to stagger toward Wallace. There he met the supervisor of the Coeur d'Alene, William Weigle, who had returned from his own misadventures an hour before. The eastern third of Wallace was afire. He told Weigle that everyone else at the Nicholson mineshaft was dead. Weigle organized a rescue mission.

By the time that party arrived, others in the shaft had roused themselves, including Big Ed himself. The creek water was hot and alkaline, too foul to drink. They sucked in deep breaths of air still heavily laden with smoke. They counted off and realized that five were missing—they had died where they passed out on the tunnel floor, probably drowned in the muck and waters that had ponded behind the fallen bodies. Pulaski suffered more than most. He was temporarily blind and his lungs were so charged with soot and seared with heat that he could breath only haltingly. Their way lit by flaming snags and logs, they staggered through the ash to Wallace.

As reports screamed across telegraph lines, it was not clear how the fires would be interpreted. Those on the ground considered the Great

The Big Blowup

Firefight as a rout. On the Lolo forest, supervisor Elers Koch labeled the summer a "complete failure." More than seventy-eight firefighters had died, the Forest Service had expended almost a million dollars over budget, and the flames had roared over the Bitterroots with no more pause than the Clarks Fork over a boulder. At national headquarters, foresters fretted whether the Great Fires might be the funeral pyre of the besieged Forest Service. In fact, those far removed from the flames saw them otherwise. They chose to see Pulaski's stand, not his flight. They saw a gallant gesture, not an act of desperation. The Forest Service's critics claimed the Service had been granted ample resources and had failed. Its defenders claimed the Service had failed only because it had not been given enough.

Quickly the political tide turned in the Service's favor. The agency successfully defended its 1911 budget. The Weeks Act that would provide for the eastern expansion of the national forests by purchase and for federal–state cooperative programs in fire control, which had been stalled for years, broke through the congressional logjam in February. In March a beleaguered Ballinger asked to resign. Foresters redoubled their efforts to crush light burning, and all it implied. It was, they sniffed, mere "Paiute forestry." Light burners belonged with perpetual motion mechanics and spoon-bending psychics.

The young Forest Service had the memory of the fires spliced into its institutional genes. The Great Fires were the first great crisis faced by Henry Graves, Pinchot's handpicked successor. The next three chief foresters—William Greeley, Robert Stuart, and Ferdinand Augustus Silcox—had all been personally on the scene of the fires, had counted the costs, and had buried the dead. They seized upon "smoke in the woods" as their yardstick of progress. Not until this entire generation passed from the scene would the Forest Service consider fire as fit for anything, save suppression. Three months after the Big Blowup, Silcox wrote that the lesson of the fires was that they were wholly preventable. All it took was more money, more men, more trails, more will.

In 1935 Gus Silcox, then chief forester, had the opportunity to reconsider. Large fires had ripped through the Selway the previous summer and sparked a review in which the Forest Service itself admitted the lands it was protecting at such cost were in worse shape than they had been when the agency assumed control. Field critics observed that the

Big Country, Big Fires

Service was unable to contain backcountry burning. Scientific critics had announced at the January meeting of the Society of American Foresters that fire was useful and perhaps essential to the silviculture of the longleaf pine. One critic observed bitterly that this was the first time such facts had become public. And a cultural criticism burst forth as well. Elers Koch noted that the pursuit of fire into the hinterlands—mostly by roads—was destroying some of the cultural value of those lands. The Lolo Pass, through which Lewis and Clark had breached the Rockies, was no more, he lamented, having been bulldozed into a highway. All this landed on Silcox's desk. His reply was to promulgate, in April, the 10 A.M. Policy, which stipulated as a universal standard that every fire should be controlled by 10 o'clock the morning following its report. The veteran of 1910 replied by attempting to squash fire, to allow it no sanctuary, to tolerate no qualifications, to apply the full force of the Civilian Conservation Corps and the federal treasury. He would refight the Great Fires, and this time he would win.

Beneath the surface storms of 1910 politics, moreover, ran a deep current of cultural sentiment. This was an activist age—of political reform, of nation-building, of pragmatism as a formal philosophy. One of its mightiest intellects, William James, published his last essay in the same month as the Big Blowup. "The Moral Equivalent of War" argued to redirect to more constructive purposes the growing militarism James saw boiling over in Western civilization. Why, he reasoned, could there not be a moral equivalent of war as there was a mechanical equivalent of heat? Why not divert those martial enthusiasms into a campaign against humanity's common enemy, the forces of nature, to replace wars against other people? The point was to do, but to do rightly.

James had written the essay in Europe. He returned to America, terminally ill, even as Ed Pulaski and William Rock and Joe Halm were standing before flames unlike any short of the Apocalypse. He hurried to his country home in New Hampshire and lay dying as the smoke from the Big Blowup passed overhead and turned the New England sun to a copper disk. The firefight as moral equivalent of war. Why not, indeed?

To an astonishing degree the Great Fires contain, virtually in all their pieces, voices, and avatars, the grand narrative of American fire. The politics. The contrast between federal and state fire protection. The controversy between fire-setting and fire-suppressing. The use of the emergency fire fund (1910 saw a twentyfold increase over previous expenditures). The mass hirings and the appeal to the military. Lavish meals in fire camps. Wholesale salvage logging. The (attempted) rehabilitation of burned landscapes. Inaccurate and self-serving reports. The confused memorializing of the dead. The stories of crews saved and crews felled. The metaphor of the firefight as battlefield. A platoon even hauled away an injured bear cub. The profound impact on persons and institutions: the Great Fires acted on the Forest Service as Valley Forge had the young American republic, or the Long March, Red China. Almost every fire story since has its rhetorical structure forged in the flames of 1910, and no fire since has harbored all the parts so completely. Nearly every incident, controversy, or idea had its rehearsal in the Great Fires. Fundamentally the same story plays out at Blackwater, Pepper Run, Mann Gulch, Rattlesnake, Inaja, Loop, South Canyon, or the next-millennial fires of 2000. The fires stayed.

Most of the people who fought them, however, did not. They moved on, transferred, climbed up the ranks. A few did hold, Ed Pulaski among them, homesteading bureaucratically in Wallace. At 40 he had been older than most. He was married and had an adopted daughter and a house and remained on the Wallace district until a car accident in 1930 forced him into retirement. Because he stayed, he never left the aftermath of the Great Fires.

He refused to become a celebrity. He wrote only once about his experiences, for an essay contest sponsored by *American Forestry*, and that because he needed money to pay for eye surgery. (Through bureaucratic fumbling, he had received no compensation for his fire injuries.) He tended the two mass graves hastily dug at the Wallace cemetery for those who had died and were otherwise unclaimed, and in fact unidentified. He pestered the Forest Service for a more fitting memorial, which finally arrived in 1921. He rebuilt the trails blocked by blowdown; assisted with timber cruising for salvage logging; helped replant the hillsides; upgraded the fire-control organization. When, a decade later, the Missoula office sought to collect the remembered stories of the Great Fires, he declined to contribute. What he had done was known. More words didn't matter.

He remained a field man, and, as those who knew him often

remarked, he remained a man who took pride in the things he could make with his hands. Practice, not theory, would decide the future. Tools, not ideas, determined what could actually happen. He had led his crew by example, not by exhortation. Meaning resided in acts, not texts. It was fitting then that, after the burns, he devised a combination tool, half ax and half mattock, to send into the field. There was not much enthusiasm when he first presented the device to forest supervisors. But he persisted, lengthening the shaft, widening the ax, shrinking the mattock, all in his backyard forge. He sent out the tool with smokechasers. Only in the field, he insisted, could its value be tested. They soon took it to heart. By 1920 so did the Northern Region of the Forest Service, which ordered commercial companies to manufacture it out of industrial steel. Along with the shovel, the "pulaski tool" became the basic implement of fire control, and the one tool both universal and unique to wildland fire.

Contemplate that tool. Three parts make it up: the ax, the hoe, the handle. It's a practical, not an elegant, tool. Cutting and grubbing don't balance easily. It's awkward. It's ungainly. Yet it works, and it embodies the saga of Big Ed and the Big Blowup as nothing else could. Every time a firefighter hefts a pulaski, he or she is retelling the story of the Great Fires.

So, too, an institution like that which governs America's wildland fires requires three things. It needs practice, poetry, and policy. It needs practice to make things happen on the ground. It needs poetry to inspire people, both those within its ranks and the general public, to make them understand and believe in its purpose. And it needs policy, like a handle, to hold those two opposite-facing edges together.

The Great Fires had it all. They had story, purpose, tools. Modern fire management does not; it holds policy like an empty handle. Fire officers know they cannot continue with the Great Firefight alone. They know fire in the West will return, either wild or by choice; but come it will. If contemporary fire agencies had the chance to replay the light-burning controversy, they would almost certainly choose fire lighting over fire fighting as a basis for wildland stewardship. They know the problem was not fire suppression, but the abolition of controlled burning, that magnificent and misguided attempt at fire's wholesale exclusion. Yet they know by now that an equally scaled reintroduction isn't possible. They should know that the issue is not fire but its regime, that fire synthesizes its surroundings, that it takes its character from its context, that flame is not a kind of ecological pixie dust that, sprinkled over land, will transform the bad and ugly into the good and beautiful. Messed-up forests only yield messed-up fires.

The truth is, policy by itself is incompetent. Contemporary fire management has policy aplenty—has had adequate policies for twenty or thirty years to do what needs to be done without seeing hard results on the ground. Turning existing policy inside-out is not likely, alone, to reverse overgrown woods and scrub-infested savannas. Pumping money into controlled fire will do no more good than sluicing money into fire control. Contemporary fire management doesn't need more policy, dumb as an empty handle. It needs a hybrid head of practice and poetry to swing at policy's end.

It needs iron, forge, flame, smith, and vision. It needs knowledge bred into the bone by long practice. It needs flames equivalent, catalytically, to those of the Great Fires. It needs someone to stand before those flames. It needs a story to explain them. It needs a site that ninety years hence someone can hack into and know that here Creation occurred. It needs a Pulaski.

Part II

Of Fire and the Landscape

Fire drives out fire.
—English Proverb

In the 1840s a new animal, the settler, intervened in the prairie battle. He didn't mean to, he just plowed enough fields to deprive the prairie of its immemorial ally: fire. Seedling oaks forthwith romped over the grasslands in legions, and what had been the prairie region became a region of woodlot farms. If you doubt this story, go count the rings on any set of stumps on any "ridge" woodlot in southwest Wisconsin. All the trees except the oldest veterans date back to the 1850s and the 1860s, and this was when fires ceased on the prairie.

—Aldo Leopold, *A Sand County Almanac,* 1949

One could not ask for a more visionary naturalist to lead the way into the next era of wildfire and writing in America than Aldo Leopold. The pioneering conservationist was years ahead of his time when he penned *A Sand County Almanac,* just as he had been twenty-five years prior in writing about the role of fire in southern Arizona. Throughout his career, Leopold was a pioneer, stubbornly challenging beliefs and values concerning wilderness and the natural environment. In writing about the grassy foothills district he watched over in the Southwest, Leopold carries forth that practice and questions many of the traditional beliefs about fire in the natural landscape. Leopold was more aware of the rhythms and patterns of nature than many of his time, and through his work, helped to usher in a new era of thoughts and feelings about wildfire.

The twentieth century would witness dramatic changes in the way Americans related to fire. Organized suppression of fires saw its start during the drastic and deadly fire season of 1910. The 1930s saw the introduction of Civilian Conservation Corps (CCC) troops and forest rangers with firefighting equipment, and by the 1940s, the first smoke-jumpers were parachuting from the sky. The sciences of forestry and fire science would sprout and grow under the tutelage of Leopold's counterparts, greatly affecting how land stewards cared for and managed public lands. Wildland firefighting would establish itself as a career, albeit a seasonal one, with challenge, excitement, and danger wrapped up in the job description.

Of Fire and the Landscape

From the mid-1920s through the mid-1980s, the way Americans related to the natural environment would undergo the most drastic changes of all. No longer was wilderness seen as untamable. This era saw the first use of pesticides, widespread clearcuts across public national forests, as well as the building of the Hoover, Grand Coulee, and Glen Canyon dams. Widespread fire suppression became the norm. As knowledge about fire's role in the environment grew, so did the value of America's forests for paper and wood products. Frequently, economic values prevailed.

The fire research of this era had its origins in the science of forestry, with emphasis on the physical study of fire behavior. The end goal was to apply scientific knowledge to fire suppression techniques and strategy. By the mid-1960s, a new movement within the field sought to understand the environmental role of fire through examining biological systems. A new day for fire management was born when fire research began to include the basics of biology, including vegetation succession, mineral release in soils, air and water quality, and the effects of fire on native plants and animals. As fire ecology sprouted into a developed science, the idea that wildfire and natural ecosystems exist side by side as intertwined entities became more commonplace and brought into question the tradition of fire suppression.

This paradigm shift resulted in accepting fire as a legitimate component of many environments, with a natural role in maintaining the health and equilibrium of ecosystems. Rightly so, as fire functions as a system disturbance factor, removing organisms and opening up space for colonization by new or different species. Disturbance is important because of the effects it has on organisms, from creating new niches and space to colonize, to recycling nutrients and "weeding out" unfit species. The power of fire is not to be underestimated; it is one of few natural events that can regularly kill mature plants and large trees. This makes fire a crucial agent in restructuring vegetation communities, as new openings provide the opportunity for drastically altering the flora of a particular ecosystem.

Consider Nevada's Great Basin, wide flat valleys spaced between rows of craggy mountain ranges. These valleys once were the home of immense and spectacular sagebrush plains, thick and pungent gray-green shrubs supporting diverse wildlife, from herds of mule deer and pronghorn antelope to the threatened sage grouse, the pygmy rabbit, and the sagebrush lizard. While the Great Basin is historically accustomed to the seasonal appearance of fire, it was on a smaller and less intense scale than the fires that sweep across the valleys today. Add cheatgrass, the nonnative species from Eurasia that has invaded and infested these fields, and witness drastic and fundamental changes in the vegetation and animal composition across the Great Basin.

Cheatgrass had a little help, in the form of wildfire, in generating all this change. Cheatgrass produces abundant seeds, spreading quickly and easily with cattle and human traffic. It competes with native grasses and brush and easily dominates with its deep roots that monopolize scarce water supplies. When a fire sweeps through, the carpet of dry cheatgrass acts as an explosive fuel, carrying wind-driven flames rapidly across a valley floor. Sagebrush on the other hand, drops its tiny seeds right around the plant, with much lower dispersal. Fire frequently kills sagebrush, and when a fire blows through a sagebrush stand, it can take more than a decade for it to return to preburn conditions. With the new presence of cheatgrass, sagebrush stands are burning every two to five years, leaving no time for a healthy recovery. As fire disturbs this ecosystem, opening space for new species, cheatgrass rushes in to take over, and eventually wins the land, establishing dominance over the troubled native plants. This loss of sagebrush is more than a loss of a plant community, it is a loss of habitat for the many animals that depend on it for food and shelter. Once again we are reminded how all living things are connected, and how important each part is to the whole.

American writers of this era captured the changing attitudes, beliefs, and knowledge about wildfire in their work. Fire no longer existed in the background, however. It took center stage as a worthy and common topic for writers from all genres. As wildland fire, fire ecology, and firefighting became integrated into the American literary consciousness; voices from all walks of life and regions of the country spoke out with their experiences and views. Norman Maclean's account of the 1949 Mann Gulch fire and the tragedy of one August afternoon would become a classic in wildland fire writing. Margaret Millar, a noted mystery writer, took time to detail the wildfires near her Southern California home. More recently, Roger Caras describes a wildfire through the eyes of a wild panther in the Florida wetlands.

Of Fire and the Landscape

These are the writers that would influence and shape the next generation of wildfire writers and firefighters. Edward Abbey takes note of his season as a fire lookout in Glacier National Park, written the year I was born. Twenty-one years later I would find myself in a fire tower, manipulating a firefinder, and pondering my new found relationship to fire and the landscape shaped by it. Ed Engle's depiction of a seasonal firefighter inspired future firefighters to chronicle their experiences on the fireline. Norman Maclean's son, John, would carry on the tradition of his father in chronicling the tragedy of a fatality fire, and the work of Leopold and his contemporaries would not only further the fields of forestry and environmental science, but would also inspire the ecological awareness of the next generation.

These writers are the crucial link in the history of American wildfire literature. Elements of conflict surface in the presentation of new ideas and the challenging of old beliefs. Distinct reactions and ecological explanations emerge as people become more involved in the study, the suppression, and the interactions of and with wildfire. Emotions expand and fluctuate, from the sorrow of Mann Gulch to the calm sense of renewal surrounding the Santa Barbara hills of Millar's home. Wildfire has become a way to relate to nature, to growth and change, and to death. These writers are interpreting nature through a growing relationship with fire, not just in observing the marks of fire on the landscape. Just as these writers influenced thinking on wildfire, wildfire influenced their lives, in subtle and enduring ways. Edward Abbey would work in more than one lookout tower, watching for rising smoke against a deep green canopy. Norman Maclean was so moved by the story of a fire in his home state of Montana that he wrote about it decades later. Ed Engle spent season after season returning to firecrews, and sadly, Aldo Leopold met his untimely death helping neighbors battle a grass fire.

Grass, Brush, Timber and Fire in Southeast Arizona

ALDO LEOPOLD

ONE OF THE FIRST THINGS which a forester hears when he begins to travel among the cow-camps of the southern Arizona foothills is the story of how the brush has "taken the country." At first he is inclined to classify this with the legend, prevalent among the old-timers of some of the northern states, about the hard winters that occurred years ago. The belief in the encroachment of brush, however, is often remarkably circumstantial. A cow-man will tell about how in the 1880s on a certain mesa he could see his cattle several miles, whereas now on the same mesa he can not even find them in a day's hunt. The legend of brush encroachment must be taken seriously.

Along with it goes an almost universal story about the great number of cattle which the southern Arizona foothills carried in the old days. The old timers say that there is not one cow now where there used to be 10, 20, 30, and so on. This again might be dismissed but for the figures cited as to the brandings of old cattle outfits, of which the location and area of range are readily determinable. This story likewise must be taken seriously.

In some quarters the forester will find a naive belief that the two stories represent cause and effect, that by putting more cattle on the range the old days of prosperity for the range industry might somehow be restored.

Of Fire and the Landscape

The country in which the forester finds these prevalent beliefs consists of rough foothills corresponding in elevation to the woodland type. Above lie the forests of western yellow pine. Below lie the semi-desert ranges characteristic of the southern Arizona plains. The area we are dealing with is large, comprising the greater part of the Prescott, Tonto, Coronado, and Crook National Forests as well as much range outside the Forests. The brush that has "taken the country" comprises dozens of species, in which various oaks, manzanita, mountain mahogany and ceanothus predominate. Here and there alligator junipers of very large size occur. Along the creek bottoms the brush becomes a hardwood forest.

Five facts are so conspicuous in this foothill region as to immediately arrest the attention of a forester.

1. Widespread abnormal erosion. This is universal along watercourses with sheet erosion in certain formations, especially granite.
2. Universal fire scars on all the junipers, oaks, or other trees old enough to bear them.
3. Old juniper stumps, often leveled to the ground, evidently by fire.
4. Much juniper reproduction merging to pine reproduction in the upper limits of the type.
5. Great thrift and size in the junipers or other woodland species which have survived fire.

A closer examination reveals the following additional facts:

First, the reproduction is remarkably even aged. A few ring counts immediately establish the significant fact that none of it is over 40 years old. It is therefore contemporaneous with settlement; this region having been settled and completely stocked with cattle in the 1880s.

Second, the reproduction is encroaching on the parks. These parks, in spite of heavy grazing, still contain some grass. It would appear, therefore, that this reproduction had something to do with grass.

Third, one frequently sees manzanita, young juniper or young pines growing within a foot or two of badly fire-scarred juniper trees. These growths being very susceptible to fire damage, they could obviously not have survived the fires which produced the scars. Ring counts show that these growths are less than 40 years old. One is forced to the conclusion that there have been no widespread fires during the last 40 years.

Fourth, a close examination of the erosion indicates that it, too, dates back about 40 years and is therefore contemporaneous with settlement, removal of grass, and cessation of fires.

These observations coordinate themselves in the following theory of what has happened: Previous to the settlement of the country, fires started by lightning and Indians kept the brush thin, kept the juniper and other woodland species decimated, and gave the grass the upper hand with respect to possession of the soil. In spite of the periodic fires, this grass prevented erosion. Then came the settlers with their great herds of livestock. These ranges had never been grazed and they grazed them to death, thus removing the grass and automatically checking the possibility of widespread fires. The removal of the grass relieved the brush species of root competition and of fire damage and thereby caused them to spread and "take the country." The removal of grass-root competition and of fire damage brought in the reproduction. In brief, the climax type is and always had been woodland. The thick grass and thin brush of pre-settlement days represented a temporary type. The substitution of grazing for fire brought on a transition of thin grass and thick brush. This transition type is now reverting to the climax type—woodland.

There may be other theories which would coordinate these observable phenomena, but if there are such theories nobody has propounded them, and I have been unable to formulate them.

One of the most interesting checks of the foregoing theory is the behavior of species like manzanita and piñon. These species are notoriously susceptible to fire damage at all ages. Take manzanita: One finds innumerable localities where manzanita thickets are being suppressed and obliterated by pine or juniper reproduction. The particular manzanita characteristic of the region (*Archtostaphylos pungens*) is propagated by brush fires, seedling (not coppice) reproduction taking the ground whenever a fire has killed the other brush species or reduced them to coppice. It is easy to think back to the days when these manzanita thickets, now being killed, were first established by a fire in what was then grass and brush. Cattle next removed the grass. Pine and juniper then reproduced due to the absence of grass and fire, and are now overtopping the manzanita. Take piñon: It is naturally a component of the climax woodland type but mature piñons are hardly to be found in the region; just a specimen here and there sufficient to perpetuate the species which has evidently been decimated through centuries of fires. Nevertheless today there is a large proportion of piñon in the woodland reproduction which is coming in under some of the Prescott brushfields.

Another interesting check is found in the present movement of type boundaries. Yellow pine is reproducing down hill into the woodland type. Juniper is reproducing down hill into the semi-desert type. This down-hill movement of type lines is so conspicuous and so universal as to establish beyond a doubt that the virgin condition previous to settlement represented a temporary type due to some kind of damage, and completely refutes the possible assumption that the virgin conditions were climax and the present tendency is away from rather than toward a climax.

A third interesting check is found in the parks. In general there are two alternative hypotheses for Southwestern parks—the one assuming chemical or physical soil conditions unfavorable to forests and the other assuming the exclusion of forests by damage. When the occasional forest tree found in any park is scrubby, it indicates in general defective soil conditions. When the occasional forest tree shows vigor and thrift, it indicates that the park was established by damage and that the soil is suitable. Nothing could be more conspicuous than the vigor and thrift of the ancient junipers scattered through the parks of the southern Arizona foothills. We may safely assume that these parks were not caused by defective soil conditions. That they were caused by grass fires is evidenced by the survival of grass species in spite of the extra heavy grazing which occurs in them and by the universal fire scars that prevail on the old junipers in them. The fact that they are now reproducing to juniper clinches the argument.

A fourth check bears on the hypothesis that the virgin grass was heavy enough to carry severe fires. The check consists in the occurrence of "islands" where topography has prevented grazing. One will find small benches high on the face of precipitous cliffs which, in spite of poor and dry soil, bear an amazing stand of grasses simply because they have never been grazed. One even finds huge blocks of stone at the base of cliffs where a little soil has gathered on the top of the block and a thrifty stand of grasses survives simply because livestock could not get at it.

The most impressive check of all is the occurrence of junipers evidently killed by a singe fire from 50 years to many centuries ago, on areas where there is now neither brush nor grass and where the junipers were so scattered (as evidenced by their remains) that it is absolutely necessary to assume a connecting medium. If the connecting medium had been brush it could hardly have been totally wiped out because neither fire nor grazing exterminates a brushfield. It is necessary to assume that the connecting medium consisted of grass. It is significant that the above described phenomenon occurs mostly on granitic formations where it is easy to think that a heavy stand of grass might have been exterminated by even moderate grazing due to the loose nature of the soil.

Assuming that all the foregoing theory is correct, let us now consider what it teaches us about erosion. Why has erosion been enormously augmented during the last 40 years? Why has not the encroachment of brush checked the erosion which was induced by the removal of the grass? Why did not the fires of pre-settlement days cause as much erosion as the grazing of post-settlement days?

It is obvious at the start that these questions can not be answered without rejecting some of our traditional theories of erosion. The substance of these traditional theories and the extent to which they must be amended before they can be applied to the Southwest, I have discussed elsewhere. It will be well to repeat, however, that the acceptance of my theory as to the ecology of these brushfields carries with it the acceptance of the fact that at least in this region grass is a much more effective conserver of watersheds than foresters were at first willing to admit, and that grazing is the prime factor in destroying watershed values. In rough topography grazing always means some degree of localized overgrazing, and localized overgrazing means earth-scars. All recent experimentation indicates that earth-scars are the big causative agent of erosion. An excellent example is cited by Bates, who shows that the logging road built to denude Area B at Wagon Wheel Gap has caused more siltage than the denudation itself. Another conspicuous example is on the GOS cattle range in the Gila Forest, where earth-scars due to concentration of cattle along the water-courses have caused an entire trout stream to be buried by detritus, in spite of the fact that conservative range management had preserved the remainder of the watershed in an excellent condition.

Let us now consider the bearing of this theory on Forest administration. We have learned that during the pre-settlement period of no grazing and severe fires, erosion was not abnormally active. We have

Of Fire and the Landscape

learned that during the post-settlement period of no fires and severe grazing, erosion became exceedingly active. Has our administrative policy applied these facts?

It has not. Until very recently we have administered the southern Arizona Forests on the assumption that while overgrazing was bad for erosion, fire was worse, and that therefore we must keep the brush hazard grazed down to the extent necessary to prevent serious fires.

In making this assumption we have accepted the traditional theory as to the place of fire and forests in erosion, and rejected the plain story written on the face of Nature. He who runs may read that it was not until fires ceased and grazing began that abnormal erosion occurred. We have likewise rejected the story written in our own fire statistics, which shows that on the Tonto Forest only about ⅓ of 1% of the hazard area burns over each year, and that it would therefore take 300 years for fire to cover the forest once. Even if the more conservative grazing policy which now prevails should largely enhance the present brush hazard by restoring a little grass, neither the potential danger of fire damage nor the potential cost of fire control could compare with the existing watershed damage. Moreover the reduction of the brush hazard by grazing is to a larger degree impossible. This brush that has "taken the country" consists of many species, varying greatly in palatability. Heavy grazing of the palatable species would simply result in the unpalatable species closing in, and our hazard would still be there.

There is one point with respect to which both past policy and present policy are correct, and that is the paramount value of watersheds. The old policy simply erred in its diagnoses of how to conserve the watershed. The range industry on the Tonto Forest represents a present capital value of around three millions. Since his is about one-third of the total Roosevelt Reservoir drainage we may assume roughly that the range industry affecting the Reservoir is worth nine millions. The Roosevelt Dam and the irrigation works of the Salt River Valley represent a cash expense by the Government of around twelve millions. The agricultural lands dependent upon this irrigation system are worth about fifty millions, not counting dependent industries. Grazing interests worth nine millions, therefore, must be balanced against agricultural interests worth sixty-two millions. To the extent that there is a conflict

Grass, Brush, Timber and Fire in Southeast Arizona

between the existence of the range industry and the permanence of reclamation, there can be no doubt that the range industry must give way.

In discussing administrative policy, I have tried to make three points clear: First, 15 years of Forest administration were based on an incorrect interpretation of ecological facts and were, therefore, in part misdirected. Second, this error of interpretation has now been recognized and administrative policy corrected accordingly. Third, while there can be no doubt about the enormous value of European traditions to American forestry, this error illustrates that there can also be no doubt about the great danger of European traditions to American forestry; this error also illustrates that there can be no doubt about the great danger of European traditions uncritically accepted and applied, especially in such complex fields as erosion.

The present situation in the southern Arizona brushfields may be summed up administratively as follows:

1. There has been great damage to the watershed resources.
2. There has been great benefit to the timber resources.
3. There has been great damage to the range resources.

Whether the benefit to timber could have been obtained with lesser damage to watersheds and ranges is an academic question dealing with bygones and need not be discussed. Our present job is to conserve the benefit to timber and minimize the damage to watershed and range in so far as technical skill and good administration can do it. Wholesale exclusion of grazing is neither skill nor administration, and should be used only as a last resort. The problem which faces us constitutes a challenge to our technical competency as foresters—a challenge we have hardly as yet answered, much less actually attempted to meet. We are dealing right now with a fraction of a cycle involving centuries. We can not obstruct or reverse the cycle, but we can bend it; in what degree remains to be shown.

There are some interesting sidelights which enter into the foregoing discussions but which could not there be covered in detail. One of them is the extreme age of the junipers and juniper stumps. In one case I found a 36-inch alligator juniper with over half its basal cross-section eaten out by fire. On each edge of this huge scar counted forty rings. Within 24 inches of the scar were two yellow pines of 20" in diameter

Of Fire and the Landscape

just emerging from the blackjack stage. Each must have been 130 years old. Neither showed any scars, but upon chopping into the side adjacent to the juniper, each was found to contain a buried fire-scald in the fortieth ring. It is perfectly evident that these 130-year pines had grown in the interval between the fires which consumed half the basal cross-section of the juniper, and the subsequent fires which resulted in the latest series of four healings. The fires which really ate into the juniper would most certainly have killed any pine standing only 24 inches distant. The conclusion is that the juniper attained its present diameter more than 130 years ago. The size of the main scar certainly indicates a long series of repetitions of scarring, drying and burning at the base of the juniper. The time necessary to attain a 36-inch diameter is in itself a matter of centuries. Consider now that other junipers killed by fire 40 years ago were found to still retain ¼-inch twigs, and then try to interpret in terms of centuries the meaning of Arizona foothills. Who can doubt that we have in these junipers a graphic record of forest history extending back behind and beyond the Christian era? Who can doubt that this article discloses merely the main broad outlines of the story?

The following instance also tells us something about the intervals at which fires occurred. I mentioned a juniper with a big scar and four successive healings of which the last counted forty rings. The last was considerably the thickest. In a general way I would say that the previous fires probably occurred at intervals of approximately a decade. Ten years is plenty of time for a lusty growth of grass to come back and accumulate the fuel for another fire. This would reconcile my general theory with the known fact that fires injure most species of grass, it being entirely thinkable for the grass to recover from any such injury during a ten-year interval.

The foregoing likewise strengthens the supposition that root competition with grass rather than fire, was the salient factor in keeping down the brush during pre-settlement days. Brush species which coppice with as much vigor as those of the Arizona brushfields could stage quite a comeback during a ten-year surcease of fire if they were not inhibited by an additional competitor like grass roots.

Whether grass competition or fire was the principal deterrent of timber reproduction is hard to answer because the two factors were always paired, never isolated. Probably either one would have inhibited extensive reproduction. In northern Arizona there are great areas where removal of grass by grazing has caused spectacular encroachment of juniper on park areas. But here again both grass competition and fire evidently cause the original park, and both were removed before reproduction came in.

It is very interesting to compare what has happened in the woodland type with what has happened in the semi-desert type immediately below it. Here also old timers testify to a radical encroachment of brush species like mesquite and cat's-claw. They insist, however, that while this semi-desert type originally contained much grass, it never contained enough grass to carry fire. There are no signs of old fires. The encroachment of brush in this type can therefore be ascribed only to the removal of grass competition.

There are many loose masonry walls of Indian origin in the headwaters of drainages both in the woodland and semi-desert types. These have been fondly called "erosion-control works" by some enthusiastic forest officers, but it is perfectly evident that they were built as agricultural terraces, and that their function in erosion control was accidental. It is significant that any number of these terraces now contain heavy brush and even timber. Since they are prehistoric, the Indians could not have had metals, and therefore could not have easily cleared them of timber or brush. Therefore their sites must have been either barren or grassy when the Indians built them. This conforms with the belief that brush has encroached in both the woodland and semi-desert ranges.

In the brush fields of California the drift of administrative policy is toward heavy grazing as a means of reducing fire hazard. If the ecology of these California brushfields is similar to the ecology of the Arizona brushfields, it would appear obvious that either my Arizona theory or the California grazing policy is wrong. The point is that there is no similarity. The rainfall of the California brushfields is nearly twice that of the Arizona brushfields. Its seasonal distribution is different, and from what I can learn there is a great deal more duff and more herbs and other inflammable material under the California brush. It would appear, therefore, that the California tendency toward heavier grazing and the tendency in the Southwestern District toward much lighter grazing are not inconsistent because the two regions are not comparable.

The radical encroachment of brush in southern Arizona has had some interesting effects on game. There is one mountain range on the Tonto where the brush has become so thick as to almost prohibit travel, and where a thrifty stock of black bears have established themselves. The old hunters assure me that there were no black bears in these mountains when the country was first settled. It is likewise a significant fact that the wild turkey has been exterminated throughout most of the Arizona brushfields, whereas it has merely been decimated further north. It seems possible that turkeys require a certain proportion of open space in order to thrive. Plenty of open spaces originally existed, but the recent encroachment of brush has abolished them, and possibly thus made the birds fall an easier prey to predatory animals.

The cumulative abnormal erosion which has occurred coincident with the encroachment of brush and the decimation of grass naturally has its worst effect in the siltage of reservoirs. The data kept by Southwestern reclamation interests on siltage of reservoirs is regrettably inadequate, but it is sufficient to indicate one salient fact, viz., that the greater part of the loosened material is at the present time in transit toward the reservoir, rather than already dumped into it. Blockading this detritus in transit is therefore just as important as desilting the storage sites. The methods of blockading it will obviously be a combination of mechanical and vegetative obstructions, and with these foresters should be particularly qualified to deal. This fact further accentuates the responsibility of the Forest Service, and indicates that the watershed work of the future belongs quite as much to the forester as to the hydrographer and engineer.

Selection from

Young Men and Fire

NORMAN MACLEAN

I N 1949 THE SMOKEJUMPERS were not far from their origins as parachute jumpers turned stunt performers dropping from the wings of planes at county fairs just for the hell of it plus a few dollars, less hospital expenses. By this time they were also sure they were the best firefighters in the United States Forest Service, and although by now they were very good, especially against certain kinds of fires, they should have stopped to realize that they were newcomers in this ancient business of fighting forest fires. It was 1940 when the first parachute jump on a forest fire was made and a year later that the Smokejumpers were organized, so only for nine years had there been a profession with the aim of taking on at the same time three of the four elements of the universe—air, earth, and fire—and in a simple continuous act dropping out of the sky and landing in a treetop or on the face of a cliff in order to make good their boast of digging a trench around every fire they landed on by ten o'clock the next morning. In 1949 the Smokejumpers were still so young that they referred affectionately to all fires they jumped on as "ten o'clock fires," as if they already had them under control before they jumped. They were still so young they hadn't learned to count the odds and to sense they might owe the universe a tragedy.

It is true, though, that no technical advance was to influence the Forest Service's methods of spotting and fighting wildfires as much as the airplane, which arrived early in the century about the same time as the Forest Service (1905). Two world wars hastened the union between airplanes and fire fighting. By 1917 chief forester Henry S. Graves was conferring with the chief of the Army Air Corps about the possibility of army planes flying patrol missions over western forests. By 1925 the Forest Service itself started using planes from which fires could be spotted more quickly and thoroughly than from scattered lookouts. By 1929 planes were dropping supplies to firefighters, and it seemed that soon firefighters themselves would be dropped, but psychological difficulties and difficulties with equipment held back the development of parachute jumping on wildfires. It was only after several years of experimenting and training that the first parachute jump on a forest fire was made, one of the two jumpers being Earl Cooley, who was to be the spotter on the C-47 that carried the Smokejumpers to the Mann Gulch fire and, as spotter, tapped each jumper on the left calf as the signal to step into the sky over Mann Gulch.

The chief psychological roadblock holding up the acceptance of parachute jumping by the government and the public itself was the belief that most parachute jumpers were at least a little bit nuts and the high probability that a few of them were. In 1935, Evan Kelley, of the Forest Service's Region One (with headquarters in Missoula, Montana, where in a few years one of the biggest Smokejumper bases was to be established), rejected the possibility of dropping men on fires from parachutes by saying: "The best information I can get from experienced fliers is that all parachute jumpers are more or less crazy— just a little bit unbalanced, otherwise they wouldn't be engaged in such a hazardous undertaking." There is no doubt that among those most visibly touched with the Icarus complex were jumpers off wings of planes at county fairs or stuntmen doing the same kind of work for movies. Only a year before Kelley had made his psychological analysis of parachute jumpers, Frank Derry, a stuntman in California and short of cash, got the idea of jumping from a plane in a parachute, dressed as Santa Claus. He made a perfect landing, pleased the local Los Angeles merchants, quit factory work for good, joined a flying circus barnstorming the West, and became one of the nine original Forest Service Smokejumpers, one of the Forest Service's finest jump instructors, and one of its best riggers, making important improvements in both the parachute and the jump suit.

Young Men and Fire

Most people have a touch of the Icarus complex and, like Smokejumpers, wish to appear on earth from the sky. In my home town of Missoula, Montana, older brothers all over town trained their younger brothers to jump from garage roofs, using gunnysacks for parachutes. The older brothers argued that the younger brothers should do the jumping because, being smaller, they would take longer to reach the ground and so give their gunnysacks more time to open and soften the landing. From the start, Smokejumpers had to have a lot of what we had a little of, and one way all men are born equal is in being born at least a little bit crazy, some being more equal than others. A number of these latter were needed to get the Smokejumpers started, and a certain number more have always been needed to keep it going.

Fortunately, many of those powered by the Icarus complex, unlike Icarus, are gifted mechanically in odd ways and have long worked on problems connected with landing safely. Even the most sublime of oddballs, Leonardo da Vinci, had studied the problem of safely landing men on earth from the sky. But it wasn't until 1783 that the French physicist Louis Sebastien Lenormand made the first successful parachute jump from a tower, and even in 1930 the parachute had many shortcomings as a means of aerial transport, some of which were eliminated or reduced by none other than Frank Derry, the Santa Claus parachute jumper who was also gifted mechanically. One of the parachute's greatest shortcomings as aerial transport had been that, being a parabolic object, it drops with a bell-like motion. As it descends, air is forced up into it and, since there are no openings in the parachute through which the air can escape, it rocks up on one side until the surplus air is released, then swings to the other side until it tips out the excess air it has accumulated on its return trip. As a result, before the parachute could be a reasonably safe means of getting from the sky to the earth, the rocking had to be taken out of its flight and some means of steering it had to be devised so Smokejumpers and their supplies could be dropped on a designated spot near a fire instead of scattered all over the nearby mountains.

The parachute developed by Frank Derry became the standard Smokejumpers' parachute for many years and is the parachute used by the crew that dropped on the Mann Gulch fire. The rocking motion had been reduced by three openings through which air could be released—an opening in the top and two slots on opposite sides. On the outside of

Of Fire and the Landscape

the chute attached to the slots were "tails," pieces of nylon that acted as rudders to guide the flow of air coming through the slots, and to them guide lines were attached so that the direction of the flight was ultimately determined by the jumper. Not a highly safe and sensitive piece of machinery, but better than Icarus had. It had a speed of seven or eight knots, and, as soon as a jumper could, he turned his face to the wind and looked over his shoulder to see, among other things, that he didn't smash into a cliff.

Frank Derry, his two brothers, and others of the early Smoke-jumpers not only greatly improved the parachute but soon were developing a safer jump suit, one designed especially for jumping in mountainous timber country—football helmet with heavy wire-mesh face mask, felt-lined suit, and "shock absorbers" such as ankle braces, athletic supporters, back and abdominal braces, and heavy logger boots (the White logger boots from Spokane, Washington, the best). Frank Derry's two brothers were helpful, but staying put was not part of their calling and they weren't long with the Smokejumpers. Frank, however, lasted much longer, then bought a bar nearby and became his own best customer.

So far it has all been the jump in smokejumping and nothing about the smoke or fire at the end. In 1949 a fair number of old-timers in the Forest Service still believed that God means there to be only one honest way to get to a forest fire and that is to walk your guts out. To these old-timers the Smokejumpers were from a circus sideshow, although in fact they were already on their way to becoming the best firefighting outfit in the Forest Service.

Basic movements in the history of the Forest Service had helped put the Smokejumpers by 1949 on their way to being the best. The United States Forest Service was officially established in 1905 by President Theodore Roosevelt and Governor Gifford Pinchot of Pennsylvania, eastern outdoorsmen who knew and loved the earth in its wondrous ways when left to itself and given a chance. Their policy of acquiring and protecting some of the earth's most beautiful remaining parts became the Forest Service's primary purpose. Then came 1910, the most disastrous fire year on record. In western Montana and Idaho 3 million acres were left behind as charred trees and ashes that rose when you walked by, then blew away when you passed. This transformation occurred largely in two days, August 20 and 21, when thousands of people thought the world was coming to an end, and for eighty-seven people it did.

I remember these two days very well. My family was on summer vacation, camped in tents on an island between forks of the Bitterroot River. The elders in my father's church had become alarmed and had come in a wagon to rescue us. A team of the elders waded out to our island, crossed hands, and in this cradle carried my mother back to the wagon. My father and I followed, my father holding me with one hand and his fishing rod with the other and I also holding my fishing rod with my other hand. It was frightening, as what seemed to be great flakes of white snow were swirling to the ground in the heat and darkness of high noon. I was seven years old and might have cried for our tent, which we had to leave behind, except I thought my mother and our two rods would make it to the wagon.

Since 1910, much of the history of the Forest Service can be translated into a succession of efforts to get firefighters on fires as soon as possible—the sooner, the smaller the fire. If a campfire left burning can be caught soon enough, a man with a shovel can bury it. If the fire is a lightning fire burning in a dead tree, a man will need an ax to drop the burning tree and will still need the shovel to dig the shallow trench into which he is going to drop and bury it. If two Smokejumpers had reached the Mann Gulch fire the afternoon it started, they would at least have kept it under control until a larger crew arrived. Before the Mann Gulch fire was finally put under control five days later, there were 450 men on it and they didn't have as much to do with stopping it as did cliffs and rock slides.

So history went from trails and walking and pack mules to roads and trucks up every gulch to four-wheel drives where there weren't any roads to planes and now to helicopters, which can go about anywhere and do anything when they get there or on the way. The Smokejumpers are a large part of this history. Graphs prove it.

The two graphs reproduced in this chapter are a part of the statistical studies by Charles P. Kern, fire coordinator of the Forest Service's Region One, and assistant fire coordinator Ronald Hendrickson of the variations in number and size of forest fires in Region One from 1930 to 1975. The first graph, "Total Number of Fires per Year," shows just what an old-time woodsman who has long fought fires would expect—that there has been no significant trend either up or down in the number of

Of Fire and the Landscape

wildfires during those forty-five years. There has been a bad fire year now and then, as in the late thirties and early sixties, and there probably always will be now and then, let's hope never as bad as 1910, but on a statistical curve lightning seems to be a fairly fixed feature of the universe, as does the number of people who are careless with campfires. The result is no discernible downtrend in the number of wildfires.

The graph entitled "Number of Fires Rated Class C and Larger" tells a very different story and shows clearly the coming and continuing presence of the Smokejumpers. The number of fires rated Class C (ten to ninety-nine acres) and larger in Region One, figured as a percentage of the total fires per year, plunged sharply as the Smokejumpers became an organization in the early 1940s, then made its last sharp rise to almost 9 percent with the coming of World War II when the Smokejumpers became a depleted operation, but plunged just as precipitously when the war was over and veterans filled up the crews of Smokejumpers, who again were stopping fires before they spread far. Since 1945 there has been no year when 5 percent of the fires became Class C or larger—thirty years is surely a trend, no doubt one that cannot be ascribed solely to the Smokejumpers but one that has to be a great tribute to them.

Although this trend has to be a tribute in part to the fixed theory of doing everything possible between heaven and earth to get firefighters on a fire as fast as possible, what also makes a world of difference is the kind of men who get there first. The requirements used in selecting the first crews of Smokejumpers give a rough profile of the kind of men the Forest Service thought were needed to join sky with fire, and those same requirements should have given the jumpers some idea of their life expectancy. They had to be between twenty-one and twenty-five, in perfect health, not married, and holding no job in the Forest Service as important as ranger. So basically they had to be young, tough, and in one way or another from the backcountry. And the Forest Service carried no insurance on them.

It is not hard to imagine why the Smokejumpers from the start have had several visible bloodlines. With their two major activities—to jump from the sky and fight fire when they land—they have always drawn professional adventurers. The three Derry brothers are good examples. They were important in giving shape and substance to the early history of the Smokejumpers, and, from the nature of things, the Smokejumpers will probably always draw their quota of adventurers. On weekends, they are likely to rent a Cessna 180 and go jumping just for the hell of it; they try to make big money in the summer and some go to Honolulu and shack up for the winter, at night passing themselves off as natives to multi-national female tourists or even to female natives. Others spend the winters as ski instructors in Colorado or Utah or Montana, colder work in the day but probably not at night.

One might assume that most Smokejumpers come from the woods and after they are finished as jumpers join up for good with the United States Forest Service or some state agency supervising public lands or some private logging company—the Smokejumper base in Missoula is a magnet for being the headquarters for Region One of the Forest Service, Missoula is also the home of the University of Montana, which has a powerful school of forestry. Any summer a highly select number of forestry students are Smokejumpers—of the thirteen firefighters who died in Mann Gulch, five were forestry students at the University of Montana and two were forestry students as the University of Minnesota. Two of the three survivors had just finished high school and were also University of Montana students. Select, very good students, trained in the woods.

At best, though, there is very little chance of a longtime future in smokejumping. To start with, you are through jumping at forty, and for those who think of lasting that long there are only a few openings ahead, administrative or maintenance. But one thing that remains with Smokejumpers, no matter where they ultimately land, is the sense of being highly select for life and of belonging for life to a highly select out-fit, somewhat like the Marines, who know what they are talking about when they speak of themselves as the proud and the few. Although many Smokejumpers never see each other after they leave the outfit, they remain members of a kind of fraternal organization that also has some dim ties seemingly with religion. Just being a first-class woodsman admits you almost anywhere into an international fraternity of sorts, and although you will meet only a few of your worldwide brotherhood, you will recognize any one of them when you see him swing an ax. Going a little up the fraternal ladder is being admitted to the Forest Service, and that is like belonging to the Masons or the Knights of Columbus; making the next step is becoming a Smokejumper, and that

Of Fire and the Landscape

is like being a Shriner or Knight Templar. This kind of talk is going too far but not altogether in the wrong direction. It is very important to a lot of people to make unmistakably clear to themselves and to the universe that they love the universe but are not intimidated by it and will not be shaken by it, no matter what it has in store. Moreover, they demand something from themselves early in life that can be taken ever after as a demonstration of this abiding feeling.

So it shouldn't be surprising that many Smokejumpers never intend to remain Smokejumpers or even to work in the woods for the rest of their lives. A good number of them are students working for M.A.'s or Ph.D.'s—even more go on to be lawyers and doctors, and even more to be dentists. These young men are first class, both as students and jumpers. They tend to hang out together but don't talk much about their university life, at least not when other jumpers are around. Later, though, when they are far away and far up the professional ladder, they get a remote look in their eyes when they talk about the tap on the calf of the left leg telling them it's only a step up to the sky.

For many former Smokejumpers, then, smokejumping is not closely tied up with their way of life, but is more something that is necessary for them to pass through and not around and, once it is unmistakably done, does not have to be done again. The "it" is within, and is the need to settle some things with the universe and ourselves before taking on the "business of the world," which isn't all that special or hard but takes time. This "it" is the something special within that demands we do something special, and "it" could be within a lot of us.

On the bottom line, this is the story of an "outfit," as men call themselves when they take on the same tough job, have to be thought a little bit crazy to try it, have to stick together and share the same training to get it done, and shortly afterwards have to go to town together and stick together if one of them starts losing a fight in a bar. They back each other and they imitate each other. It should be clear that this tragedy is not a classical tragedy of a monumental individual crossing the sword of his will with the sword of destiny. It is a tragedy of a crew, its flaws and grandeurs largely those of Smokejumpers near the beginning of their history. Their collective character counts, and being young counts, it especially counts, but only certain individuals emerge out of the smoke and roar that took in everything. Eldon Diettert counts; he was the fine research student who was called from his birthday dinner to make this flight and told some of the crew that he almost said no—only recently a scholarship in the forestry school at the University of Montana has been named in his honor. David Navon was already something of a four-dimensional adventurer; he had been first lieutenant in the 101st Airborne Division and had parachuted into Bastogne and in about an hour would be taking snapshots on his way to death. William Hellman, squad leader and second-in-command, was handsome and important and only a month before had made a parachute landing on the Ellipse between the White House and the Washington Monument. At the end he wished he had been a better Catholic, and men wept when they saw him still alive. Then there were the three survivors. R. Wagner ("Wag") Dodge, the foreman, gifted with his hands, silent on principle, and fastidious, who invented a fire and lay down in its ashes, lived only a few years more. Walter Rumsey and Robert Sallee, the other two who survived, spent years trying to forget the fire. Part of our story will be to find them and to bring them back to Mann Gulch with us to discover how well they remembered and forgot. In this part of the story there are living ghosts and characters, and the story doesn't come out quite the way either the ghosts or the non-ghosts expected.

But even in the memories of those who knew them, the dead Smokejumpers have a collective character. When you ask any one of them what he knew of any one of the dead, you always get the same answer, which is undoubtedly true: "He was a great guy." And when parents can bring themselves to speak of a son, they always say, "He was a wonderful boy." Of the fifteen who jumped on the fire, thirteen were between seventeen and twenty-three, and were still so young they didn't like the taste of hard liquor but drank beer, gallons of beer. Being that young, they were in good part what their training made them, and maybe with their girls—maybe especially with their girls—they acted mostly like Smokejumpers. Important in becoming a Smokejumper is learning how to act like one.

First-year Smokejumpers believed women were largely what second- or third-year Smokejumpers told them women were, and, having few chances to see women of the world while they were on the job in the woods, they had a very small body of fact to correct what they were told. Probably the "woman of the world" they knew best was at the near-

Of Fire and the Landscape

est bar, about a four-and-a-half-mile walk down the road from their training base at Nine Mile, and sometimes, especially after returning from a jump, they wouldn't get to the bar until nearly 1:30 at night, which was closing time, but they would make the owner stay open until dawn. No matter the time, there was always this same tall dame on a stool waiting to accommodate herself to their beer. She was tall and silent, but after a couple of hours her trunk would begin to sway, and, as she finally toppled like a tree from her stool, the Smokejumpers would all stand and yell, "Timber." Then they would walk four and a half miles back to the base and be ready to jump.

A few such glimpses of women when mixed with verbal images of them drawn by experienced jumpers must have left first-year jumpers picturing "women of the world" as part tree, probably part sheep, and certainly part deer, because almost without doubt they had branches and antlers.

What most first-year jumpers really knew about women was only one girl, the girl back home. She had been a junior in high school when he had been a senior. He took time off in the summer to be with her at the creamery picnic back home, and he took at least another weekend off during the summer just to be with her. Then they went on a long pack-trip together. She always carried at least forty pounds in her packsack, and they would stay out overnight. Like him and other great walkers, she walked slightly stoop-shouldered. At night after he returned to his job of smokejumping he would float into her dreams from the sky looking for a fire, and as he floated by always he stopped for a look at her. If he had to go on before he found her, she would wake up deeply disturbed, but, believe it or not, she never thought of him as tough.

It is hard to realize that these young men would be dead within two hours after they landed from parachutes no longer made of silk but of nylon, so they would not be eaten by grasshoppers.

So it was a young outfit, of necessity young as individuals and barely started as an organization. As individuals, they would soon go the way of prizefighters—all washed up when their reflexes began to slow by fractions of a second and when they no longer could absorb a beating and come back to win. Few have ever made it to the age limit of forty. As an organization, the outfit also was young, only nine years old in 1949, and some of those nine years were war years when the development of the Smokejumpers was slowed down. The war, though, had positive after-effects on the history of the Smokejumpers. For instance, of the fifteen who jumped on the Mann Gulch fire, twelve had been in the armed services and the other three had been too young to enlist.

In 1949, then, this was an outfit of great power and to us, but not to them, of some apparent weaknesses. Although modern graphs demonstrate the effectiveness of the Smokejumpers in carrying out their major purpose of putting out fires so fast they don't have time to become big ones, nothing initially—at least not before the Mann Gulch fire—made visible any weakness in adhering too exclusively to this purpose even when it would have made sense to enlarge it.

One danger of making almost a sole specialty of dropping on fires as soon as possible is that nearly all such fires will be small fires, and a tragic corollary is that not much about fighting big fires can be learned by fighting small ones. Small fires, remember, most frequently are put out with a shovel and an ax, to which, for the sake of the record, a Pulaski should be added, a Pulaski being a double-bitted ax with one of the bits made into a little hoe. As for big fires in the early history of the Forest Service, a young ranger made himself famous by answering the big question on an exam, "What would you do to control a crown fire?" with the one-liner, "Get out of the way and pray like hell for rain." Another weakness that might show up from a specialization of dropping on small fires in otherwise inaccessible country is that there aren't enough of them in a usual season to make them into a profession. In 1949, when there were big critical fires that could be approached on the ground, the Forest Service continued its original practice, as it was to do with the Mann Gulch fire, of going to the big towns—Spokane, Butte, Missoula, or Helena—and picking up what they could find sitting at bars or lined up outside employment agencies, maybe with one good pair of walking shoes among the whole bunch which one barfly passed to the other in the alley when it came his turn to be interviewed. In these early times, when Smokejumpers were not actually on fires, most of which were small, they were either at their base picking dandelions out of the lawn while waiting for their names to come to the head of the jump list or out in the woods on what were called "projects," building trail, stringing telephone wire, or thinning dense timber and not learning much if anything

Of Fire and the Landscape

about what to do when a fire gets big enough to jump from one side of a canyon to the other.

The Smokejumpers are now the crack firefighters of the Forest Service, the shock troops. Whenever fires are critical, which practically always means big, that's where they are, from Missoula, Montana, to Minnesota to New Mexico to Alaska, and they don't care how they get there—by plane, bus, horse, or on foot, just so it is the fastest way. They are professional firefighters, for a living taking on fires of all sizes and shapes.

A Class C fire (10 to 99 acres) has a special place in this story, although as forest fires go it is no great fire. But many of this crew had never been on a fire as big as a Class C fire. Wag Dodge, the foreman of the crew and a Smokejumper foreman since 1945, had led one crew of Smokejumpers to one Class C fire in 1948 and to one Class D fire (100 to 299 acres) the year before but to no fire larger than that.

When the crew landed on the Mann Gulch fire, it was a C. Then suddenly it blew, and probably no one there had ever been on a "blowup" before. A blowup to a forest fire is something like a hurricane to an ocean storm. When 450 men finally got the Mann Gulch fire under control, it had burned forty-five hundred acres, between seven and eight square miles.

The primary purpose of the first Smokejumpers, then, was still primary to the Smokejumpers of 1949—to land on a forest fire in difficult or otherwise inaccessible country before suddenly the universe tried to reduce its own frame of things to ashes and charred grouse. When the Mann Gulch fire was first spotted from the plane, the pilot, the crew foreman, and the spotter sized it up as a fairly ordinary fire—they reported it was just a "ground fire" that had "crowned" in one place where it had already burned out. None of the three saw any "spot fires" around its edges, and that meant the fire had been advancing slowly on the ground and was not playing leapfrog by throwing small fires ahead of the fire's main front.

The words in quotation marks above and undoubtedly some that are not are those of firefighters, and we had better be sure of the meaning of these key words in the Basic English of firefighters so that when the tragic race between the firefighters and the fire begins it won't have to be stopped for definitions. It is not enough to know the word for this or that kind of fire; to know one fire is to see how what was dropping live ashes from a dead tree at the end of one afternoon by next afternoon had become one kind of fire after another kind of fire until it had become a monster in flames from which there was no escape.

Of the two main kinds of forest fires distinguished by their causes, man and nature itself, the Mann Gulch fire was lightning fire, as 75 percent of the forest fires in the West are. Lightning fires usually start where lightning gets its first chance to strike—high up near the tip of a ridge but slightly down its side where the first clump of dead trees stands, and the start of the Mann Gulch fire fits this description. The fire in the dead snag may drop live ashes for several days before starting a fire on the ground, for the ground near a mountaintop is likely to be mostly rocks with at best only a light covering of dead leaves, needles, or grass. But the lightning storm that started the Mann Gulch fire passed over the gulch on August 4, and by the end of the next afternoon on the hottest day ever recorded in nearby Helena thirteen Smokejumpers were dead.

Once started on the ground the lightning fire became simply a "ground fire," a term that includes most fires, and so ground fires are of many sizes, shapes, and intensities, and practically all man-made fires such as campfires and fires set to burn slash or brush but allowed to get away at least start as ground fires. A ground fire may become dangerous, even murderous, but most often it is just a lot of hard work to get under control. Until an hour before the end, that is what the Smokejumpers expected the Mann Gulch fire to be—hard work all night but easing up by morning.

The job of controlling most ground fires starts with the job of scraping a "fire trench" of fire-line around it or its flanks so as to force it onto rocks or open meadows. A fire trench or fire-line is some two to three feet wide, is made with a Pulaski and shovel, and is nothing more than the surface of the ground scraped down to mineral soil. Nothing flammable, such as fallen trees or hanging branches, can be left across it.

The chief danger from a ground fire is that it will become a "crown fire," that is, get into the branches or "crowns" of trees especially where the trees are close together and the branches interlace. So a crew has to be careful that a ground fire doesn't burn in to a jack-pine thicket where the branches are close to the ground and can be set afire by low flames. But there is still a very different way for an ordinary-looking fire to explode. A fire doesn't always need flames to advance. A fire may seem under control, burning harmlessly under tall trees with branches too high to be touched by ground flames, but the fire is burning with such intensity that most of the oxygen has been burned out of the air near it, which is heated above the point of ignition. If the wind suddenly changes and fresh air is blown in loaded with oxygen, then the three elements necessary for a fire are suddenly present in the lower branches— flammable material, temperature above the point of ignition, and oxygen. An old-timer knows that, when a ground fire explodes into a crown fire with nothing he can see to cause it, he had not witnessed spontaneous combustion but the outer appearance of the invisible pressure of a "fire triangle" suddenly in proper proportions for an explosion.

The crown fire is the one that sounds like a train coming too fast around a curve and may get so high-keyed the crew cannot understand what their foreman is trying to do to save them. Sometimes, when the timber thins out, it sounds as if the train were clicking across a bridge, sometimes it hits an open clearing and becomes hushed as if going through a tunnel, but when the burning cones swirl through the air and fall on the other side of the clearing, starting spot fires there, the new fire sounds as if it were the train coming out of the tunnel, belching black unburned smoke. The unburned smoke boils up until it reaches oxygen, then bursts into gigantic flames on top of its cloud of smoke in the sky. The new firefighter, seeing black smoke rise from the ground and then at the top of the sky turn into flames, thinks that natural law has been reversed. The flames should come first and the smoke from them. The new firefighter doesn't know how his fire got way up there. He is frightened and should be.

A fire-line, unless a river or a wide right-of-way on a trail is being used as a line, is not much good when a crown fire is off and running. It usually takes a "backfire" to stop a big crown fire, and the conditions are seldom right for the foreman to start one. He has to build piles of fast-burning twigs, shavings, or dried bunch grass in front of the main fire and, before starting his backfire, must wait until the wind blows back toward the main fire, and often it never does. When you fool with a backfire, you are really fooling with fire—you are counting on the wind to continue to blow your backfire toward the main fire. If the wind changes again and blows toward you, your backfire may only have given the main fire a fatal jump on you.

Young Men and Fire

It's perhaps even more unpredictable if there isn't much of a wind to begin with, because a big crown fire can make its own wind. The hot, lighter air rises, the cold, heavier air rushes down to replace it in what is called a "convection effect," and soon a great "fire whirl" is started and fills the air with burning cones and branches which drop in advance of the main fire like the Fourth of July and start spot fires. The separate spot fires soon burn together, and life is trapped between the main fire coming from behind and the new line of fire now burning back toward it.

Then something terrible can happen. The space between the converged spot fires as they burn close to the main fire can become hotter than the point of ignition. If the convection effect or a change in the wind blows fresh oxygen between the two fires, suddenly replenishing the burned-out air, there can be a "blow-up," although a blowup can be caused in still other ways. Not many have seen a blowup, even fewer have seen one and lived, and fewer still have tried afterwards to recover and record out of their seared memories exactly what happened. Later on in Mann Gulch we shall try to re-create a blowup seen by almost no one who lived to record it, and it might help as preparation if we turn briefly to the great pioneer in the science of fire behavior, Harry T. Gisborne, who was one of the first to observe and describe a blowup accurately.

In 1929 Gisborne was on what was up to then Montana's largest man-caused fire, the ninety-thousand-acre Half Moon fire in Glacier National Park (640 acres being a section or a square mile). As he says, measured "runs" show that even a big crown fire advances not much faster than a half-mile to a mile an hour.

Returning two days later, he found the perfectly balanced body of a young grouse, neck and head "still alertly erect in fear and wonder," the beak, feathers, and feet seared away. Within a few yards was a squirrel, stretched out at full length. "The burned-off stubs of his little hands were reaching out as far ahead as possible, the back legs were extended to the full in one final, hopeless push, trying, like any human, to crawl just one painful inch further to escape this unnecessary death."

Although young men died like squirrels in Mann Gulch, the Mann Gulch fire should not end there, smoke drifting away and leaving terror without consolation of explanation, and controversy without lasting settlement. Probably most catastrophes end this way without an ending, the dead not even knowing how they died but "still alertly erect in fear and wonder," those who loved them forever questioning "this unnecessary death," and the rest of us tiring of this inconsolable catastrophe and turning to the next one. This is a catastrophe that we hope will not end where it began; it might go on and become a story. It will not have to be made up—that is all-important to us—but we do have to know in what odd places to look for missing parts of a story and a wildfire when we see one. So this story is a test of its own belief—that in this cockeyed world there are shapes and designs, if only we have some curiosity, training, and compassion and take care not to lie or be sentimental. It would be a start to a story if this catastrophe were found to have circled around out there somewhere until it could return to itself with explanations of its own mysteries and with the grief it left behind, not removed, because grief has its own place at or near the end of things, but altered somewhat by the addition of something like wonder—wonder, for example, because now we can say that the fire whirl which destroyed was caused by three winds on a river. If we could say something like this and be speaking both accurately and somewhat like Shelley when he spoke of clouds and winds, then what we would be talking about would start to change from catastrophe without a filled-in story to what could be called the story of a tragedy, but tragedy would be only a part of it, as it is of life.

After the Fire

MARGARET MILLAR

F IRE . . . IS A NATURAL condition of life in the chaparral regions of southern California, and an essential condition if vegetation is to remain young and vigorous. Without an occasional clearing out, the underbrush gets so thick and high that deer and other mammals can't penetrate it and ground-dwelling birds have trouble foraging. When this happens the chaparral, normally rich in wildlife, becomes incapable of supporting its usual share. Fire occurring at twenty- to twenty-five-year intervals is a benefit, a cleaning-out of dead and diseased wood and groundcover. (Before any nature lover sets off into the hills with a pack of matches, it should be noted that more frequent fires result in the destruction of chaparral, and its conversion to a different and less interesting type of vegetation.)

Some forty or more plant species are grouped together under the name chaparral. Chaparral is the Spanish word for scrub oak; it also means a short, stocky person, and perhaps this gives, to someone who has never seen it, a better idea of chaparral. Chaparral is short, stocky, tough vegetation, capable of withstanding a yearly drought for six months or more.

Throughout the centuries a number of ways have evolved for chaparral plants to survive burning. Some, like green-bark ceanothus, sprout new leaves directly from the "dead" stumps. Some have woody crowns or burls at ground level, like toyon, or underground, like Eastwood manzanita, which is back to full size in a few years. Others have seeds with a hard coat that must be split open by fire, or else soft-coated seeds which

Of Fire and the Landscape

need very high temperatures to trigger their internal chemistry. Among the plants with seeds requiring fire in order to germinate are some of the most dominant and important in the chaparral group of the region—chamise, big berry manzanita, laurel sumac, hoary leaf ceanothus, big pod ceanothus, sugar bush, and lemonade bush. All but chamise are frequently used in cultivated gardens.

After the Coyote fire I hiked around the burned areas, observing as bird watcher, not a botanist. But I couldn't help noticing that greenery started to reappear almost as soon as the earth had cooled. This applied especially to a certain vine, rather similar to a grapevine, which spread along the ground, as lush a green as ever graced a rain forest, and wrapped its tendrils around the blackened stumps of trees and shrubs. This was a chilicothe, or wild cucumber. Its appearance had been neither delayed or hastened by the fire, by the rain that followed, or by any external circumstances at all. When its cycle of growth was ready to begin again, it began: everything necessary for the complete process—leaves, flowers, fruit, seeds—was contained in a giant tuber buried underground.

An example of the chilocothe's self-containment and independence of the outside world was accidentally provided by the local Botanic Garden. To show the public the size of the tubers, one weighing about fifty pounds was dug up and placed in the information center. At Christmas time it started sprouting, and within the next few weeks it went through its entire growth cycle while in a display case. Again the following year, still in the display case, it grew leaves and tendrils, it flowered and fruited and went to seed. It was only during this second cycle that the tuber becomes noticeably smaller and wrinkled as its water content decreased.

The emergence of the chilicothe was unimportant as far as food or shelter for wildlife was concerned. Yet it appeared to be a signal for the forest to come alive again. After a December rainfall of four and a half inches, oaks that looked ready for the woodpile and seemed to be still standing only because nobody had leaned against them, suddenly burst out with a cluster of leaves here, and a cluster there. No two trees refoliated in quite the same way. These native oaks are accustomed to fires and make strong comebacks, as do the sycamores. Not so the pines, which lack the regenerative powers of other species. The pines that looked dead were dead. Although a few of them put out new needles at the top; these soon withered and dropped, and nothing further happened.

Such debility on the part of the tree itself must, in order to account for the species' survival through centuries of periodic fires, be compensated for by durability for the seed or the seed's protective device. Some pines, such as Bishop, knobcone, and to a certain extent Monterey, are equipped with closed cones which open and drop their seeds only when exposed to very high temperatures. There is a stand of Bishop pines near Santa Barbara which passersby assume to be a state or county planting because the trees are all exactly the same size. The actual reason is that the seeds all germinated after the same fire.

During the Coyote fire the eucalyptus trees, especially the most widely planted variety, blue gum, burned very quickly. This was partly because of their natural oil content, which caused a great deal of black smoke, and partly because they were very dry. The deep underground water which carried many large trees through the summer drought was unavailable to the shallow-rooted eucalyptus. But their comeback was also quick. In fact, the adaptation for these imports from Australia to California fire provided one of the oddest sights of spring and summer. Normally, eucalyptus leaves grow like other leaves, out of branches and twigs. When the branches and twigs, however, were consumed by fire, the leaves grew instead out of the trunk of the tree. They looked like telephone poles which had suddenly started to sprout leaves from top to bottom.

Certain trees took a long time to show signs of regeneration. These included the redwoods in the center of the Botanic Garden and the olive trees on the slopes of a canyon adjoining the Botanic Garden. The grove had been planted for the commercial milling of oil in the 1880s, about the time the first daily newspaper was established in Santa Barbara and the first free library and reading room was opened. The olive oil project was abandoned when cheap Mexican labor became scarce. One of the methods used to keep the workers on the job would be frowned on by present-day union officials; whenever the braceros gave evidence of wanting a siesta, a barrel of wine, carried on a donkey-drawn sled, passed between the rows of trees, and the braceros were bribed with booze on a considerably more generous scale than the British seamen with once-a-day grog.

Of Fire and the Landscape

This olive grove, left untended for years and with a heavy growth of underbrush between the trees, was severely damaged by the fire. The underbrush was the main reason for the destruction, not, as some people believed, the oil content of the wood or leaves. When I walked through the area a week after the fire ended, all the trees looked dead, and continued to do so for a long time. Yet on a visit in mid-January, sixteen months after the fire, I noticed that nearly every blackened stump was showing some greenery at the base. The heavy rains in November and December had caused the various kinds of grasses to grow thick and tall, and there were birds everywhere: house finches, white-crowned sparrows, golden-crowned sparrows, and lesser goldfinches foraged in flocks, with the sparrows providing the dinner music, assisted by two or three invisible wrentits. The brown towhees took part with an occasional chink, reminding me of grade school monotones who are allowed to accompany their musical classmates by "playing" percussion pie plates or cake tins. Dozens of quail, securely hidden, ticked and talked, discussing the intruder among themselves without bothering to lower their voices. They made it plain that they considered me a yark and a kookquat; since I didn't know what a yark or a kookquat was, I couldn't very well contradict them.

The same visit provided an unexpected bonus, a pair of black-chinned sparrows, male and female, resting on the burned branch of an olive tree. These birds are normally seen only during the late spring and summer in stands of chamise-dominant chaparral in the mountains or foothills. Finding them in January near the city limits was highly irregular. Perhaps the Coyote fire had something to do with their appearance, since the species is known to be partial to burn areas where the new vegetation is only half grown.

On my next visit to the olive grove in mid-July, most of the trees gave evidence that they would recover completely in time. Branches growing out of the woody crown were as long as six feet and covered with silver-green leaves.

Even without the braceros and the wine wagon to keep them on the job, there will someday be another crop of olives for the white-crowned sparrows, robins, and California thrashers.

After the Fire

The forest was turning green again. For residents of the fire areas the change was gradual. For those who only visited from time to time it was incredibly fast and far, from death to life. At the higher altitudes the white-bark ceanothus had a fresh growth of the tough, wiry stems and sharp spikes that kept predators away from such guests as the green-tailed towhee and the mountain quail. Closer to sea level the green-bark ceanothus was performing a similar function for the lazuli bunting and California quail, the wrentit and lark sparrow.

Soon manzanita apples would again be ripening for the cedar waxwings, toyon berries for the purple finches, and mistletoe for the phainopeplas. Oak buds were already appearing for the band-tailed pigeons, and there was promise of a fresh crop of chaparral currants for the hermit thrushes, mountain cherries for the Townsend solitaires, nightshade for the grosbeaks. Through the picture window beside my chair I watched the mountains recover from the fire, each day bringing a new patch of green that turned to violet when the sun set.

As each day of recovery came and went, and each new flight of birds landed on the ledge to feed, I was continually reminded of a letter John Keats sent to a friend in 1817.

"The setting Sun will always set me to rights," he wrote, "or if a Sparrow come before my Window I take part in its existence and pick about the Gravel."

Selection from

Panther!

ROGER CARAS

TURTLES ABOUNDED ON Bitterroot, thousands of them, and Panther found these easy to tear apart and eat. On one occasion, as he tore into some debris in which he thought a turtle was hiding, he heard an angry *whirrrr* and flew backward almost too late, just in time to avoid the strike of a badly irritated diamondback rattler who was escaping the midday heat.

There were very few alligators in the island's waters, for the poachers had been there many times. Those few that were left were small and not likely to survive the attrition natural to the area. There were other amphibious creatures, though, uncountable thousands of frogs and toads, at least nine kinds of turtles, and snakes of which more kinds were harmless than dangerous. All of the small mammals that had been found on Billy Buck were on Bitterroot as well, only more of them because of the island's larger size. It would have been all but impossible for even a less experienced animal than Panther to have starved and he settled down to check the hammock out in detail. There were deer on the north end of the island, more or less permanent residents, and several areas where raccoons were in plentiful supply. There were tens of thousands of crayfish to be found in the waters around the hammock and in its pools, and upon these the small hunters thrived. There were skunks on the island, too, and in a pinch these could be taken with a little special care. There were no permanent wild-pig residents, but signs abounded to

Panther!

prove that they came there regularly. The hammock was one of the very few areas within the Everglades where the nine-banded armadillo had become established. Probably descended from imports brought eastward from Louisiana by men with some purpose or other in mind, these small armored mammals managed to get a substantial foothold in a number of areas on the peninsula. Bitterroot, for better or for worse, was one of these, and armadillo holes were everywhere to be found.

As might be expected of so rich a larder, bears were not unknown to the island. However, the island had been hunted so often and bears so frequently taken in the preceding decades that those that had survived had a bad memory of the place and generally stayed away. But there were always old tramp bears moving through that part of the Glades, big old bears beyond their prime and filled with resentment, and they found Bitterroot and stopped there often enough to bring back an occasional bear hunter for a "look-see an' a sniff a' the old place."

Because of its great size and the way in which it loomed up out of the flats, because it sat hard by a major north–south slough carrying water from Okeechobee to the sea, and because the dense thickets that crowded its beaches promised safety to many a threatened animal, panthers included, Bitterroot had a highly mobile transient population. In fact it was a crossroads. On the one hand, that was good for the hunter—a varied diet was always available—and on the other hand, bad. Other predators knew about the hammock as well and more than one bear, more than one panther, had died there in violent battles and had sometimes been eaten. The numbers of both species shot and skinned could not even be reckoned. Just as many had been shot and allowed to crawl away to die. At best, the hammock known as Bitterroot Island was a dangerous and violent place. But then, to all of the natural inhabitants of the Everglades, Panther was a dangerous and violent animal. He and Bitterroot Island suited each other.

The world of the Everglades has two seasons, not four. The average summer temperature varies from the winter by only eighteen degrees. Monthly precipitation, however, varies from 1.4 to 9 inches. The two real seasons are the *wet* and *dry*.

It was November, the dry time, a time of danger in a world where water is the fulcrum of the natural balance. In the shallowest places out on the flats, dry ground was showing and the smaller pools no longer fed by either surface water from the north or by precipitation were drying out. Fish were dying by the thousands and so were frogs and turtles.

Ironically, those smaller aquatic and semi-aquatic animals that did survive would do so in many cases because of the alligator. It had dug many a hollow in the mud and here available water collected and life lasted longer. The alligators that had survived the poachers gathered at ever smaller pools and here the wading birds accumulated as well. It was stark, sere, a bad time.

The slough west of Bitterroot still had water, but it was markedly less than in the other season and steep banks showed that had been completely submerged when Panther first found the island. Of course, there was water to drink, for the hammock had pools and small ponds that survived the drought. The water wasn't as sweet and the number of snakes that gathered near this supply was dangerously high. It was now that Panther, in a single careless moment, was struck in the left foreleg by an eighteen-inch ground rattler.

When the snake struck, Panther flew straight up in the air as if his legs had been coiled springs. The pain was immediate and grew rapidly in intensity. The snake, one of dozens in the immediate area, had struck out from behind a small pile of debris as Panther stepped across it and had caught the careless cat just above the elbow. Luckily, a blood vessel had not been hit, but well-blooded muscle tissue was involved.

A very sick cat crawled away into a sheltered nest he had found beneath a windfall, a nest where a now dead panther mother had once raised her young, and lay there for several days. He shifted his position constantly in an effort to find a way of alleviating the pain. In four days a very hungry cat was limping out to hunt again, but it would be months before his leg would heal. He was lucky to have survived not only the envenomation but the secondary infection that followed.

In the few days that Panther was incapacitated by the bite of the small rattler, things had deteriorated even further in the world of the Everglades. No rain had fallen anywhere on the entire peninsula of Florida or on any of its islands in several weeks. The spillage from Lake Okeechobee had all but stopped completely and the groundwater that remained was fast disappearing. There was a constant, a discernibly frantic movement among the animals of the area. The otters were all gone,

gone to where there were still flowing rivers where they could survive. The birds that depended on aquatic life had also moved away for the most part or had gathered along the drainage ditches that men had built and that had helped endanger the area by carrying off too much water in a way that did no one any good.

Then it started, over to the west, but how, no one will ever know. At first there was only a hint of a black thread drifting up and away into a cloudless sky, but then there was another and another. In a matter of minutes there was a cluster of black smoke bunched up to the southwest, then another to the northwest. In less than half an hour they were joined and the light was changing its value. A full-blown saw-grass fire was underway and moving across the Glades of its own free will. There had been no wind at first, but now there was, a wind that carried the stink of the fire with it because it was fire-born, fire-bred and fire-reinforced.

Panther had never smelled fire before, but like all living creatures who may ever face the possibility of smoke and flame, he had an instinctive dread of its scent. At the first hint of it in the wind, he raised his head and stared off toward the west. He moved down to the shore as the first flights of ducks moved closer, the birds increased in number and variety. Egrets that had not yet moved off streamed past. Snipe and smaller birds, many of them newly arrived visitors from the north, bunched up overhead, exploded into ever-changing patterns, reconsolidated into tight flocks and burst outward again as they pulsed their way across the sky.

Panther was distracted for a moment when the first deer streamed into view, their dainty little hooves beating a distinctive tattoo on dry land where only weeks before water had flowed. There were two deer, then two more, then six, then ten. Dark little humps out on the flats moving toward Bitterroot took shape. There were raccoons, skunks, rats of all kinds and grizzled opossums. They were moving toward Bitterroot, around it, and on the eastward side of the island, fire-wise survivors of other droughts were moving off the island and away.

Now, from where Panther stood, a bright red-orange line could be seen below the black pall that all but filled the sky. There was a new noise, too, a *whoooosh* that seemed to promise that it would soon become a roar. The flames could be seen clearly and sparks and bits of burning matter were being carried on the wind. In the trees overhead these small incendiaries were being caught in the Spanish moss and

Of Fire and the Landscape

clumps of it were beginning to smolder. Panther turned and fled to the hammock's interior, for he was no less panicked than all of the other animals. Here was a threat against which there was no counterthreat. Here a blow of the paw could gain him nothing; there was no purchase for his claws in the fire winds.

The fire, only minutes old, had already consumed millions of lives, billions upon billions, really if the insects were included. Small pools had been sucked dry in seconds as the fire passed overhead. With a sizzling, snapping sound, water vanished and the mud curled and cracked and turned ash-gray. Birds rising late from grassy hides were snatched up by the heat and smashed to the ground, where they kicked convulsively for a second or two, no more. Fish stared upward in disbelief as the heat stripped their cover of water away and filled their gills with soot. They kissed the wind with foolishly puckered mouths for an instant and began to cook. Snakes coiled convulsively by the thousands, for they had neither the legs nor the wings that could carry them away from danger. All across the seared landscape they could be seen thrusting their coils in loops to the sky in the grotesque postures of the dead and the damned. Turtles, slower yet, baked in their own ovens.

The heat was suffocation on the hammock, and oxygen needed to support the flames that now were moving across the flats like a flood, was being drawn from the air, making it poorer and less sustaining. The noise was now incredible, and the stink sickened the cat and all the other creatures that had remained on the island. Streams of fire had flowed past the hammock on the south and a freshet from the south had pushed these fingers of fire toward the north. Animals that had fled from Bitterroot were being killed where they were caught in the open. Few even managed to cry out; they just curled and contorted and cooked. Thousands upon thousands of crayfish had already been boiled and abandoned; millions of frogs and toads had had their skin blister before their bodies popped and spilled out onto the ashes to become in the ensuing seconds little but ash themselves.

Only minutes remained before Panther would lose consciousness and his hide would begin to steam. He had waited too long. He didn't have the strength to flee and the air didn't have the oxygen left to help him muster any last bit of energy. On the westward shore three ancient docks that hunters had made for their punts had already passed the

Panther!

steaming point. The moisture that had gathered there for generations was gone and the wood, now like paper, would turn to flame in another minute or two with a slight explosive sound. In fact, there were a thousand places where the island was ready to burst into flames. The last moisture from its leaves, the last sap for its trunks, the last drops of water from the humus underfoot were evaporating. In minutes all of the hammock, all of Panther's new world, would vanish.

Since fires were blazing independently of each other in a hundred different places in Florida at that moment and since rain had to fall in each of these places eventually, and since it had to start somewhere, it would be stretching a point to say that the cloudburst was a miracle. It was one, perhaps, for Panther, because it saved his life, and seven of his kind had already died in fires that day.

At any rate the rain fell.

It came in torrents; it came from clouds too masked by soot and smoke to be seen. Fire speck after speck sizzled out of existence and a billion places saw ash and fire dust pocked by drops in the first seconds. In ten minutes the fire was out and small flowing streams were beginning to wash the dead into the sloughs that would float them away toward the Gulf.

With the water came a drop in temperature and with the wind came air and life. Panther and millions of other creatures that had survived limped off to rest and just to breathe. They now carried the seed for those that had perished. They now carried the past, and the future. Water and wind, air and life, flowed across the scarred land and repaired it and called down to those that still panted in the steaming destruction to repair themselves as well, because after the fire, as after all things that come and go in the lives of the wild, there is life, there is life, and that is all there is, all there ever was.

Fire Lookout: Numa Ridge

EDWARD ABBEY

July 12, Glacier National Park

We've been here ten days before I overcome initial inertia sufficient to begin this record. And keeping a record is one of the things the Park Service is paying us to do up here. The other, of course, is to keep our eyeballs peeled, alert for smoke. We are being paid a generous wage (about $3.25 an hour) to stay awake for at least eight hours a day. Some people might think that sounds like a pretty easy job. And they're right, it is an easy job, for some people. But not for all. When I mentioned to one young fellow down at the park headquarters, a couple of weeks ago, that I was spending the summer on this fire lookout he shuddered with horror. "I'd go nuts in a place like that," he said, thinking of solitary confinement. I didn't tell him I was cheating, taking my wife along. But that can be risky too; many a good marriage has been shattered on the rock of isolation.

Renee and I walked up here on July 2, packs on our backs, two hours ahead of the packer with his string of mules. The mules carried the heavier gear, such as our bed-rolls, enough food and water for the first two weeks, seven volumes of Marcel Proust, and Robert Burton's *Anatomy of Melancholy*. Light summer reading. Renee had never worked a fire lookout before, but I had, and I knew that if I was ever going to get through the classics of world lit it could only be on a mountain top, far above the trashy plains of *Rolling Stone*, *Playboy*, the *New York Times*, and *Mizz* magazine.

Fire Lookout: Numa Ridge

The trail is about six miles long from Bowman Lake and climbs 3,000 feet. We made good time, much better time than we wished because we were hustled along, all the way, by hordes of bloodthirsty mosquitoes. We had prepared ourselves, of course, with a heavy treatment of government-issue insect repellent on our faces, necks, arms, but that did not prevent the mosquitoes from whining in our ears and hovering close to eye, nostril, and mouth.

We also had the grizzly on our mind. Fresh bear scat on the trail, unpleasant crashing noises back in the dark of the woods and brush, reminded us that we were intruding, uninvited, into the territory of *Ursus horribilis*, known locally as G-bear or simply (always in caps) as GRIZ. It was in Glacier, of course, only a few years ago, that two young women had been killed on the same night by grizzlies. We clattered our tin cups now and then, as advised, to warn the bears we were coming. I was naturally eager to see a GRIZ in the wild, something I'd never done, but not while climbing up a mountain with a pack on my back, tired, sweaty, and bedeviled by bugs. Such an encounter, in such condition, could only mean a good-natured surrender on my part; I wasn't *about* to climb a tree.

Bear stories. My friend Doug Peacock was soaking one time in a hot spring in Yellowstone's backcountry. Surprised by a grizzly sow and her two cubs, he scrambled naked as a newt up the nearest pine; the bear kept him there, freezing in the breeze, for two hours. Another: Riley McClelland, former park naturalist at Glacier, and a friend were treed by a GRIZ. Remembering that he had an opened sardine can in his pack, Riley watched with sinking heart as the bear sniffed at it. Disdaining the sardine lure, however, the bear tore up the other man's pack to get at a pair of old tennis shoes.

Sacrifice, that may be the key to coexistence with the GRIZ. If we surprise one on the trail, I'll offer up first my sweat-soaked hat. If that won't do, then cheese and salami out of the pack. And if that's not enough, well, then nothing else to do, I guess, but push my wife his way. *Droit du seigneur a la montagne,* etc.

We reach the lookout without fulfilling any fantasies. The lookout is a two-room, two-story wood frame cabin at timberline, 7,000 feet above sea level. On the north, east, and southeast stand great peaks—Reuter, Kintla, Numa, Chapman, Rainbow, Vulture. Northwest we can see a bit

Of Fire and the Landscape

of the Canadian Rockies. West and southwest lie the North Fork of the Flathead River, a vast expanse of Flathead National Forest, and on the horizon the Whitefish Range. Nice view: 360 degrees of snow-capped scenic splendor, lakes, forest, river, fearsome peaks, and sheltering sky.

We remove the wooden shutters from the lookout windows, shovel snow from the stairway, unlock the doors. The pack string arrives. The packer and I unload the mules, the packer departs, Renee and I unpack our goods and move in. Except for a golden-mantled ground squirrel watching us from the rocks, a few Clark's nutcrackers in the subalpine firs, we seem to be absolutely alone.

July 14 (Bastille Day!)

The Great Revolution was a failure, they say. All revolutions have been failures, they say. To which I reply: All the more reason to make another one. Knocking off "work" at five o'clock (the transition from work to nonwork being here discernible by a subtle reshading in the colors of the rock on Rainbow Peak), my wife and I honor this day by uncorking a bottle of genuine Beaujolais. With Renee's home-baked crusty French bread and some real longhorn cheese from the country store down at the hamlet of Polebridge, it makes a fitting celebration.

A golden eagle soars by *below us,* pursued by—a sparrow hawk? My wife the bird-watcher is uncertain; but it must have been. Looking unhurried but pursuing a straight course, the eagle disappears into the vast glacial cirque above Akakola Lake, followed steadily, slightly above, by the smaller bird. More Clark's nutcrackers. Chipping sparrows. Mountain chickadees. Oregon juncoes. Clouds of mosquitoes whining at the windows, greedy for blood. A doe, a fawn, a yearling buck with velvet horns jostling one another at our salt deposits on the rocks outside. The doe is dominant; the young buck retreats. Women's Lib has reached out even here, for God's sake, all the way from Washington Square to Numa Ridge. Depressing thought. Striving to uphold the natural superiority of the male, I have beaten my wife—at chess—five games straight. Now she refuses to play with me. You can't win.

What *do* people do on a lookout tower when, as now, the season is wet and there are no fires? Aside from the obvious, and reading Proust and *The Anatomy of Melancholy,* we spend hours just gazing at the world through binoculars. For example, I enjoy climbing the local mountains, scaling the most hideous bare rock pitches step by step, hand by hand, without aids, without rope or partners, clinging to fragments of loose shale, a clump of bear grass, the edge of an overhanging snow cornice, above a nightmarish abyss, picking a route toward even higher and more precarious perches—through these U.S. Navy 7 x 50 lenses. The effortless, angelic, and supine approach to danger.

It's not all dreaming. There are some daily chores. Ever since arrival I've been packing snow to the lookout from a big drift a hundred yards below, carrying it up in buckets, dumping it into steel garbage cans, letting it melt in the sun. Now we've got 120 gallons of snow water in addition to the drinking water brought up by muleback. Then there's firewood. Although we have a propane stove for cooking, the only heat in the lookout comes from an old cast-iron cook-stove. And with the kind of rainy, windy weather we've been having, heat is a necessity. Even in July. So a couple of times a week I go down the trail with ax and saw, fell one of the many dead trees in the area—fir, whitebark pine—buck the log into eighteen-inch lengths, tote it up the hill armload by armload.

Three times a day we take weather observations—wind speed and direction, temperature, relative humidity—or my wife does, since she is the scientist in this family. We wash windows, occasionally. We patch and repair things. We listen to the Park Service radio and the Forest Service radio, ready to relay messages if necessary. I entertain the deer and the squirrels with my flute. Renee bakes things, studies the maps, memorizes the terrain. But mostly we sit quietly out on the catwalk, reading about aristocratic life in *fin-de-siecle* Paris and looking at northwestern Montana in the summer of '75.

This is a remote place indeed, far from the center of the world, far from all that's going on. Or is it? Wherever two human beings are alive, together, and happy, there is the center of the world. You out there brother, sister, you too live in the center of the world, no matter what you think you are.

July 16

Heavy cloud buildup in northwest. Lightning likely, fire danger rising, humidity dropping. The haze lies heavy over yonder Whitefish Range, obscuring the farther peaks. Looks like smog, but is only water vapor, dust, the smoke from many campfires along the North Fork. They tell us.

Of Fire and the Landscape

One longs for a nice little forest fire. We need some excitement around this joint. Nothing healthier for the forests than a good brisk fire now and then to clear out the undergrowth, give the moose and bear some living room. Besides we need the overtime pay. If that idiot Smokey the Bear (the noted ursine bore) had *his* way all us firefighters would starve to death.

We see a Townsend's solitaire, abundant here. Hermit thrush. Swallowtail butterflies. Little spiders hanging on threads from the attic trapdoor. A six-legged spider (war veteran) on the outside of the windowpane chewing on a mosquito. Good show! mate. One snowshoe hare loping into the brush.

Gordon the Garbage Man, one of the park's seasonal employees, comes up the mountain for a visit, leaves us two big Dolly Vardens fresh from the lake. Fried by my frau, filleted and anointed with lemon, they make a delicately delicious supper. If I weren't so corrupt and lazy, I'd take hook and line myself, drop down to Lake Akakola 1,200 feet below, and catch a similar supper every evening. According to the old logbooks here, at least some of the previous lookouts used to do that.

Officially, all measurements at Glacier National Park are now given in meters. All road and trail signs, all park maps, show distances and heights in meters and kilometers, without their Anglo-American equivalents. The Park Service, no doubt at the instigation of the Commerce Department, is trying to jam the metric system down our throats whether we want it or not. We can be sure this is merely the foot in the door, the bare beginning of a concerted effort by Big Business—Big Government (the two being largely the same these days) to force the metric system upon the American people. Why? Obviously for the convenience of world trade, technicians, and technology, to impose on the entire planet a common system of order. All men must march to the beat of the same drum, like it or not.

July 17

Still no real fires, aside from a few trivial lightning-storm flare-ups in the forest across the river, soon drowned by rain. But we are ready. Perhaps I should describe the equipment and operations of a lookout.

We live and work in the second story of the cabin. The ground-floor room, dark and dank, is used only for storage. Our room is light, airy, and bright, with windows running the length of all four walls. Closable louvred vents above each window admit fresh air while keeping out rain. In the center of this twelve-foot by twelve-foot room, oriented squarely with the four directions, stands the chest-high fire finder. The Osborne Fire Finder consists essentially of a rotating metal ring about two feet in diameter with a handle to turn it by and a pair of sights, analogous to the front and rear sights of a rifle, mounted upright on opposite sides. When the lookout spots a fire, he aims this device at the base and center of the smoke (or flame, if discovered at night) and obtains an azimuth reading from the fixed base of the fire finder, which is marked off into 360 degrees. By use of the vernier scale attached to the rotating ring, the lookout can get a reading not only in degrees but precisely to the nearest minute, or one-sixtieth of a degree.

Having determined the compass direction of the fire from his own location, the lookout must still establish the location of the fire. To do that he must be able to recognize and identify the place where the fire is burning and to report its distance from his lookout station. A metal tape stretched between front and rear sights of the fire finder, across a circular map inside the rotating ring, gives the distance in kilometers. Another aid is the sliding peep sight on the rear sight, by means of which the lookout can obtain a vertical angle on his fire. Through a bit of basic trigonometry the vertical angle can be translated into the distance. Or if another lookout, at a different station, can see the same fire, the line of his azimuth reading extended across a map of the area intersects the line of the first lookout's reading to give the exact point of the fire. Assuming both lookouts are awake, fairly competent, and on duty at the same time.

If these procedures sound complicated, that is an illusion. The technical aspects of a lookout's job can be mastered by any literate anthropoid with an IQ of not less than seventy in about two hours. It's the attitude that's difficult: Unless you have an indolent, melancholy nature, as I do, you will not be happy as an official United States government fire lookout.

Anyway, having determined the location of his fire, and being reasonably certain it is a fire and not a smoking garbage dump, a controlled slash burn, a busy campground, floating vapors, or traffic dust rising from a dirt road, the lookout picks up his radio microphone or telephone and reports his discovery to fire-control headquarters. After that

Of Fire and the Landscape

his main task becomes one of assisting the smoke-chasers in finding the fire, relaying messages, looking for new and better fires.

July 20

Bear claw scratches on the wooden walls of the ground-floor storage room. Last thing before retiring each night I set the bear barrier in place on the stairway leading to our quarters. The bear barrier is a wooden panel with many nails driven through it, the points all sticking out. Supposed to discourage *Ursus stairiensis* from climbing up to our cat-walk balcony. In a previous lookout's log we had read this entry:

Woke up this morning to see a big black bear staring up at me thru window, about six inches from my face. Chased him off with a Pulaski.

The Pulaski is a fire-fighting tool, a combination ax and pickax. I keep one handy too, right under the bed where I can reach it easy. I'd keep it under the pillow if my old lady would let me.

Thinking about GRIZ. Almost every day, on the park or forest radio, we hear some ranger report a bear sighting, sometimes of grizzly. Campers molested, packs destroyed by hungry and questioning bears. Somebody was recently attacked and mauled by a GRIZ north of the line, in Waterton Lakes. Bear jams on the park highway, though not so common here as they used to be in Yellowstone, before so many of Yellowstone's bears mysteriously disappeared, do occur in Glacier from time to time.

No doubt about it, the presence of bear, especially grizzly bear, adds a spicy titillation to a stroll in the woods. My bear-loving friend Peacock goes so far as to define wilderness as a place and only a place where one enjoys the opportunity of being attacked by a dangerous wild animal. Any place that lacks GRIZ, or lions or tigers, or a rhino or two, is not in his opinion, worthy of the name "wilderness." A good definition, worthy of serious consideration. A wild place without dangers is an absurdity, although I realize that danger creates administrative problems for park and forest managers. But we must not allow our national parks and national forest to be degraded to the status of mere public playgrounds. Open to all, yes of course. But—*enter at your own risk.*

Enter Glacier National Park and you enter the homeland of the grizzly bear. We are uninvited guests here, intruders, the bear our reluctant host. If he chooses, now and then, to chase somebody up a tree, or all the way to the hospital, that is the bear's prerogative. Those who prefer, quite reasonably, not to take such chances should stick to Disneyland in all its many forms and guises.

July 22

Bowman Lake 3,000 feet below looks more like clear Pennzoil than water. A milky turquoise green color, strange to my eyes. The North Fork even more so. The cause is not man-made pollution of any sort, but what is called "glacier milk," a solution of powdered rock washed down from under the bellies of the glaciers hanging all around us under the high peaks.

Toy boats glide up and down the lake, trailing languorous wakes that spread across the oil-smooth water in slow-subsiding ripples. Anglers at work. The fishing is poor this summer, they say; weather too wet, too much insect life in the air and floating down the streams.

Too wet? You can say that again. This is the foggiest, boggiest, buggiest country I have ever seen in my life. Everywhere I look, below timberline, the land is clothed in solid unbroken greenery. Damp, humid green all over the place—gives the country an unhealthy look. I guess I really am a desert rat. The sound of all these verdant leafy things breathing and sweating and photosynthesizing around me all the time makes me nervous. Trees, I believe (in the ardor of my prejudice), like men, should be well spaced off from one another, not more than one to a square mile. Space and scarcity give us dignity. And liberty. And thereby beauty.

Oyster stew for lunch. Out of a tin can. Had buckwheat cakes for breakfast, with wild huckleberry syrup by Eva Gates, Bigfork, Montana.

Enormous clouds with evil black bottoms floating in from the Pacific, great sailing cities of cumulo-nimbus. Lightning plays among their massy depths. Will it bring us fire? God, one hopes so. What are we up here for, perched like condors on this mighty mountain, if not to conjure up a storm? The children need shoes. All those fire fighters down at headquarters need overtime. The forest needs a rebirth, a renascence, a weeding out.

Of Fire and the Landscape

July 23

Down the mountain I go, returning same day with mail, wine, cheese, other essentials. I sing, as I march along, songs I hope will warn the GRIZ of my approach. But what kind of music does the GRIZ like? Suppose he *hates* old cowboy songs? Or Puccini?

All the way up the mountain, under a dark and grumbling sky, a personal cloud of hungry mosquitoes envelopes my head. I am relieved and glad when the first lightning strikes begin to bounce off the crags above. Am less glad when I reach the open ridge at timberline with jagged high-voltage bolts crashing all around. No place to hide now; I keep going for the relative safety of the lookout cabin and reach it just as the storm bursts out in all its awful grandeur.

We cower inside in the dark, Renee and I, trying to stay away from all metal objects, as instructed. But, of course, the lookout is crowded with metallic objects—iron stoves, fire finder, steel cots, water cans, buckets, ax, dishpan. We can feel the next charge building up: we stand on the negative terminal of a high-powered electrical system, the positive pole directly overhead. Our skin prickles, our hair stands up. We hear a fizzing noise above us, on the roof of the cabin where the lightning rod sticks up. A crackling sound, like a burning fuse. I know what's coming now, and an instant later it comes, a flash that fills the room with blue-white light, accompanied simultaneously by a jarring crash, as if the entire cabin had been dropped from the sky upon our rocky ridge. No harm done. The building is thoroughly grounded, top and sides, and Thor's hummer blow passes on safely into the heart of the mountain. Lightning strikes many times in the same place. As every lookout learns.

That evening we spot a couple of small flare-ups across the river in the national forest. But both are soon drowned out by rain and never go anywhere.

July 27

The bird list grows slowly. Add barn swallow, cliff swallow, water pipit, raven, blue grouse, white-tailed ptarmigan, rufous hummingbird, brown creeper, gray jay, evening grosbeak, red-shafted flicker, loon. *Loon!*— heard from the lake far below—that wild, lorn, romantic cry, one of the most thrilling sounds in all North America. Sound of the ancient wilderness, lakes, forest, moonlight, birchbark canoes.

Fire Lookout: Numa Ridge

The flowers have been blooming, on and off, ever since we got here. We've identified the following so far: purple-eyed mariposa, false asphodel, valerium, harebell, blue penstemon, arnica, fleabane, mountain penstemon, bear grass, sulfur flower, stonecrop, Indian paintbrush, alum root, glacier lily, prince's pine, mountain gentian, forget-me-not, bluebonnet, alpine buttercup, yellow columbine, elephant head, blanket flower, alpine aster, swamp laurel, fireweed.

The bear grass, with its showy panicle of flowers on a two- or three-foot stalk, is the most striking flower in Glacier. It reminds me of pictures of the giant lobelia on the slopes of Mount Kilimanjaro. The deer eat the flower stalks.

Bear sighting reported on park radio: A ranger reports one grizzly sow with two cubs in "Moose Country," along the Going-to-the-Sun Highway. The bear, he says, is reared up on her hind legs, roaring and waving her arms at tourists as they surround her, their cameras clicking. He breaks it up. Nobody hurt. This time.

The park radio is our chief amusement. Over a million people visited the park last summer, most of them driving through by way of the Going-to-the-Sun. Many traffic problems every day, much police work.

Exempli gratia 1: 1961 converted schoolbus at Logan Pass, brakes burned out, driver thinks he can bring bus down mountain by driving in low gear, requests ranger escort. Not allowed. Tow truck dispatched.

E.g. 2: Ranger reports distraught wife and children at Lake McDonald campground. "Woman is very upset," he says. Cause? Her husband, the children's father, went off on a hike with a fifteen-year-old baby-sitter, been gone for hours. (Family is reunited later in evening.)

E.g. 3: Rookie ranger reports five bikers camping under highway bridge and smoking a controlled substance. "I think they're smoking dope," he says, "although, of course, I don't know what dope smells like."

Our friend Gus Chambers up on Swiftcurrent Lookout in the center of the park spots the first genuine park fire of the season. (And the only one as it turns out.) He gives his azimuth, the UTM (Universal Transverse Mercator) coordinates, locates it one kilometer south-southeast of Redhorn Lake. No one can see the fire but Gus; we other lookouts are sick with envy and rage. One snag burning in a small valley, remote from any trail; too windy for smoke jumpers, firefighters are flown to scene by helicopter.

Fire caused by lightning. When Smokey Bear says that only You can prevent forest fires, Smokey is speaking an un-truth. A falsehood. Ninety percent of the fires in the American West are lightning-caused, as they have been for the last 20,000 years, or ever since the glaciers retreated. Yet the forests survived. And thrived. Hard to explain this to some old-time foresters, who often feel the same passionate hatred for fire that sheepmen feel for coyotes. Now, after fifty years of arduous fire-suppression effort, the useful role of natural fire in the forest ecosystem is becoming recognized among foresters. But the public, indoctrinated for so long in the Smokey Bear ethic, may not be easy to reeducate.

No one disputes the fact that it will always be necessary to quell forest fires that threaten lives, homes, business establishments, or valuable stands of timber scheduled for logging.

July 30

Renee bakes a prune pie. An experiment. I read Burton on "Heroical Love." The days sail by with alarming speed; why this headlong descent into *oblivion?* What's the rush? Sinking comfortably into the sloth and decay of my middle middle age, I am brought up short nevertheless, now and then, by the alarming realization that all men, so far, have proved mortal. Me too? Each day seems more beautiful than the last. Every moment becomes precious. Thus are we driven to the solitary pleasures of philosophy, the furtive consolations of thought.

Gus's fire is out. Burnt only five acres. Snow slides in Logan Pass again, traffic halted. Hiker killed on Snyder Lake trail, trying to climb cliff. Child lost and found. Woman, sixty-seven, lost for three hours near Bowman Lake. Found. GRIZ trees three hikers at Trout Lake.

More bugs. Mosquitoes as numerous as ever, soon to be augmented by swarms of flying ants. And now another enemy, the moose fly, appears, the bloodsucking *Muscas horribilis sangria.* Mean, vicious Draculas with wings. About the size of bats. We stay inside when the wind dies and all these flying plagues come forth together.

I read the old lookout logs. First of all Numa Ridge lookouts was Scotty Beaton, who worked here twenty-two years summers, beginning in 1929. Unlike all succeeding lookouts, whose logbook entries tend (like mine) to rant and ramble, Scotty kept his notation terse, laconic, to the point. Viz.:

Aug. 2, 1945: hot & dry done my usual chores

July 28, 1946: Very warm—Hugh Buchanan the ranger came up with a Paper to have me Pledge I wouldn't overthrow the government that never entered my mind in the fifty five years I been in this country.

July 5, 1948: Moved up today the bears had moved into the lower part of the Lookout & took a few bites out of the upper story. The lower part a hell of a mess.

July 12, 1949: Done usual chores

Sept. 11, 1950: Found mud in bottom of water barrel put there by youngster from McFarland's dude ranch. Same kid who broke crosshairs on firefinder, tramped down nails in bear board and set my binoculars on the hot stove.

According to the logbooks, every lookout since Scotty found Numa Ridge a delightful place—but only one of the twenty-four (including many couples) came back for a second season, and the second was enough for him. In the fire lookout's vocation many are called, few chosen. The isolation is too much for most. This is my seventh summer as a lookout; I guess I like it.

Down on Loneman Peak in the southern part of Glacier sits Leonard Stittman. This is his fourteenth summer on Loneman. In all those summers he has had a total of eight visitors, all of them rangers.

We've had a ranger-visitor too—Art Sedlack, the man who shot the snowmobile.

It happened one night in December 1974. Sedlack, on duty at Walton Ranger Station in Glacier, caught a snowmobiler buzzing around in an area where snowmobiles are not supposed to be. This sort of thing had been going on for a long time, and the operator of this particular snowmobile was a repeat offender. Suddenly inspired, Sedlack drew his trusty .38 Ranger Special and shot the snowmobile right through the head. "One snowmobile, immobilized," he reported by radio. Sensation! For a while Sedlack's rear end was in a sling as the owner of the snowmobile and other local motorized recreationists demanded blood, a

Of Fire and the Landscape

head for a head. Sedlack might have lost his job but for an outpouring of public support, phone calls and letters from all over western Montana. Reconsidering, the park administration suspended him for one week without pay, then sent him to the service's police-training school in Washington, D.C. Now he is back in Glacier, an unrepentant and even better ranger.

Art talks about the bear problem in the national parks. Really a human problem. Too many humans crowding the roads and trails, conflict inevitable. Solution: Reduce population. Which population? Ah yes, indeed, that is the question.

A bear, when caught in mischief, is tranquilized and tagged on the ear. Caught again, it is tagged on the other ear. A bear with both ears tagged is in trouble. It may be transported to a locality remote from human activity, but this is not a solution. There are no vacant areas in nature. The newcomer bear is not welcome among established inhabitants, is harried, fought, driven out by native bears, becomes a loner, an outlaw, a rogue—doomed. If caught in trouble a third time he or she will likely be "taken away" for good. That is, shot dead.

August 2

Fog and rain. Foul is fair and fair is foul. Cut more wood, keeping the bin full. When I go down the hill to the john in the morning I find the mosquitoes huddled inside, waiting for me as usual. As usual I light up a Roi-Tan, a good cheap workingman's cigar, and the mosquitoes flee, choking and swearing. I sit there and contemplate, through the smoke, the dim shapes of fir tree and mule deer through the mists. On clear mornings, sunshine on my lap, I can look right down on the pearly, oily, iridescent surface of Bowman Lake in all its incredible rich blueness. I think, if I think at all, about simplicity, convenience, the advantages of what I call Positive Poverty.

There is of course no flush toilet on a fire lookout. But the pit toilet is a perfectly adequate, comfortable, and even pleasant substitute for the elaborate bathrooms of the modern home. A little lime or wood ashes keep down the odors, discourage flies. In cold weather one kerosene or Coleman lamp keeps the outhouse warm enough. What more does one need? And no freezing pipes, no water pump, no septic tank to worry about, no awful plumber's bills. And the basic good sense of it: Instead of flushing our bodily wastes into the public water supply, we plant them back in the good earth where they belong. Where our bodies must go as well, in due course, if we are to keep the good earth productive.

Nor is there running water up here. Or electricity. I carry the water by the bucketful up from the barrels in the cellar. We heat the water on the wood stove, wash and scald-rinse the dishes in a pair of dishpans, bathe (when we feel like it) in a small galvanized tub set on the floor or out on the catwalk when the sun is shining. Before the big drifts melted, Renee and I sometimes scrubbed ourselves with handfuls of snow, standing naked on the dazzling snowbanks, in the heat of the sun.

Hauling water, cutting firewood, using a pit toilet seem like only normalcy to me, raised as I was on a backwoods Pennsylvania farm. For Renee, a city girl, these methods are new, but she adapts at once, without difficulty, to such minor deprivations. No problem at all. Most of what we call modern conveniences are no more than that at best. They are far from being necessities. And what a terrible price most of us have to pay for our tract homes, our fancy plumbing, our automobiles, our "labor-saving" appliances, the luxuriously packaged ersatz food in the supermarkets, all that mountain of metal junk and plastic garbage under which our lives are smothered. Men *and* women trapped in the drudgery and tedium of meaningless jobs (see Studs Terkel's *Working* if you don't believe me), and the despoliation of a continent, the gray skies, the ruined rivers, the ravaged hills, the clear-cut forests, the industrialized farms, all to keep that Gross National Product growing ever grosser. Madness and folly. Untouched by human hands. Unguided by human minds.

Not that technology and industrialism are evil in themselves. The problem is to get them down to human scale, to keep them under human control, to prevent them from ever again becoming the self-perpetuating, ever-expanding monsters we have allowed them to become. What we need is an optimum industrialism, neither to much nor too little, a truly sophisticated, unobtrusive, below-ground technology. For certainly science, technology, industrialism have given us a number of good things. Not many, but some. My list begins with the steel ax. Matches. Nails, hammer, handsaw. Writing paper and pen and ink. The birth-control pill. Or the condom. (Forget-me-not.) Galvanized bucket—no, strike that item; the old oaken bucket is good enough. The cast-iron stove. Electricity. And solar heating. Windmills and suction pumps. Candles, Aladdin lamps, pianos, and platinum flutes. The coal-burning locomotive, transcontinental train service, the horse collar, the pneumatic-tired wagon, bicycles, the rocket-powered spaceship. But not automobiles. (What? Spaceships! Yes. Why not? I believe space exploration is a worthy human adventure.) Radios and record players, but not BHT, sodium nitrate, monosodium glutamate, or artificial coloring. The democratic rifle and the egalitarian revolver, but not the authoritarian B-52. And so on.

But we cannot pick and choose this way, some technophiles may insist—it's the entire package, plagues and all, or nothing. To which one must reply: If that is true then we have indeed lost control and had better dismantle the whole structure. But it is not true: We *can* pick and choose, we can learn to select this and reject that. Discrimination is a basic function of the human intelligence. Are we to be masters or slaves of the techno-industrial machine?

My cigar has gone out. The mosquitoes come sneaking back. They whine around my ears like the sirens of commerce, like bill collectors, like the National Association of Manufacturers. The sound of greed.

Time to sharpen the old ax. A chill wind is blowing and the fog rolls in again. Dark birds flap through the mist, croaking for blood.

August 3

Done usual lookout chores.

August 4

Done usual lookout chores. To wit: woke, ate, answered radio check, looked, chopped wood, carried water, read Burton ("Of all causes of this affliction," he writes, meaning romantic love, "the most remote are the stars"), looked, re-leveled fire finder, washed dishes, played chess then flute, watched sun go down, went to bed.

In the evening after sundown an owl flies round and round the lookout, swooping silent as a moth through the fog and gloom, checking out our chipmunks. Barred owl? Short-eared owl? Hard to tell in this darkness. A spooky bird of ill import.

August 5

My wife looks prettier every day. By God, a man begins to get ideas in a place like this.

Fire Lookout: Numa Ridge

August 7

High winds all day, clear sky, scudding clouds. The surface of the lake below, stirred by the wind, looks like brushed aluminum, has the color of my knife blade. The peaks round about stand forth in startling, blazing, preternatural brilliance. A cold, immaculate clarity. Shall we climb Rainbow Peak one of these days? Ever see Goat Haunt? Belly River? Mount Despair? Loneman? Gunsight Pass? Rising Wolf Mountain? Spirit Lake? Two Medicine Mountain? Almost a Dog Mountain? Vulture Peak?

August 11

Storms. Fog and drizzle, brief blaze of sun—a rainbow floats in the fog below.

Lightning again, flashing through the mist; the thunder rumbles in at a thousand feet per second. Pink lightning. Heaven and earth link nerves in illuminated ecstasy—or is it pain? Once, in another place, I saw lightning score a direct hit on a juniper tree. The tree exploded in a burst of flame.

Now comes another direct hit on our lookout. First the buzzing sound, the eerie *hiss* and *fizz* directly overhead. That sinister touch, God's fingertip upon our roof. Light, deadly, an almost dainty touch, you might say. Followed by the flash of light and the *crack!* of a great whip. The building vibrates.

When the hard winds blow the cabin creaks and groans, tugging at the cables that keep it anchored to the rock. On our east side the ridge drops off at fifty degrees down a tree-less slope to the bottom of the cirque 600 feet blow.

In the evening things settle down a bit. We go for a walk down the trail, down through the drifting fog. The huckleberries are ripening now, but it looks like a poor crop. The bears will be roaming and irritable. Mushrooms bulge through the damp duff under the pines—fat, brown, speckled domes of fungoid flesh. Delicacies for the deer. The mushrooms remind me of bitter days at another lookout post, 2,000 miles away and a decade in the past. I was enduring the agonies of unrequited love, exactly as Burton describes them, and in my misery I contemplated with interest some of the mushrooms growing all about the tower of that other lookout; the rosy hoods of *Amanita muscaria* suggested the possibility of flight beyond the sorrows of this sublunar sphere. But I refrained, not from fear of hallucination or death, but because I was becoming accustomed to the realization that I enjoyed my sufferings more. So the girl I loved had betrayed me by running off with her husband. What of it? I survived.

Men have died and worms have eaten them, but not for love.

August 15

Been gone three days, leaving Renee to man the lookout on her own. She was willing and ready and is in fact a better fire lookout than I. Much more conscientious, not so corrupted by subversive notions of fire ecology, etc.

Down from Numa Ridge, the first thing I did was go to Logan Pass, hike the Highline Trail to Granite Park and up Swiftcurrent Peak to visit Gus at his fire lookout. Late in the evening I returned to Logan Pass. Nineteen miles round trip. On the way I had passed a group of mountain goats, six of them, grazing not fifty feet from the trail, indifferent to my presence. Returning at twilight, I encountered five big-horn rams bunched up right on the trail, blocking my way. They showed no inclination to move and I wasn't going to climb around them. I approached to within twenty feet, waved my arms and whistled; grudgingly they got up and let me through. That's the way it is in the Peaceable Kingdom, the wildlife so accustomed to hikers they won't even get out of your way.

I had timed my walk badly. The dark settled in while I was still five miles from Logan Pass, the road, and my car. The trail wound through thickets of alder brush, with a cliff on my left and a drop-off on my right. A cloudy, starless night. Hard to see more than ten, fifteen feet ahead. Odd noises off in the thickets. I began to think about GRIZ again. What to do if I met one now? No climbable trees in sight and my only weapon a pocketknife. Words of wisdom, often heard at Glacier, whispered through my brain: "Anyone who hikes alone, after dark, is asking for trouble." Bears are omnivorous, have no pride at all, will eat anything, even authors. Even if the GRIZ hears me coming, I realized, he will have difficulty getting out of my way on this mountain trail. We'd have to sidle past one another, smiling apologetically, like strangers in a narrow doorway. I walked on, singing loudly, feeling foolish, half amused by my own fear. Yes, I did want to meet a grizzly in the wild—but not just yet. Nothing happened that night. I saw nothing but shadows, heard nothing but the wind and those obscure crashing sounds, now and then, below the trail.

August 16

Old magazines on the shelves under the fire finder, left here by former lookouts. I leaf through *Field and Stream, Outdoor Life, Hook & Bullet News*. Here's an interesting item:

> *Stock taking.* California has a new procedure for scattering the trout it stocks in streams in an attempt to foil hatchery-truck chasers. The fish are not released until dusk or after dark and are placed in one spot rather than in several. Wardens report that the fish are well scattered by daylight and the night stocking stymies the truck followers.

And another:

> *Pump Priming.* In an effort to stimulate the lagging fishing and subsequent business decline caused by the ban on keeping fish caught in Lake St. Clair, the Michigan Marine and Snowmobile Dealers Association is trying to raise $50,000 to $100,000 to finance the tagging of thousands of fish that would be worth anywhere from $100 to $10,000 apiece to the anglers catching them. The ban resulted from mercury contamination tests run on some of the lake's fish.

So it goes, sportsmen.

Reflections on hunting. My father was a hunter. During the Great Depression and the war years, he killed dozens of deer, hundreds of cottontail rabbits, in order to put meat on the table for his hungry family. My mother would can the extra rabbit, putting it up in jars. During the fifties and sixties, as the times got better, my father gradually gave up hunting. Never in his life has he killed another living thing for sport. Except, that is, during his boyhood. Before he grew up. Hunters, he would explain, never kill for sport.

All those red-coated men we see out in the field during deer season—what are they up to? Well some of them are hunters, engaged in the ancient, honorable, and serious business of providing meat for kith and kin. The majority, however, outnumbering the hunters and the deer as well by ninety-nine to one, are not hunters but merely gunners. Sportsmen.

The sportsman's pursuit of game is incidental to his primary purposes, which can be defined as follows, in descending order of importance:

1. Get away from wife and kids for a few days
2. Get drunk and play poker with cronies by the light of a Coleman lamp in tent, lodge, or Winnebago
3. Swap lies with same
4. Maybe shoot some legal game
5. Failing that, shoot some illegal game—cow, horse, chicken, game warden, etc.
6. Failing that, shoot *something*—side of barn, road sign, his own foot, whatever's handy.

How do I know about this? Because I was there. I too was once a sportsman. But I grew up. In that one respect anyhow. Like my old man, Paul, who beat me to it.

August 18

Somebody falls into McDonald Falls again. "Bring the wagon," radios ranger. The hurry-up wagon. Happens every year. As at North Rim, Grand Canyon, where somebody disappears every summer.

Whole family mauled by a grizzly on Grinnel Glacier trail. Father, mother, two children. Apparently the children had been walking far ahead of their parents, got between a sow and her cub. Children attacked. Their screams bring father running to the scene, who attempts to fight off the GRIZ with his bare hands. Reinforced by mother, the bear knocks them both about, then wanders off. Entire family hospitalized with serious injuries. Rangers close trail to further hiking for time being.

Might be hard to explain to those people why the grizzly bear is a vital part of the Glacier wilderness. But it is. The parks are for people? Certainly. And for bears also? Absolutely. How do we resolve the inevitable conflict? Are we going to ration the wilderness experience? Probably; that process has already begun at Glacier National Park, where backcountry camping is restricted to certain sites, requiring written permits and advance reservations. A sad and ominous but unavoidable expedient.

Fire Lookout: Numa Ridge

One calamity after another. One mishap after another. A ranger's work is never done. And more and more, in every national park, that work consists largely of police work. The urbanization of our national parks. All through the summer bumper-to-bumper auto traffic crawls up and down the Going-to-the-Sun Highway. I've said it before and I'll say it again, we've got to close the parks to private cars if we want to keep them parks. The parks are for people, not machines. Let the machines find their own parks. Most of America has surrendered to them already, anyway. New Jersey, for example. Southern California.

On the forest radio, the weather report concludes as usual with the daily firefighting capability report: "We have available in Missoula today fifty-two smoke jumpers, two B-16s, one Neptune, two twin Beechcraft, two helicopters, four DC-7s, etc." All on standby, in readiness.

There used to be ten active fire-lookout stations in Glacier. Now there are only four. My old lookout tower on North Rim was deactivated five years ago. More and more lookouts are superseded by aircraft patrols. Part of the national industrializing pattern, human beings put out of work by machines. Labor-intensive jobs (so to speak) made obsolete by capital-intensive substitutes. One hour of an airplane's time costs more than two or three days' pay for a human lookout on a mountaintop. But no doubt it is, as they say, more efficient. And what happens to all the displaced fire lookouts? They swell the ranks of the unemployed. They wander the streets of small western towns, kicking beer cans around, getting in trouble.

Who cares? Most fire lookouts are crazy anyhow. Once from a peak in southern Arizona, at sundown, with the western sky full of smoke, dust, and clouds, I looked straight at the sun with my lookout's binoculars. I knew it was a foolish thing to do. Could have ruined my eyes forever. At the very least might have impaired my night vision. But the haze seemed so extremely dense, the sun so blood-red behind it, that I thought it might be safe, just this once. All I wanted was one quick glimpse of those plasmic bonfires 10,000 miles high leaping into space from the rim of the roaring sun. So I looked. And I saw them. It was a sublime and terrifying spectacle, which I can never forget. And my eyes survived apparently unharmed, although a few years later I began to have trouble reading numbers in a phone book, and my arms seemed too short to hold a newspaper far enough away from my eyes to make it readable.

Of Fire and the Landscape

"You need glasses," the eye doctor said. "You're far-sighted."

"Why?"

"Middle age."

I told him about the time I stared at the sun face to face.

"You were lucky," he said.

August 22

Renee takes off for a three- or four-day tour of the park, leaving me here alone with my dirty dishes and the unswept floor. Two old-time park naturalists arrive, sit around drinking my coffee and telling what they call North Dakota jokes.

"Why won't a North Dakotan eat pickles?"

"Can't get his head in the jar."

"What does it say on the bottom of Coke bottles in North Dakota?"

"Open other end."

Etc. They do all the laughing.

Fog and rain, rain and fog. The fire season is shot to hell. Word from headquarters is that we're to be "terminated" (without prejudice) on September 5. Lookout completely socked in. Black bear with two cubs seen near Moose Wallow during my evening walk. Huckleberries, whortleberries, raspberries all ripening, but few of them.

The short-eared owl comes back at dusk, circling my glass-walled home. Perhaps it is me that silent bird is looking for. All my superstitions rise to the surface. At midnight under the full moon, dip your hand in the punky water of a hollow stump if you want to rid it of warts. Etc.

Cut and stack wood, refilling bin. Install new stovepipe. Caulk window frames. Repair broken shutters. Won't be here much longer.

One young punk showed up at nine-thirty this morning, jogging up the trail. Gasping for breath, before he even said hello he asked what time it was. So he could time his hike. A goggle-eyed bore with hairy legs, wearing track shorts and tennis shoes. Outward Bound type. He hung around for a few minutes, saw little of interest in me or the lookout, and trotted down the trail again, vanishing into the clouds below.

Days now getting perceptibly shorter. Full moon rising over Rainbow Peak. Grand, gorgeous, shocking-pink sunset. Feel of autumn in the air. In August! Two golden eagles hovering on the sky, high above my cabin. God Bless America—Let's Save Some of It. Long live the weeds and wilderness yet.

August 23

Rain, wind, rain, and fog. When the storm clears I see fresh snow on Kintla, Rainbow, and Reuter peaks, down to the 8,000-foot line. Temperature was 34 degrees F this morning at 0630. Everything was wet and slimy. Expect to see snails and other Mollusca crawling up the windowpanes. Horny octopi...

August 24

Awoke this morning, after a long cold night, to find two inches of snow on the catwalk railing, on the pines, on everything in sight. Wet, fat snow, clinging to every twig and needle.

Renee returns, but only briefly. Has to leave at once for Vancouver. Her grandfather's dying. I am alone for the final week of this cold, dismal, rain- and snow-soaked mountain. I get so lonesome I wash the dishes for diversion. Loneliness. Mount Despair. Wintertime in August.

August 26

Termination date has now been advanced to August 28. I go for long walks in the evening, hoping for one clear sight of GRIZ. The silence of the woods. No birds speak except one woodpecker, far below, hammering on a snag. But 1,000 feet below, under the snowline, the weather is late summer. Tufts of moss, like scalp locks, dangle from the branches of the lodgepole pine, the larch, the spruce. This is the forest primeval. Elaborate spiderwebs hang face-high across the trail, each with a tiny golden spider waiting at the center. Damp smells of fern and pine bark, the distant drumming of the woodpecker. Sounds like Red Norvo at the vibraphone. Bluebells still in bloom down here, wild roses trail. I pause on the way back up to drink a handful; the sweet, cold, piney flavor reminds me of boyhood, the Allegheny Mountains back in old Pennsylvania. Lost at twilight in the green depths of the Big Woods.

Back to the cold darkness of the lookout cabin. I build a fire in the stove, sit with my feet on the open oven door and play the flute. The deer outside lift their heads to listen for a moment, then resume their feeding.

Of Fire and the Landscape

Down in Arizona I used to rouse the coyotes at dawn, playing certain high notes on this silver-plated instrument. I'd play our tune and wait and after a few moments their wild cries came floating back to me across the desert, mimicking my song.

August 27

Last full day on the mountain. Sun shining for a change. Many deer hang about, fighting over my various urine-supplied salt deposits. Obvious pecking order among them: One old battle-scarred six-point buck is clearly dominant; the others keep their distance from him but jostle one another roughly.

Always looking and listening, these deer. Even the fawns have that wary look. Danger everywhere. Nor do they look well-fed, even now in late summer. Gaunt and ganted, lean and bony deer, how will they ever get through the coming winter? A tough life. Always hard times for deer. The struggle for existence. All their energy goes into survival—and reproduction. The only point of it all—to go on. On and on and on. What else is there? Sometimes I am appalled by the brutality, the horror of this planetary spawning and scheming and striving and dying. One no longer searches for any ulterior significance in all this; as in the finest music, the meaning is in the music itself, not in anything beyond it. All we have, it seems to me, is the beauty of art and nature and life, and the love which that beauty inspires.

Smell of cooking rubber. I withdraw my booted feet from the oven.

August 28

Raining again. Storm predicted. The packer with his mules is coming up the mountain this morning. I clean the lookout, put everything away, bolt the shutters back on the windows, pack our baggage, sign off on the radios. "This is Numa Ridge Fire Lookout going ten-seven [out of service] for about ten months. Have a good winter everybody."

The packer arrives. Followed by the wind. We load the mules in a driving rain and start down the mountain.

Fire

ED ENGLE

THE PICTURES WERE ALL over the national TV news. There was a squad of Forest Service firefighters standing in front of a house somewhere in southern California. The brush for as far as the camera panned was blacked down into piles of smouldering ash. They had saved the house. They grinned into the camera and the ecstatic homeowners hugged and kissed them. Dan Rather smiled.

I noticed that one of the firefighters clutched a small note pad in his hand. It was the standard issue three-by-five-inch tablet. The pages are gridded in blue quarter-inch squares. There are 216 squares on a page and the top is perforated so each page can be neatly torn off if required. The acquisition clerks would know that this is the 1300-18a(3-66). To most of us it is simply known as the Idea book. This comes from the message emblazoned fully across the cover:

Innovate
Develop
Encourage
Activate
Suggest

It is a simple acronym meant to guide us along our way. In the upper right hand corner of the cover are the italized words, *"Work Safely Don't Get Hurt!"*

Of Fire and the Landscape

I know why that firefighter was holding so tightly to his Idea book. From the second he had received the fire call from wherever he was stationed he had been keeping track of his fire time. He had carefully noted his regular hours and the quarter time hazard pay he would get until the fire was declared controlled. There was another column for night differential.

Time and three-quarters is what can make a grunt's day on the fireline. At any given moment that firefighter who was standing out in the ash and smoke could probably give you an exact figure in dollars and cents of how much money he had coming. It helps encourage him to activate when he is dirty, tired, thirsty, and bored.

I don't know what makes Dan Rather smile, but I do know what makes firefighters smile.

Most seasonal forest firefighters get started on their home districts. At the beginning of the season there is an orientation that explains how the district is operated. A couple of days is usually devoted to fire training. Firefighters learn how to size up "smokes" and hopefully put them out. The basic notion in most wildfire suppression is that the fire must be deprived of fuel by cutting a fireline around the burning area.

There are hundreds of refinements to fireline theory, but it always works down to clearing away anything that might burn from the fire's path. This means a "line" dug down to mineral soil all the way around the fire. It might be two feet wide or the width of six or seven D-9 cat blades depending on the size of the fire. Other options include taking the heat from the fire by cooling it with water, if water is available. Still, the mainstay is always the fireline. This is sacred.

The tools that a firefighter uses are basic. A shovel to scrape and dig fireline and throw soil on hot spots to cool them and the Pulaski, which is a combination ax and grubbing hoe, to break up the soil and cut small trees and brush. Other more specialized tools like chainsaws, brush hooks, and the rake-like McCleod sometimes come into play, particularly on the larger fire crews.

The working organization of a fire suppression crew is similar whether it is a two- or three-man "initial attack" crew or a standard twenty-man hand crew. The firefighters line out with Pulaskis in the lead and "brush" out the fireline and break up the sod or duff. The shovels follow and scrape the line down to mineral soil. Sometimes a chainsaw man will lead off if there are trees or a lot of brush that needs to come out. Brush hooks may also work along with the Pulaskis. McCleods may be used in conjunction with the shovels.

The idea, particularly in the larger twenty-man crews, is for each firefighter to give the line a "lick or two" then move on and let the next guy do the same. If the crew is "well oiled," they will have built a perfect fireline, down to mineral soil, by the time the twentieth man puts his licks in. If it isn't, either the firefighters up front will do all the work or the ones in the back will. A good crew can build a lot of line quickly because, theoretically, no one firefighter gets too tired.

The entire fire organization is set up to deal with a much broader spectrum of eventualities. The direction is mostly oriented toward the very big, or project, fires. These fires often employ thousands of individual firefighters and an array of equipment.

On a big fire the twenty-man crews might be organized into divisions and sectors. Some of those crews might be hotshot or interregional firefighting crews whose main function is wildfire suppression—sort of the Green Berets of firefighters. Specialized engine crews lay hose, supply water, and protect structures that might be threatened. Fixed-wing aircraft might be used to drop slurry. Helitack crews utilize helicopters to transport firefighters, scout out the fire, and drop buckets of water on hot spots. There may be overhead teams, Dozer bosses, tree felling bosses, supply bosses, transport bosses, information officers, reconnaissance teams, field observers, planners, tacticians.... It has all the beauty of a war except nobody's shooting at you. Actually, it's amazing that as few people get hurt or killed as do on the big fires.

Despite the technology of it all the bottom line still comes down to the basic fact that everyone, either directly or indirectly, is trying to remove the fuel or the heat or maybe even the oxygen from the wildfire. And it could be that the wildfire, on some weird level, is a life itself. Something to be called by name. Sometimes, "Sir."

Most firefighters don't get their start on the big ones. It's seldom the kind of blazing inferno that makes its way to the nightly news. Most often, at least in the Rockies, it is a lightning strike that has managed to nail a single pitchy snag. One burning tree can puff up a lot of smoke and the district will dispatch a couple of firefighters out to the area. Although the smoke is easy to see from the air or maybe from a fire

Of Fire and the Landscape

tower posted off on some distant ridge, it can be a different story when you are looking for it on the ground in the jumble of the forest.

Smoke does funny things when it is gliding across the land. If it's early in the morning when the wind is coming down the draws, smoke can carry miles from the source and layer into a hollow of cold air. When you are new at it you will think things are quite simple when you see a concentration of smoke like that and dive off a ridge and follow it. Maybe after searching for an hour or two you learn a first lesson—where there's smoke there isn't always fire.

I remember a burning snag on the Pikes Peak ranger district in Colorado. The fire tower had spotted it late in the evening and they called us up and told us to be ready to go after it first thing the next morning. There was a new forester on the district and he was going along. He was straight out of college and had all the course work in fire management. His skills on the ground were limited, but the Forest Service figured this was a good way for him to learn—they made him the boss.

We gathered at the office at dawn and headed out. The night before we'd pulled the air photos of the area and found a road that would get us close. It took about an hour to wind our way up out of town and into the area. When we got out of the truck and had a look we saw a small draw about half a mile off that was filled with smoke as far down it as we could see.

This is when we learned that the forester had apparently had some leadership training, too. He took the show over in a characteristic military sort of way. This isn't unusual on a fire because a para-military type chain of command and mode of action is well suited when you have to move lots of firefighters and equipment as quickly and efficiently as possible. On these smaller smoke-chasing deals we usually would forego some of the formalities, but we figured this guy was green.

He barked some orders out, we grabbed our tools, and busted double time over to the draw. We didn't talk it over when we got into the smoke and headed down the draw. I knew where the fire was and so did the other grunts with me, but we followed. After about forty minutes we were working hard not to giggle when we left the chainsaw and some hand tools leaning up against a tree. The forester didn't even notice as he raced around searching for the fire.

Finally, we broke out laughing when he asked us where the hell our

Fire

tools were. We told him they were up the draw toward the fire and his pupils began to dilate. Sweat was pouring out from under his hard hat. We pointed all the way back up the draw. A single ponderosa pine was puffing smoke on a ridge not more than a thousand feet from our truck. He took it well and even choked out a muffled laugh as we headed back. It has happened to all of us and we never told anyone in the office about it.

Fighting district wildfires is the best kind of apprenticeship for a firefighter. Sometimes they turn out to just be a snag, but in other cases it could be three or four acres or maybe upwards of twenty. We learned how to size each smoke up and decide what to do about it. Sometimes if the fire was just crawling along in the duff we took our time digging line around it.

If the fire was hotter and walking or even trotting a little we often decided to hotline it, which meant we went right to where the fire was moving the fastest and tried to get a line around that area. If things worked out it meant that we stopped the advance of the fire at the head and then could take our time finishing the fireline out around the areas that had already burned or weren't burning very hot.

It was good training in the basics of how to safely carry the tools over rugged terrain and pace ourselves for the long haul when we used them. We picked up tricks from other more experienced firefighters, like how to push the shovel with a knee while scraping line and conserve our strength. We learned how to anchor the fireline into a creek or rocks or roads so that we knew the fire wouldn't get behind us.

The details were critical, like making sure to throw any twig or branch that had burned in toward the fire but anything that was totally green outside the fireline. This prevented the possibility that even an ember might get outside the line and start up some trouble. The saying went, "green to green and black to black."

When there was a line around the entire fire, the dirty, boring, and absolutely crucial mop-up work began. On the smaller fires this meant going to every log, every stump, every ember, and every pine needle that had any fire in it and putting it dead out. Most of the time we did it by "dry-mopping," which meant we chopped the embers off logs, then mixed dirt with them and spread them until we could hold a hand to them and feel no heat. We did the same for anything else that held any heat. They called it "cold trailing."

Sometimes we carried five-gallon backpack pumps with water that we used to cool the embers and duff down before we stirred and spread. The backpack pumps, or "piss bags," were miserable and heavy to carry but greatly speeded up the process. We used the same mop-up techniques—it was just quicker with the water. The rule of thumb was that if you didn't know how to dry-mop, then you couldn't wet-mop, either. Just spraying water on a hot spot won't put it out—it needs to be broken up, stirred, fiddled with.

Most importantly we learned that fires and firefighters keep some odd hours. We learned about telephone calls in the middle of the night and sticking with things even though we were going to have to work through the entire night following the light from our headlamps. We learned that you could be more tired than you ever thought was possible and keep digging fireline. We learned how to take care of ourselves and watch out for the occasional fire that the wind would throw into the crowns of the trees where it could take off into an uncontrollable run. We learned that you don't always stop them and that the little fires can get big in a hurry. And that sometimes people get hurt.

All of it prepared us for the big fires, the project fires, where the call might come at two in the morning and before you knew it you were on an airplane heading out to some monster fire in California, Idaho, Montana, Wyoming, Nevada, Virginia…a fire that would have camps with hundreds, even thousands of tired firefighters sprawled out, sleeping on the ground or trying to get to a telephone to let someone know where they were. It can get into your blood.

I would like the project fires for no other reason than the going. Aside from the adventure of it all and the mystery of where you might end up and what you might see and the money you might make I would settle for the simple pleasure of being constantly in motion. During the fire season most firefighters have a packed bag standing by the door or in the trunk of their cars. It's an everyday reminder that at any moment a call might come and you will be on the road.

It is travel stripped bare. There are no photo stops, no educational sidesteps, no chance to get a feel for anything other than the wind over a truck's windshield or an airplane's wing. The idea is to just get there. Your meals are covered. You throw a sleeping bag out wherever you end up when you can't continue. You catnap. You keep moving. I was born with a feel for it.

The fire crews that mobilized for the great California fires in the fall of 1987 did it so well that the Army came by and asked how it was that they could get five or ten thousand people and their equipment on the road and headed out in just a day or two. They'd been trying to find the answer for years. The Israeli and the Swiss armies and apparently the American firefighters know the answer. It's simple enough—they have all their gear at home, ready to go, actually just waiting, almost hoping to go. The Army tends to draw the line at M-16s stashed in every soldier's home.

I was called to the California fires that year and in a lot of ways they were like most of the other big project fires I've worked on. There was one exception, though. We drove a strike team of five fire engines from Colorado to California. It seemed like most of the engines in California were the big jobs and the need for the small, mobile, four-wheel-drive type of initial attack "pumpers" that we use in the Rockies was recognized. We left Durango, Colorado, at two in the morning, two firefighters to a truck, one driving and one wedged in that dreamy zone this side of unconsciousness—the place where the little green men live—and we drove for thirty hours with a three-hour nap in Ely, Nevada.

I know fatigue much better than I know the other phantoms in my life and I can thank firefighting for the friendship. The rulebook says they can work you for the first 24 hours straight when you get the fire call and after that you're entitled to 12 hours on duty and 12 hours off. It seldom works that way, at least in the early stages of a big fire. Figure some stretches at 18 or 20 hours a day, figure 100- maybe 120-hour work weeks if things get ugly. Figure on no relief. Figure on making exhaustion a friend rather than an enemy. Make it a give and take relationship and hope that you're "on" if things get hot. The little green guys dancing across the road, or the fireline, or in the mess line are all right, but draw the line at the little blue guys.

I was working night shift on a big fire near Fairplay, Colorado. My job was simple—just make sure that a Pacific Marine pump located by a small stream kept the water coming to the firefighters up on the line. There wasn't much to do other than gas it up every few hours and listen for any break in the mechanical hum that might mean things were going wrong. After three or four days of it I got to where I could doze next to the pump and wake up instantly when it started to sputter for lack of gas. Sleeping off shift, during the day, wasn't going well. The fire camp was noisy and too bright. We were getting three or four hours a day.

One night I figured to break up the boredom and walked over to talk to another firefighter that I'd noticed rummaging around in the back of a nearby pickup. It turned out that all that was there was a broom, stuck up in the bed of the truck by its handle. I don't think I talked to it for very long before I realized...

The language conveys something of a chromatic scale—tired, dog-tired, fatigued, bushed, beat, worn out, weary, exhausted, goneness, dead tired, spent—but these are only the notes in a fugue. You can come to understand the orchestra, the composer, and even the performance.

They put us up in a motel when we pulled into Redding, California. It wasn't part of the plan. The dispatcher had figured to head us straight up to the fireline, at least, until our strike team leader told him that the crew wasn't going to move a goddamn inch until they got some sleep. We'd been seeing the little blue guys.

At four the next morning we left for the fire. We made the district ranger station in Hayfork, California, at dawn, just in time for chow at a fire camp that had been set up nearby. The place was chaotic. A huge storm full of lightning, but no rain, had torched eighty percent of the district. They didn't even know how many fires they actually had burning. They dispatched us to another fire camp farther to the west. Smoke filled all the valleys.

The fire camp had been up in the mountains, but when we arrived they were in the process of moving it to a huge field near Hyampom, California, which they figured would be big enough to hold the expected two or three thousand firefighters who were on their way. We grabbed the best campsite we could find in the new fire camp and set up shop. Word was that we would be pulling night shift. We left for work at six that evening.

At first it was easy duty. We'd been charged with protecting a fireline that had been backfired on the previous night shift. Backfiring is a form of wildfire control that you see a lot of on the bigger fires. Generally a fireline is dug, or in our case a road is located that is in a position ahead of the direction that the wildfire is moving. Controllable fires are delib-

Fire

erately set at the fireline with the intention of burning out the fuel ahead of the fire. When the wildfire meets with the backfired area it is deprived of fuel and theoretically stopped. It's a way of creating the *very* wide firelines necessary to hold huge wildfires that can jump over any line dug by firefighters or bulldozers.

A lot can go wrong with a backfire. If the wind changes and it gets out of hand it can jump your fireline and you're right back where you started. If things go right the backfire can eliminate the fuel from the oncoming fire and even change the direction or force of the fire's convection column and turn it back into itself. Most backfiring is done on the night shifts when the humidity is a little higher and conditions don't favor the kind of blowups that can occur during the day shifts.

They like having pumper trucks like the ones we'd brought from Colorado to follow the firefighters who are lighting the backfires. If the thing gets out of hand and spots over the fireline, the water is available immediately to put it out. Spot fires are the firefighter's enemy. If they get out of control not only do they mean that all the work put into the fireline is worthless but that you may end up having wildfire on both sides of you. This isn't considered sporting.

The section of line we were patrolling was in good shape. The backfire had gone as planned and there were just a few hot spots, here and there, that we figured were too close to the line and put out. It looked like an easy shift that held the potential for a catnap. An experienced firefighter will always sleep when he can, because he knows that at any minute he may be called on to go full out at one hundred percent if something blows up. We laid back.

It didn't last. Around one in the morning they dispatched us to a couple of spot fires that had jumped the line on another part of the fire. From the beginning it was what firefighters call a watch-out situation. In fire training they give you a little book with a skull and crossbones on it. The title is *Fire Situations That Shout Watch Out.* There are thirteen of them. What they are trying to get across is that if you don't watch out you may get your ass burned.

As axioms for survival go, they are pretty simple. Take number seven—"You are in country you haven't seen in the daylight"; number ten—"You are getting frequent spot fires over your line"; number eight—"You are in an area where you are unfamiliar with local factors

Of Fire and the Landscape

influencing fire behavior"; number one—"You are building a fireline downhill toward a fire." I like number thirteen—"You feel like taking a little nap near the fireline." All of these and a few more applied. There was that wonderful jolt of adrenaline that watch out situations can provide. The kind that can get you through an entire night shift. We checked for our fire shelters.

Yes, the Fire Shelters. They are neatly packaged outfits that look like an aluminum pup tent when deployed. The idea is that a firefighter who has run out of options can find a spot relatively clear of fuel, hopefully a purposely created wide spot in the fireline called a safe zone, set up his fire shelter, and get into it with his feet pointed toward the oncoming wildfire. The aluminum and fiberglass lined fire shelter will reflect the intense heat of the fire away from him while he breathes the cooler air an inch or two above the ground. He can crawl around in the shelter to get away from any unbearable heat if necessary. He must hold the shelter down tightly when the fire and its accompanying cyclone of winds goes over him. The shelters are proven and there are a number of firefighters alive today thanks to them, but it still doesn't keep us from calling them, "Shake and Bakes."

Things *do* happen. Years before I'd been on a project fire in southern California. The fuels there are flashy to the point of being explosive. I was on a hand crew that was backfiring a section of line out. The squad doing the firing was using flare guns. The key when backfiring with flare guns is to shoot the flare in from the fireline twenty or maybe thirty yards. When it ignites the fuel the fire doesn't have enough time to get a head on it before it meets up with the preconstructed fireline and can be controlled.

This particular squad got to screwing around and was shooting the flares too far down a steep slope of heavy fuel. The fire took off and overran them. I managed to run down the fireline to safety, but some of the crew had to deploy their shelters. It was over as quick as it started and we ran up to them. Everyone was okay except for one firefighter who'd had his sleeves rolled up. The shelter, which he had to hold down with his forearms, had gotten so hot that it burned his arms. It wasn't as bad as it could have been.

Another time in southern California I was on a twenty-man crew along with four other twenty-man crews on a narrow ridge away from

Fire

the main fire—a watch out situation. We were there awaiting instruction from Command. The main fire, which was still a couple of miles off, kept coming, but we could hear it even that far away. People started getting edgy. The crew bosses called in again and were given the same instructions. The fire began to run.

That's when the crew bosses began looking for spots to deploy our shelters and come to the conclusion that the country was so steep there wasn't enough room for the 100 firefighters on that ridge to put out their shelters if they needed to. We were backed up to a steep, almost vertical slope on one side. The fire was boiling when they called Command and requested a slurry drop to try and slow the fire so they could think.

The planes came in low and made their drops. There was no talk because even us grunts knew things were getting tight. Less experienced crews might have bolted and that would have been the kiss of death. The slurry slowed the fire just a little, but it was enough for us to pull up a hose lay that was on the fireline, tie it into whatever we could find, and go hand over hand down the steep slope to safety. That's when we started the banter, yelling at the crew bosses to call in for 100 pairs of clean shorts.

Those are the exceptions. Most of the time the firefighting is boringly routine. If you are going to get hurt it's more likely to occur when you're flying, or being transported by the National Guard, or by the sudden randomness of a huge burned out snag that falls out of nowhere. The snags may be the most feared because there is absolutely nothing you can do if your time is up. It takes some getting used to.

Those spot fires when we were on the pumpers in northern California? Well, we didn't do too well. They got away from us. Another crew came up but refused to help because they thought the situation was too dangerous. We pulled back when the flames started racing into the crowns and lit backfires to try and slow it, but it was too close to morning and the sun heated things up. The whole thing blew up on us. We went back to camp after being up twenty-five or thirty hours. As they say, "That's show biz!" The pay really is the same.

Eventually, the crews did get a handle on the fires, which were collectively called the Gulch Complex. Our lives turned into an endless string of patrols and backfires—all night shifts. The smoke hung in thick and once or twice the carbon monoxide took its toll in the form of nausea and delirium, but we just figured it was fatigue. One shift it was so bad that when a division boss came to talk to one of our engine bosses, he found him completely incoherent. The division boss asked, "How long have you people been out here?" We couldn't tell him. We became the walking dead.

I remember the rest of that time in California more like the two-minute sound bites you get on the nightly news. It is all in fragments and the story line is hard to find. I remember sitting around a warming fire that Frankie Maestas and I built one cold night on the fireline and talking about how we would stop at Reno if they ever let us go home. It struck us as funny and we laughed until the tears rolled down our cheeks and we slid into that deep, dark kind of fatigue that even scares the little blue guys away.

I remember getting released from one fire only to be dispatched to another. Fire camps that looked all the same in the Seiad Valley, Happy Camp, North Elk, Norcross, Forks of the Salmon...and endless night shifts. There was R&R for a day or two in Yreka, California, and the feeling that I would never get enough sleep. Our strike team leader was going nuts trying to get us relieved. One morning I looked over at one of the firefighters on the crew and I realized how bad it was. There was no light to be found. Her eyes were dull. I figured that we all must have the thousand-mile stare. We were sick and coughing from the smoke.

Finally after thirty-five days they sent us home. We made it to Reno, but when the leggy bargirl came over and asked what she could do for us, we just stared into space.

"Somebody say something," she said. We told her we'd been on the fires for a very long time.

The crew split up after Reno and we all drove home our separate ways. We'd had our fights and reconciliations the way all crews do on a long run, but most of it was forgotten. We were family whether we liked it or not.

I ended up driving alone for the final leg of the trip from Grand Junction to Durango. Try it after you've been with ten other firefighters day and night, good and bad, for thirty-five days. It's a new kind of aloneness. The best month in Colorado is September and it was over, but the air was clear and some of the aspen were still brilliant and yellow as I drove over Red Mountain Pass. It was nice to see mountains that I knew. It was a lot like home.

Fire

I read later that the Fire Siege of 1987 involved 22,000 firefighters in California and Oregon. In California 775,000 acres burned. Enough timber was burned to build homes for a city the size of San Francisco. Fire suppression costs in California alone were over $100 million. An interesting footnote gave the results of a study on the crews that pulled night shifts on the fires—they averaged three to four hours of sleep a day. Ten firefighters lost their lives.

And none of it, with the exception of the lost lives, would hold a candle to what was to happen in the Yellowstone National Park area in 1988.

Wildfire fighting, at least the grunt work that most of the seasonals do, is a job for young men and women. Needless to say, the hours are long, but the money is good although there comes a time on the big fires where even the money doesn't matter.

After twelve years of firefighting I've gotten to the point where on any project fire I go to I'll see a firefighter that I've met on some other obscure jumble of topography that was burning. In many cases it could be that the wildfire was the best thing that ever happened to the landscape. But we were there anyway, whatever the politics of nature are.

I could say that after having worked on somewhere close to a couple hundred wildfires, both large and small, that I'd had enough and it would be almost true. But there is another part of me, the part that just lives to be on the move, that is always looking for the next fire call, the next column of smoke over the next ridge, and wondering what the fire will be doing. Will it be crawling in the duff or roaring up some ridge? Will it be the kind of fire that charges me full of adrenaline and wonder? Will it be the kind of fire that has a life of its own?

I'm still no different than all the other grunts. I'm still in it for the rush and the cash.

Part III

Fire as Foe, Fire as Friend

This universe is an ever-lasting fire,
kindling itself by regular measures and
going out by regular measures.
—Heraclitus, sixth century B.C.

IN THE SUMMER OF 1996, I came across a portion of the Matthes burn, a 1,000-acre fire from the previous year on an eastern portion of the North Rim of the Grand Canyon. As I stepped from the engine, off the dirt road and into the burn, pale grasshoppers leaped around my boots. Sooty ash blackened the lower halves of the ponderosa trunks, and half-consumed chunks of heavy downed logs lay scattered around. Knee-high grass swept against my pants, and tufts of fleabane, white and purple daisy-like flowers, dotted the ground. It was quiet, the brown needles still clung to some of the lower branches, and dry. Walking the burn, I noticed the absence of the pine needle carpet and duff common to the rest of the Walhalla Plateau, and a clearing, a calm inside the quiet ponderosa grove. I remembered thinking that on a small scale, this must be what Yellowstone is like, green grass and young flowers among the darkened trunks and deadfall, birds chirping, blue sky stretching away, and the peace that comes after destruction.

The fires of Yellowstone will be remembered forever as a revelatory event for America's wilderness resource managers. The conflagrations of 1988 captured the world's attention and brought wildland fire to the forefront of natural resource management. The 1988 fires proved to the general public and resource managers alike that not even a protected landscape could withstand nature's plans and the natural cycles every environment must experience. Wildfire in Yellowstone's ecosystem had been suppressed for over 100 years, a considerable portion of the ecosystem's natural burn interval of 100 to 300 years. It was only a matter of time before the forests would reach critical mass and burn with a fury never before witnessed in recent American history. Recently, the story of Yellowstone's renewal is as common as stories of the fires that changed the face of the Park forever. Over a decade has passed since the storm clouds of smoke passed over Yellowstone National Park. The years have seen a rebirth of spirit, a renewal of hope, and the reintroduction of other elements of nature once withheld from their rightful place. Packs of reintroduced wolves now frolic among the grizzlies, and we are once again reminded that Nature will have her way.

Fire as Foe, Fire as Friend

The last fifteen years of the twentieth century saw a shift in the ways fire was used in the land management community, and in the way the general public perceived it. Prescribed fire is now an essential component of many federal and state agencies' land management policies. Knowledge of the critical role fire plays in many ecosystems is widespread among the American public, as is recognition of Smokey Bear, an icon of fire prevention. Wildfire, as an ecological force, is beginning to receive the credit it has been due ever since fire suppression took hold in American wild lands. And not a moment too soon. A century of fire suppression has changed the face of America's forests and, where once a fire may have crept along the ground, huge conflagrations now rage, consuming the collected forest litter and debris and destroying all in their path. The modern dilemma lies in allowing natural healthy fire into an ecosystem that hasn't seen flame in seventy-five years, without losing control.

Allowing fire to return to the natural landscape is a delicate topic. Suppression has been so ingrained in American culture that it is hard for most people to see past the initial shock of charred trees and blackened prairies to the inevitable renewal of life after the flames pass through. With the additional complication of increased residences in rural areas, protection of property is an issue where once fires would have been free to burn. From this environment emerge various management policies. The let-burn policy is meant to allow a naturally ignited fire to burn in certain areas, where fire is a needed natural component and there is low risk to human life and property. Prescribed fires are introduced into areas to clear out high accumulations of forest litter and vegetation before a wildfire can sweep through and ignite a large and uncontrollable area. An alternative to prescribed burning is mechanically thinning jumbled overgrown woodlands. This disturbance provides some necessary ecological changes, such as increased sunlight, lower canopy density, and increased growth of ground cover, without the unpredictability and danger of igniting fire. It doesn't however, provide the necessary chemical changes and ecological pressures under which many plant communities evolve. As public land management moves forward, our choices may widen, but fires, both wild and ignited, will never be excluded from the natural environment.

Introduction

Following the Yellowstone event and framed by a new ecological scheme, wildfire literature carried more focus and purpose than any previous fire writing. Pointed tales of firefighting, of fire, and of environmental awareness and respect for nature surfaced apace with the newspapers' chronicles of the latest "destructive" fire. Every summer since, with the drought effects of global warming, fire has become a central crisis in the American West, and increasingly in the Southeast, the Upper Midwest, and Texas. Occasional stories of runaway fires make headlines from unexpected places like Long Island and Minnesota, reminders that wildland fires can and do happen in nearly every part of the country, from the Jersey suburbs to the slopes of Hawaii's volcanoes to the sawgrass prairies of South Florida. Whole industries have sprung up around firefighting and fire prevention. Many western economies depend on a busy fire season for year-round viability. Wildfire has inspired feature films and made-for-television movies of fictional smokejumpers. Fire has also become a central issue in environmental awareness. As global warming takes hold of our ecosystems, more frequent and widespread fires will blaze across the forests and grasslands. Flora and fauna will be forever changed, as will the landscape and the lives of the people who call it home. American writers have kept pace with such developments, relating them to environmental issues, personal meditations, and ecological happenings, trying always to make sense of wildfires for their readers.

These essays move wildland fire from the edge into the central core of nature writing, capturing the experiences of those most exposed and affected by wildfire, including firefighters and those just outside the fireline. Modern-day fires frequently spawn great drama and tragedy, tales of lessons hard learned. The South Canyon fire in 1994 proved once again that some fires cannot be outrun, and some lives will be lost in the struggle to protect others. A new element of emotion surfaces in these works, reflecting a personal relationship to fire, a sometimes private reflection on how wildfire has shaped not only the landscape but lives and personalities as well. Homeowners, resource managers, ecologists, and firefighters are all personally involved with the flames and heat, the smoke and the ash. These works capture their thoughts and experiences and leave us with permanent impressions of wildfire's effects on human life.

Incineration of Yellowstone

TED WILLIAMS

E VEN WITHOUT WILDFIRE, the 70-mile-per-hour winds that tore through Yellowstone National Park on August 20, 1988, would have been a major ecological event. Trees, particularly the lodgepole pines that once cloaked about three-quarters of the park's 2.2 million acres, would have sustained heavy damage. As it was, a few million of them were turned to black skeletons by a running crown fire that expanded on this day by 165,000 acres.

Already desiccated by a hot, rainless summer, the forest sucked up the 300-foot-high flames as fast as the gale could push them. They jumped dirt firelines, asphalt roads, and the Madison River. Two miles ahead of the front, new fires sprang up as embers spiraled down from a sky made almost indigo by the thin mountain air. Boulders exploded and scattered shrapnel around their bases. At times I could hear muffled reports like distant artillery as conifers reached tinder point and as the even more violent winds generated by the firestorm ripped up trees by their roots and slammed them into the earth.

Enormous pillars of smoke hung on all horizons as if the park had been hit by a cluster of hydrogen bombs. To the west a moon-bright, bloody sun cut through the white convection column of the North Fork Fire. Such smoke clouds look like prairie thunderheads, except bigger. They form their own ice crystals, produce their own lightning, and top the cruising altitude of commercial jetliners. The fire bosses classified what they were dealing with as "fire behavior out of the Twilight Zone."

Fire as Foe, Fire as Friend

Even veterans for forty years had seen nothing like it. "Black Saturday," they called it.

I spent the afternoon of Black Saturday up to my armpits in the Yellowstone River, seeking to escape. But only from the megalopolis of the East where the few beautiful places I know about have had the wildness managed out of them, where the trout eat pellets and wear tags that say things like "Make it in Massachusetts," and from which, with my wife and two children, I had departed ten days previously.

Now, in the lee of a little island, I waded out on a lava bar, through floating flecks of ash, bubbling, malodorous sulfur vents, and ripples lit by the crimson sun. It might have been someone else's vision of hell, but at that moment there was nowhere else that I preferred to be. Two-pound cutthroat trout followed me like hungry urchins, picking up nymphs dislodged by my boots, almost getting underfoot. In the deep glides half a cast beyond the lava, other cutthroats took number 18 Olive Duns, bulging the surface or breaking it with their golden backs and flaglike dorsal fins. A white pelican cruised through the rising fish, tucked its head down between its wings in a futile attempt to hide, then lunged and missed. A bald eagle sculled by, fighting the wind. Behind me a herd of bison grunted, wallowed, and grazed. Even now, late in the rutting season, last year's winter fur was sloughing off in thick mats.

For virtually all of the twentieth century, scientists have been aware that forests evolved with fire and that, therefore, fire has a place in forests. The sequoias for California's Sierra Nevada, for example, were observed to have a thick, asbestos-like bark almost impervious to flame. But if natural ground fires were artificially suppressed, lesser trees such as white fir would grow underneath the sequoias, eventually reaching a height where they could transfer flames to the sequoias' lofty crowns. To reduce this danger, managers at California's General Grant National Park (now part of King's Canyon) conducted the nation's first prescribed burn in 1904.

But in 1910 there came a summer like that of 1988. Five million acres of western forestland burned. Americans hated fire more than ever, and the U.S. Forest Service launched a campaign to banish the phenomenon from the northern Rockies. In 1927 the American Forestry Association unleashed its "Dixie Crusaders," who tub-thumped through the South whooping it up about the evils of wildfire. Eight years later the Forest Service instituted a policy it called "10 A.M. Fire Control" because every wildfire that showed itself was to be extinguished by ten the next morning.

In the late 1930s the Forest Service got tougher still, employing an anti-fire lecturer—one H. N. Wheeler, described by Jack Shepherd in his book *The Forest Killer* as "a bellowing demagogue who had little knowledge of forest management...but who whipped up emotions and fundamentalist fervor, incorporating scripture with Forest Service Gospel." The Forest Service even hired a fire psychologist and deposited him in the Alabama woods, where he promptly established that the use of fire as a management tool reflected "the defensive beliefs of a disadvantaged culture group."

Then came Pearl Harbor and raids on U.S. timber reserves in which balloon-borne incendiary bombs were flung to the east wind by the Empire of Japan. These worked about as well as the bat-borne incendiary bombs the Allies were preparing for the Japanese. Which is to say not at all. But they taught the American public that to support the fire in the forest was to support the Axis in the war.

In 1942 there came a truly tragic forest fire—by far the worst that mankind has ever witnessed. Crazed, screaming animals flew, galloped, ran, and crawled from hideous tongues of flame, stopping only long enough to warn their friends. Some were burned. Many wept. They lost their families and their beautiful, happy homes. This was the conflagration in Walt Disney's animated motion picture, *Bambi*—a work identified by Roderick Nash, professor of history and environmental studies at the University of California at Santa Barbara, as "the most important document in American cultural history bearing on the subject [of fire management policy]."

Helping Bambi spread the word was Smokey, the fire-scarred, shovel-slinging black bear who chanted, "Remember, only you can prevent forest fires," and who eventually became so popular that the U.S. Postal Service granted him his own zip code. In the late 1970s my own children, who were not at all traumatized by their close encounter with the Yellowstone fires, could often be heard singing loudly: "He can smell a fiah before it starts to fain..." But even then they understood that Smokey, like Pooh, was a bear of very little brain.

Fire as Foe, Fire as Friend

As the general public went off in one direction, science proceeded in another. To those who knew how to look, it became patently obvious that fire not only had a place in the natural landscape but that many plant communities absolutely required it. Data poured in from the Everglades, where fires renewed the great sea of grass, and from California's sequoia country, where cool ground fires continued to preserve the big trees. In Michigan, Smokey was caught with his dungarees down, having almost stomped the Kirtland's warbler to extinction along with the fires that had previously created and maintained its habitat. For the bird nests only under small jack pines, a tree which cannot reproduce unless fire opens its hard cones. In the Selway-Bitterroot Wilderness of Montana, researchers discovered that fires had burned through some stands of ponderosa pine about once every ten years, ever since the advent of ponderosa pine.

It seemed more than coincidence that most plants which prospered after fire were extremely flammable. In Yellowstone National Park scars were found along the growth rings for ancient lodgepole pines, suggesting that these forests had been razed by major burns once every 200 to 400 years. In the northern section of the park the fire cycle appeared to be something like twenty-five years. Within lodgepole stands that had burned a quarter-century earlier there was seen a three-fold increase in species of birds, small mammals, and ground plants.

Burn sites all over the northern Rockies were monitored, beginning when embers still flickered and ending with complete revegetation. Minutes after a fire, rodents moved back in or back up. Mountain bluebirds and black-backed three-toed woodpeckers came quickly to the new insect mines in dead trees. Sunlight greened new openings. Dwindling meadows regained lost ground. Wildflowers and berries flourished. By the third growing season the earth was 70 percent covered with such plants as fireweed, lupine, leafy aster, elk sedge, and heart-leafed arnica. Tender forage. New growth. Diversity. Renewal.

The more researchers looked for fire-intolerant plants, the fewer they could find. By the early 1970s even the Forest Service was admitting that Mother Nature knew more than the chanting bear. Thus was born in the National Park System and wilderness areas administered by other federal agencies the "let-burn policy."

Incineration of Yellowstone

Something told me not to use the term "let-burn policy" in the presence of John D. Varley, Yellowstone's director of research. Varley is a quiet, thoughtful man, a fine scientist but with not much of the clinical detachment that most scientists aspire to. Unstylishly passionate in his advocacy of wildness, he is the sort of bureaucrat that has taken over the National Park Service of late and steered the agency toward the role of national conservator of nature. The radical change in course hasn't been so popular as one might suppose. The vast majority of Americans and all other federal agencies believe to varying degrees that nature can't quite be trusted to do her own thing, that man has an obligation to coax, cajole, improve, and assist.

That's what they used to believe in the Park Service, too. This was back in the days when they killed predators to protect prey and then killed prey to protect it from starvation; when they stocked semi-tame trout from the East Coast, the West Coast, and Europe; and when they put out, or tried to put out, every forest fire no matter what.

If I had to thank an individual for the wonderful fishing I had enjoyed on the Yellowstone River, it would be Varley. Above his desk at Park Service headquarters in Mammoth Hot Springs, Wyoming, is a painting of his hand pointing at something, in Jehovah-like fashion, with an index finger that doesn't look exactly right. Closer inspection reveals that it has mutated into an exquisitely rendered cutthroat trout, a native of the Old West that has nearly been swept away in a tidal wave of alien, hatchery-bred trout. While the Park Service was being kicked about in the popular and scientific press for weaning park grizzlies of garbage "too quickly," Varley and his ilk were scuttling traditional, hands-on fisheries management.

The parade of hatchery trucks to park trout water was cut off. Soon you couldn't use bait on any major watercourse. If you were a beginner and didn't know how to cast, tough. You had to use the flies and lures favored by the elitists or not fish. If you were hungry and wanted to eat a native trout, tough. You had to throw them back to die of old age or be eaten by some non-tax-paying animal that could just as easily have eaten something else. "No Fishing" signs went up on Fishing Bridge—an American tradition where moms, dads, and kids had joyfully lined up shouder-to-shoulder to haul out the big ones. Fishermen and concessionaires were outraged. "Parks are for people," they said.

Fire as Foe, Fire as Friend

Meanwhile, with the flow of alien trout eliminated and with fishing mortality dramatically abated, the native cutthroat populations expanded to a point no living human had seen or dreamed possible, a point where they again provided a major food source for the supposedly garbage-starved bears. Human fishing activity picked up, too, and as Yellowstone became a mecca for serious trout fishermen from all over the world, the local economy boomed. Nature ran a pretty good hatchery program herself, it seemed, and no one really cared about killing trout when the price for doing so was the kind of fishing you got everywhere else.

"So," a usually tactful reporter-friend inquired of John D. Varley, "how do you suppose all this fire flap will affect your let-burn policy?" It was the only time I'd ever heard a hint of pique in Varley's voice. The summer had been a long, hard one in which he had been forced to lay aside science and take up media relations. He did it well, too, never using scientific mumbo jumbo, and day after day after day patiently dispensing to reporters the same, basic information they could have gleaned from the handout sheets at the visitor center. Now he said:

"There is no such thing as our 'let-burn policy.' It's a natural-fire program. You will never hear 'let-burn' out of the mouth of a greenblood. It connotes that we sit back with our heels kicked up and read magazines." He went on to explain that the program is flexible and based on common sense. Only lightning-caused fires go unfought, and only when they don't threaten things like commercial timber in the five surrounding national forests, Indian burial grounds, buildings, and people. Spring had started out wetter than usual. In early summer eleven of twenty natural fires fizzled on their own, indicating that, for yet another year, nature had postponed the inevitable 200- to 400-year major fire cycle.

Then, for the first time in the park's 112-year weather record, rain didn't fall during June and July. Natural fuels had piled up in unnatural quantity from 1886, when the U.S. Cavalry began suppressing fires, until the Park Service implemented its natural-fire program in 1972. Now these fuels dried at unheard-of rates. In mid-July, when the danger to life and property became apparent, the Park Service went into what it calls the "suppression mode" of its natural-fire program, fighting all new fires regardless of origin. On July 23rd, under a much publicized let-nothing-burn order from Interior Secretary Donald P. Hodel, it set up a "unified area command" with the Forest Service, attacking all fires in expensive and dramatic fashion.

"Of all the resource issues that we deal with here in Yellowstone," Varley told me, "there is no policy more firmly rooted in science than the fire program. It goes back here almost seventeen years. It goes back in western forests almost thirty years. We've got a lot of good research. It's not like we're groping around in the dark with this stuff."

Varley had to rush off for yet another emergency meeting with the superintendent. So I ambled over to the Hamilton Store to get a beer and a book that I'd been looking for. Near the pre-cooked cheeseburgers I found cases of cold, sweating Budweiser. I peeled a can off the plastic birdchoke. But this Bud wasn't for me. The concessionaire pointed to a little, hand-written note taped to the glass: "Sorry the Park Service has asked that we not sell alcoholic beverages." Nothing in the regs, though, about displaying lots of them and thereby illustrating to thirsty writers and firefighters all the bliss that might be possible without the current Gestapo-like rule. Park Service bashing has long been a popular sport with people in and around Yellowstone who make their living from the park.

"Have you got *Playing God in Yellowstone?*" I asked the lady who was standing near the bookshelves. "No," she said apologetically, "we're all sold out. But here's a book that's almost as good." She passed me a thick, green volume published in 1987 entitled *Stealing the National Parks.*

So I bought it, went out into the hot, smoky afternoon, found a spot free of elk sign on the lush Kentucky bluegrass, and read. The book had been written by Don Hummel—former mayor of Tucson and chairman of the Western Conference of National Park Concessioners. Representative Morris Udall of Arizona, sounding as if he couldn't wait to get off the dictaphone and carefully recording that he did "not agree with everything," had contributed a one-page foreword.

The first subtitle that caught my eye was "Parks Are for People." Regarding some perceived plot to deprive concessionaires of something or other, Hummel wrote: "What cunning manipulation of national park policy. What consummate skill in co-opting power! You have to hand it to the environmentalists. Or they'll take it from you....The arrogant Park Service, as I have pointed out, is an independent fiefdom within the

Department of the Interior that listens politely to everyone and then proceeds in its own direction." He got nasty after that.

A few days later I did manage to turn up a copy of *Playing God in Yellowstone*. It's a more scholarly work of Park Service bashing that raises some interesting points, especially about the old agency before it became so trustful of nature. The author is Alston Chase, a retired philosophy professor who believes that nature can't be trusted to do her own thing, that man has an obligation to coax, cajole, improve, and assist. Garbage was snatched away from park grizzlies too quickly, he argues. Where the Park Service believes that fire *is* nature, Chase believes that "fire improves nature."

Unlike Hummel's polemic, *Playing God in Yellowstone* is a huge commercial success. And it has become the main reference book for politicians and reporters as they desperately try to sort out what happened last summer in Yellowstone. Unfortunately for them and the Park Service, many of the author's conclusions are based on old and/or incorrect information. For example, Chase refers to the "Kaibab tragedy" as "a textbook example of playing God." Here, according to Chase, is what happened early in the century on the Kaibab Plateau on the North Rim of the Grand Canyon: Managers ban hunting. Managers kill predators. Mule deer irrupt. Mule deer destroy their own range. Mule deer starve.

Until the early 1970s, environmentalists and game departments had adored the Kaibab story because it so neatly illustrated that predators (with four legs or two) help prey by controlling it. The trouble with nature, however, is that it is rarely neat, and the trouble with control of prey by predators is that it usually works the other way around. There aren't enough hawks to limit mice, for instance, but mouse numbers determine hawk survival.

What Chase and the old biology texts he consulted didn't figure into the equation were the thousands of domestic sheep—more than all the deer at the peak of their abundance—that also grazed the Kaibab Plateau. When these were suddenly removed, more grass became available to the deer, which then irrupted.

Just as there were too many deer on the Kaibab Plateau, submits Chase, there are too many elk in Yellowstone. Managers have an obligation to assist weather, microbes, and predators in reducing them. Elk are destroying their own range.

Incineration of Yellowstone

Up until about twenty years ago biologists were saying more or less the same thing. From 1935 to 1968 the Park Service reduced by rifle and relocation the northern elk herd (by far the park's biggest) to what was presumed to be a balanced 4,000 animals. During the next twenty years biologists watched the uncontrolled herd expand to 20,000 and also watched plants inside big, elk-proof fences called "exclosures." By 1988 the vegetation inside the fences still looked remarkably like the vegetation outside; the Kaibab formula wasn't working. Of thirty-seven scientists studying elk in Yellowstone, thirty-six have been unable to uncover any evidence of the dangerous elk irruption that Chase thinks he sees.

"Effects of large numbers of elk simply have not registered on the landscape in the way people were predicting in the early 1960s," park research interpreter Norm Bishop told me. "Some of the old-timers are still frustrated and adamant that something dreadful is going to happen." Meanwhile, the garbage-starved grizzlies have enjoyed feasting on elk, which, as in ancient times, are now a major food source for them.

Since the fires, former philosophy professor Chase has risen to minor-celebrity status, dispensing biological observations and could-have/should-have critiques of the Park Service to TV audiences and newspapers, including the *Los Angeles Times,* which misidentified him as an "ecologist." His influence is apparent everywhere.

"Yellowstone may well have been destroyed by the very people who were assigned to protect it," Senator Alan Simpson of Wyoming informed his fellow legislators. (The wording Chase had used on the cover flap of his book was: "Yellowstone, America's first national park, is being destroyed by the very people assigned to protect it.") Simpson went on to call the incineration of Yellowstone "a startling, devastating, and dramatic disaster." "Let me tell you, colleagues," he cried, "the ground is sterilized. It is blackened to the very depths of any root system within it....Prescribed burns [set on purpose] could have reduced the fuel loads in order to prevent the inferno rate we see this summer....So I think that it is time to quit playing God in Yellowstone."

The trouble with prescribed burns in Yellowstone, according to biologists, including those independent of the Park Service, is that in order to start them you need very dry, very windy conditions; in fact, you need a summer like that of 1988. And if you were to touch off such fires in such conditions you would get fuel reduction on a summer-of-

Fire as Foe, Fire as Friend

1988 scale. At one time it did appear possible to reduce fuel in such big, mature lodgepole forests by burning them on purpose. But that is a very old notion, soundly discredited about twenty years ago. Yellowstone Superintendent Robert Barbee ("Barbee-Q Bob," as he is called by some of his local critics), is probably less objective and definitely less polite. According to him, anyone who believes that planned burns could have prevented the summer fires "is chewing lotus seeds."

But Chase believes it. "The Park Service," he writes in the *New York Times,* "should embark on aggressive programs of prescribed burning, before more wildlands are engulfed by fire."

I guess I didn't mind the worst of the summer's smoke because I knew that all I had to do each day was fish and hike and that in two weeks I'd be leaving the fires and the flammable cabin at Yellowstone's north entrance a thousand miles behind me. I never even coughed. But for those whose lives were rooted in the gateway communities, the summer was pretty tough. In Corwin Springs, Montana, Elizabeth Clare Prophet, world leader of the Church Universal and Triumphant (and known to her followers as Guru Ma), lamented:

"We could never open our windows. Our newborn children had never breathed fresh air until they were three months old. Smoke levels in our area were the equivalent of three packs of cigarettes a day. The National Park Service has a cavalier attitude, an arrogance. Barbee says that he has nothing to apologize for."

According to Louisa Willcox of the Greater Yellowstone Coalition (an organization of fifty groups and some 2,000 individuals whose mission is to promote coordinated management for the Greater Yellowstone ecosystem), the smoke was creating an atmosphere that seeks scapegoats. "People are angry," she said. "They can't breathe; they're sick. They need someone to blame for it, and the Park Service is an easy target."

The locals weren't quite ready for natural fires that looked as if they might incinerate their houses or for "let-burn" biologists, doubtless with their feet kicked up on their desks and flipping through magazines, who kept saying things like: "Ecologically, these fires are the event of the century. It's very exciting."

Nor did environmentalists much oil the chop with some of their public remarks. For example, at the end of August Earth First! co-founder Howie Wolke was quoted by the *Jackson Hole News* as saying that not enough of Yellowstone had burned, that he would "like to see a nice wildfire take out everything at Fishing Bridge" and that it was a "real shame" that Grant Village hadn't gone up, too. And on September 24th, National Audubon Society board member Scott Reed of Coeur d'Alene, Idaho, made this comment to the Idaho Conservation League: "In my view the greatest environmental disaster coming out of the Yellowstone park fire was its failure to burn up West Yellowstone. In the fierce competition between Wyoming and Montana for the ugliest town, West Yellowstone [Montana] is the easy winner. What a wonderful thing it would have been to reduce all of that neon clutter and claptrap to ashes."

"Arson," is how Montana outfitter Edwin Johnson described the natural-fire program in the *Cody* (Wyoming) *Enterprise.* But Guru Ma's husband, Edward Francis, disagreed. It was, he said, more like "pyromania."

The natural-fire program, editorialized the *Billings* (Montana) *Gazette*, "says burn baby burn....Barbee rode a dead policy into hell."

The fire year was also an election year, so politicians added to the smoke and heat. Senator Malcolm Wallop of Wyoming, who sits on the Senate subcommittee that oversees the National Park Service, announced to the press that the agency had "changed the let-burn policy… at my request" (although it had not) and then called for the resignation of its director, William Penn Mott.

"I believe that the policy of wilderness lands, of 'lock it up and let it burn' is in fact a policy of ruin and ashes," said Representative Ron Marlenee of Montana, vice-chairman of the House subcommittee that oversees the Park Service.

Senator Orrin G. Hatch of Utah chalked it all up to "too much extremism in the environmental area."

Commented Wyoming State Representative Carroll Miller: "Now we're told that great benefits are there. Well, I guess then that the bombing of the poor districts of London and Berlin were beneficial because those areas needed to be torn down anyway."

Other legislators, both state and federal, and a posse of western governors condemned the "let-burn policy" and called for sweeping review. Especially shrill was the voice of Idaho Governor Cecil Andrus, who had been President Jimmy Carter's Secretary for the Interior when the natural-fire program was coming into its own in Yellowstone and on other federal lands. Now he called the program "a prescription for disaster."

This and other pronouncements by Andrus set Louisa Willcox rummaging through historical documents. She told me this: "After he said the 'let-burn' policy was nothing that he would have supported or ever did support and that he was shocked and chagrined at the way things had gone this summer, I went back and looked at how much federal land burned naturally under the existing policy when he was Interior Secretary. It was nearly 30,000 acres."

Finally, the noise reached President Reagan, who allowed that it was the first time he'd ever heard of such a thing as a natural-fire policy. Nevertheless, he dispatched Interior Secretary Hodel, Agriculture Secretary Richard Lyng, and Deputy Defense Secretary William H. Taft IV to Yellowstone where, trailed by generals, colonels, majors, and the high brass of the Park Service and Forest Service, they put on a media event.

The play was for Hodel to speak to the assembled national wire services, TV and radio networks, magazines and newspapers just as Old Faithful vented its column of hot water and steam. But Old Faithful wasn't faithful.

Although Hodel had previously supported the natural-fire program, he now called the fires "a disaster" and "devastating." According to the *Billings Gazette*, members of the media "interviewed everyone and anyone who would stand still and spoke English. They even interviewed each other." It was not the sort of climate in which accurate new coverage flourishes.

And the news that poured out of Yellowstone all summer and fall—even from sources one normally can trust—was stunningly inaccurate. For example, the *New York Times* reported that "the Park Service is planning to feed some of the park's wildlife, like elk and bison, to prevent them from migrating out of the park and looking for food on cattle ranches." It was utterly untrue. And the Associated Press reported that the "fires have blackened most of the 2.2-million-acre park." Also false.

On September 20th, exactly one month after Black Saturday, I apprehensively returned to "Yellowstone National Tree," as I'd heard it called, and moved back into the old wooden cabin in Gardiner, Montana. It and all the other buildings had come through without a paint blister, although the town had been poised for evacuation. There was light snow on the mountains, and the air was cold and wet. Up in the park smoke still hung in the valleys and lots of live embers glowed in roots and deadfalls, but the fires were essentially out. Bull elk bugled in the frosty meadows, making their own steam vents, and the sky was full of hawks hunting refugee rodents.

Other than about 250 roasted elk (some last seen vanishing down grizzly gullets), several dead bison and mule deer, a black bear, and a well-done red squirrel, whose tail fell off when I tried to pick it up, I turned up no evidence of serious casualties among the park's wildlife. But Guru Ma assured me that things were lots worse than they appeared, that the animals had taken a dreadful beating. She'd seen bison that must have been horribly burned because their fur was sloughing off in thick mats.

Animal behavior I'd observed while the park was burning in August had been strikingly dissimilar to animal behavior I'd observed during the Disney fire. A sign at Grant Village had warned firefighters to beware of running bears. But no running animals of any sort were sighted. The elk, in fact, appeared singularly unmoved and uninterested. Sometimes they grazed within fifty feet of the flames ("a lot closer than I would have dared to get," offered one observer), then wandered into the burned area even before it cooled. Bison stood around licking the ashes. A family of trumpeter swans watched the fire approach their lake and encircle it, declining to fly away or even cease normal activity.

The real effect of wildfires on wildlife comes after, not during. If diversity of plants and animals is "good," the reduction of the lodgepole desert, as the biologists call it, and the accompanying renewal of low growth and meadows, have been "good." If you are a Yellowstone elk, the fires may be "bad" or "good," depending on your age, your condition, and the severity of the coming winter. If you make it to the spring of 1989, which is a big if, you likely will find living easier than in the past.

Had winters in Yellowstone been normal, the park indeed would have "too many" elk for the available winter habitat. But the last seven winters have been freakishly warm; elk have wintered on summer range, and the herd has expanded accordingly. Even in these mild winters mortality has run eight to ten percent, and now because the drought has deprived elk of succulent forage, they are not so well fleshed as they might have been. A harsh winter could bring a spectacular die-off.

"We've had the worst drought since the Dust Bowl years," says Varley, "and now we've had some winter range burned. So it's going to be a mighty interesting winter, one in which I'll probably wish I was in Tahiti."

Unfortunately for Varley and his associates, Yellowstone elk have a habit of dying along the riverbottoms—where the road system is. Bears, coyotes, songbirds, magpies, ravens, eagles, and the like love dead elk; but humans abhor them. Such is the fear of natural ungulate mortality in Yellowstone that the Park Service is coming under heavy pressure to assist nature by setting up artificial feeding programs. Even the scientifically minded Foundation for North American Wild Sheep has launched Project FAWN (Funds Available for Wildlife Now) to assist organizations in efforts to "reseed burned watersheds and provide necessary habitat and winter feed."

Artificial feeding hurts wild animals more than it helps them, especially in the case of ungulates. By the time a herd shows signs of stress, the possibility of successful feeding has long since passed. Having built up the right intestinal bacteria to digest natural forage, the animals are suddenly confronted with 22-percent-protein alfalfa hay. It passes right through them. And artificial feeding sties create artificial crowding, facilitating the spread of parasites and disease. For example, the rate of brucellosis in the artificially fed elk at Jackson Hole, Wyoming, is about 50 percent, while the rate in Yellowstone's naturally fed northern herd is 1.5 percent.

Although the thought of feeding wild animals is anathema to the sort of people who have taken over the Park Service, they refuse to discount the possibility. "It would be unprecedented for the park, but everything else is unprecedented this year," says Varley. Still, I got the impression that what really is unprecedented is the political pressure to coax and cajole nature to where the politicians and the public suppose it ought to be.

I know very little about soils, but even where the fires had burned most furiously I couldn't find much dirt that looked as if it had been "sterilized." In fact, some of it already was supporting a carpet of new grass lush enough to attract elk and bison. So I drove back to Mammoth

Incineration of Yellowstone

Hot Springs and tracked down soil scientist Henry Shovic. "Where's all the sterilized soil they're talking about on the Senate floor?" I asked.

"Well," he said, "there isn't any. It's kind of odd that we didn't get some."

"Good," I said.

But it wasn't good. It wasn't bad either. "Number one," said Shovic, "it doesn't matter if the soil is sterilized; seeds fall right back onto it, and microbes repopulate it. And number two, it isn't sterilized. There are lots of bugs left, except maybe in the top centimeter, and what we've got on top of that is ash, nature's way of fertilizing the soil. People see these big flames, and they say, 'Oh, the soil is heating.' But it isn't. Most of the heat goes straight up."

Another soil scientist, Ann Rodman, and wildlife biologist Roy Renkin let me accompany them to the top of the steep hill opposite Roaring Mountain where, two weeks before, a hot fire had burned through 300-year-old lodgepole pines. Even as the flames approached, Renkin had marked off study plots with steel spikes. Now he was checking for small-mammal activity, and Rodman was taking soil samples.

I had visited the area before it had burned and was amazed at the difference. The scene called to mind photos of Hiroshima taken in the fall of 1945. There was no sign of life except a few ants, chipmunks, birds, and fresh elk and deer tracks. In some places the ground really did appear to be "blackened to the very depths of the root system within it," as Senator Simpson had stated. Or at least there were large, deep holes where roots had been. The earth was strewn with rock fragments and the skeletons of uprooted trees. Standing trees had been charred and stripped of their crowns. What, I asked Renkin, were those funny yellow lines on the surface ash? They were where downed trees "used to be." he said. The soil looked very black; for all I knew it might be sterilized. Was it?

"No," said Rodman, almost apologetically as she dropped a trowelful into a plastic bag.

In these and other soil samples is a new forest, visible to those who wish to look. Where the lodgepole pines were oldest the Park Service had found 50,000 seeds per acre; elsewhere up to a million. The cones, like those of jack pines, open in the heat, and yet politicians, including Hodel, are pushing for artificial planting. "We don't need [outside] seeds," Director Mott patiently explained to western senators who had called a hearing in order to vent their complaints about the natural-fire program.

One bright morning when steam and a few wisps of smoke were rising from the woods, Renkin drove me in his pickup truck to the aspen study area on Bunsen Peak that had burned twelve days earlier. I have always admired aspens, especially on campfires and when their dancing leaves turn yellow in the fall; but I cannot say that I am obsessed with them. Roy Renkin is obsessed with aspens. He talks about them constantly, sometimes with hand gestures.

As we bounced up the dirt road, two coyotes trotted through a scorched meadow, and half a dozen Clark's nutcrackers bobbed through the elk exclosure.

We walked the trapline. Only one pocket gopher, but Renkin expected more now that the weather was improving. On the higher slopes burned patches of lodgepole looked like cloud shadows, and splashed on distant hillsides were brilliant, golden clumps of aspen. The air smelled like a hunting shack after someone forgets to open the damper on the woodstove.

Here the fire had been relatively cool, traveling mostly on the ground. Some of the aspen trees on the brow of the hill were standing, but they'd been burned almost through at the trunks. Lower down, many were alive and in green or golden leaf. Most of the sagebrush had burned away.

The best thing that can happen to aspen is a forest fire. It stimulates the root system to send forth suckers so that where you had one tree in 1988 you may have 500 in 1989. By July some will be chest high. However, one should think of an aspen not as an individual tree but as a single root system—sometimes thirty-two tons to the acre—that can underlie a whole hill. You can shoot a radioactive tracer into one tree and it will show up in another, maybe a hundred feet away. The root is the organism and, as Renkin puts it, "it doesn't matter much to the aspen if it maintains itself by sending up trees or shrubs."

It is said by Alston Chase and others that aspen is vanishing from Yellowstone and that the proliferating elk are eating it away. While Renkin acknowledges that this might be possible, he notes that the plant doesn't seem to do well in Yellowstone even when elk are not abundant.

Incineration of Yellowstone

The climate is too dry and hot. But somehow aspen got started in the park. "When was the last time you had cool, wet conditions here?" he asked, not waiting for an answer. "I keep thinking about that, and I keep coming up with the Ice Age." So, if Renkin has it right, some of these aspen roots might be the oldest living things on Earth, older even than bristlecone pines.

Photos taken in the late 1800s show big aspen stands at well-known locations in the park which are now said to be devoid of aspen—Mammoth Hot Springs, for example. But those who say the species had died out haven't bothered to poke around on their hands and knees as Renkin has. Whenever he checks out these alleged die-out areas he finds lots of tiny aspen shrubs that no one else noticed. Maybe what the aspen roots in Yellowstone National Park have been waiting for is the 200- to 400- year fire.

As Yellowstone burned, the Park Service kept passing out fire maps on which the black splotches kept getting bigger until there was scarcely any white space for the ink. And when the *New York Times* published them all together, the progress of the fire from July 15th to September 18th looked like the progress of the Third Reich through Europe. What most newspapers, including the *New York Times,* failed to notice or to report was the writing on the back of the map: "Only about half of the vegetation had burned within many fire perimeters."

From the fire-command helicopter it seemed to me that even this was an exaggeration. For two hours we flew over the areas inked solid on the September 18th fire map, and we found them to be mostly green. To be sure, there were vast burns that took five or ten minutes to traverse; but there were even vaster tracts of unburned forest, much of it ravaged by mountain pine beetles. The Forest Service has this theory that beetle-killed lodgepole is a fire hazard, but I saw lots of it that the fires had skipped over because the flammable crowns were missing. Meadows looked like torched hayfields.

In some places the fire had traveled along the ground and hadn't killed the trees. Elsewhere it had left random winding trails or sent out long tendrils. And where wind-driven embers had fallen on the living forest there were brown-rimmed circles of black ranging from perhaps half an acre to fifty—"spotting," the firefighters call it. The net result was

Fire as Foe, Fire as Friend

a mosaic managers might design if they were creating firebreaks or "edge" for wildlife.

I tried to tally all the green and all the black I'd seen and guessed that there was 10 percent black. The Park Service's official estimate was 20 percent, and infrared photos studied in late November reveal that (1) fire perimeters in the entire Greater Yellowstone area enclosed only 1.4 million acres (200,000 acres fewer than reported); (2) within these perimeters, 30 to 70 percent of the vegetation was untouched; and (3) some plant life (other than seeds) remained in all but one-tenth of one percent of the 1.4 million acres.

While the fires in and around Yellowstone did no ecological damage, they destroyed three houses, thirty-one cabins, thirteen mobile homes, two park dormitory rooms, two bridges, a TV transmitting station, some power and phone lines, and assorted sheds and outhouses. They also damaged the economy, although it is difficult to ascertain to what extent. "People who have been supporters of wilderness programs and natural-fire programs got clobbered," says Bob Turner, Rocky Mountain regional vice-president of the National Audubon Society. "We need to have some compensation for them. That's where I'd like to see positive action."

Visits to the park were down 12.5 percent from 1987, and nearby towns were definitely hurt. Yet many of the people who didn't go to Yellowstone went instead to Glacier National Park, so that the entire Montana economy was down only five percent. In Idaho and Wyoming the loss of tourists was made somewhat less painful by the influx of fire-fighters. Many towns got their fire trucks paid for. And even before the fires were out the Park Service was getting calls from tour companies wanting to organize see-the-burned-park trips for next year. "People love disasters," observes a snow-tour entrepreneur from West Yellowstone.

The major damage associated with the fires came from man's attempt to put them out. Aerial application of fire retardant caused a few minor fish kills, and miles of firelines disrupted topsoil. The rehabilitation of the firelines will be a big undertaking. "It can be done," says Park Service District Ranger Steve Frye, head of firefighting operations. "We certainly have the technology to do that and do it well, but it's going to be a prolonged effort. It will take all of next summer and maybe then some."

Scars in this kind of terrain are slow to heal (140-year-old wheel ruts are still visible on the Oregon Trail, for instance). So during the joint firefighting the Park Service discouraged the use of bulldozers to make firelines in Yellowstone. Rangers even refused to allow fire trucks to cross meadows; and in one case, when their orders were flouted, they threatened citations. For this coddling of the landscape the Park Service came under bitter attack. "It's like going into a butt-kicking contest with your ankles tied together," complained one firefighter to a reporter from the *Billings Gazette*. "The politicians would kill us if we fought fires like this in California," said another. As a result, Yellowstone is not nearly so hacked up as the surrounding national forests.

"The fire-suppression people wanted to bulldoze the bejesus out of everything," Roy Renkin told me. "But there's no bulldozer line man could construct that would have stopped those fires." Bulldozer lines outside the park hadn't even slowed them, nor had the sprawling, rock-rimmed Yellowstone River.

The local public has believed right along that the fires could have been extinguished if back-to-nature sentimentalists hadn't held back. "People talk about firefighting in the context of nuclear war," says Ed Lewis, director of the Greater Yellowstone Coalition. "They think everything is insufficient, that we should have brought in the entire SAC force."

There was a time, however, when even the fire-behavior experts believed that man was in control. In early August they fed all their combined wisdom into a computer and hatched a worst-burn scenario for Yellowstone of 250,000 acres. Just a little over a month later the fires had burned 440,000 acres. Before the unified area command was established the Forest Service had its back up about "accepting" Yellowstone fires, as if it had a choice. The Targhee National Forest vehemently refused to "accept" so much as a spark. But then a spark from a logger's chainsaw touched off the North Fork fire in the Targhee and, ripping through clearcuts, it entered the park. Neither would the Shoshone National Forest "accept" a Yellowstone fire, but then, on Black Saturday, the Clover-Mist Fire decided otherwise. The Gallatin National Forest wouldn't and didn't "accept" Yellowstone fires, but it gave Yellowstone the Hellroaring Fire. The Bridger-Teton National Forest allowed that it would be pleased to "accept" Yellowstone fires, but it didn't get any.

Fire as Foe, Fire as Friend

Instead, Yellowstone got the Mink Creek Fire from Bridger-Teton. And so it went, with humans scurrying around on the attack with chainsaws, spades, Indian pumps, and water buckets slung under helicopters.

If firefighting operations had been effective, one would expect the eight major man-caused fires (fought from the beginning) to have made significantly less progress than the five major lightning-caused fires (left alone until July 21st). But they didn't.

Seemingly as effective as any firefighting operation—more so, according to Guru Ma—was that mounted by the Church Universal and Triumphant. As the wall of flame approached to within several thousand feet of the sacred, subalpine meeting ground near Mol Heron Creek, members, in rotating brigades of 300, faced it with outstretched arms and chanted a non-stop, high-speed mantra. The mantra is unintelligible to the untrained ear, but it translates to "reverse the tide; roll them back; set all free." It worked. "The press saw it," Guru Ma told me.

But during the next month the fire traveled all the way around the sect's 30,000 acres and came in from the other side, near Gardiner. So members gathered in a barn and, channeling commands through sundry celestial beings, including angels and archangels, called in cold fronts. "We got one," said Guru Ma.

The cost of the more conventional firefighting methods in the Greater Yellowstone ecosystem came to about $115 million. Other than partial appeasement of fire-haters, what really was gained by this expenditure? I put the question to Frye, who had typical Park Service trust of nature but who, as head fireman, obviously didn't like the suggestion that he might have wasted his summer. He said there were suppression efforts that "worked and worked well" and that they did a good job at saving buildings.

But, from all the reports, it appeared that the big efforts deep in the woods had infinitely less to do with saving the buildings than the close-in work, such as hosing them down. And of those that did burn, eleven of the cabins, eight of the sheds, and the TV transmitting station were lost to a backfire lit by firefighters in the vicinity of Montana's Cooke City and Silver Gate (now called "Cooked City" and "Cinder Gate"). The owner of one of the cabins is taking legal action against the Forest Service.

"What if you'd just let the fires go?" I asked. Frye allowed that they might have burned through an additional 10 or 20 percent of forestland. One reason Americans so frequently fail in their efforts to coax, cajole, improve, and assist nature is that they have so few control areas where they let nature do her own thing. They want to take nature somewhere, but they don't know where to pick her up. Yellowstone is—or was—such a control area. Other natural-fire programs—even those in other national parks—are more restrictive. In wilderness administered by the Forest Service, fire plans are based on energy-release components. When the component is above a certain window, managers try to put out the fire. When the component is below the window, and the fire has little chance of doing much, they let it burn.

During the summer of 1988, 70,000 wildfires cut through 4,000,000 acres in the western states and Alaska. But Americans got really worked up only about the fires in Yellowstone. The others were much smaller and just burned "the woods." Yellowstone, on the other hand, was a special place, a place they loved, their first-born national park.

The point they missed was that, for the most part, all 70,000 fires, including those in Yellowstone, burned about everything they could. However, the Yellowstone ecosystem (the largest temperate nature preserve on the planet) is the only patch of sub-Alaskan America where you can still get wildfire on the scale seen last summer.

Now there is a strong movement to scuttle natural-fire programs in Yellowstone and elsewhere, but it seems doubtful that it can succeed. Those conducting the reviews are scientists, and there is not a legitimate scientist anywhere who favors Smokey Bear–style fire suppression. There will be plenty of modifications that won't substantially change the basic approach but will silence the politicians who don't understand it anyway. In Yellowstone, at least, it doesn't matter what people decide to do about fires, because there won't be enough fuel for another major one until the twenty-second century.

What does matter is the gathering offensive against the whole wildlands movement. As one Park Service employee who requested anonymity put it, "You see these different groups lining up and coalescing—the Wyoming Farm Bureau, the Wyoming Heritage Society, congressmen. In my opinion, they're seeing a jugular vein and going for it."

"This summer Montana Governor Ted Schwinden banned tourism recreation but allowed mining and logging to go on," notes an official with the Montana Department of Commerce. "That's when many of us realized industry was organizing to take advantage of the situation."

Guru Ma, Senator Steve Symms of Idaho, and Barry Cullen, president of the National Forest Products Association, are saying that the Park Service needs to start "harvesting" timber before it burns up. The Church Universal and Triumphant, it turns out, is planning a colossal housing development—"an archetypal community for the Aquarian Age"—that could severely damage Yellowstone's cutthroat trout, bighorn sheep, moose, antelope, bison, mule deer, bald eagles, and grizzly bears as well as ruin some of the geothermal features. And up on sacred Mol Heron Creek a church fence along the park's north boundary is injuring animals and impeding migration. Guru Ma partially attributes negative reaction from the Park Service to "religious prejudice."

Editorializing against a bill that would add land to our national parks, the *Wall Street Journal* used the fires this way: "With Yellowstone Park a smoke-blackened ruin because of failed federal forest-management policies, one might think it highly embarrassing to propose that still more of America's scenery be trusted to the same bunglers....Some environmentalists—ourselves, for example—are appalled at what happened in Yellowstone. We see little reason to reward mismanagement with more responsibility over national treasures."

Bill Mott made himself *persona non grata* with the Reagan Administration by vigorously supporting the wildlands movement. Currently, he is under investigation by Interior's Inspector General for misconduct which, apparently, consists of advocating greater spending on public lands. And he got into trouble with Hodel, well-heeled ranchers, and Reagan team players in Congress for pushing wolf reintroduction (as required by the Endangered Species Act) in Yellowstone.

Montana Representative Marlenee had asserted that "environmentalists must be salivating [as they think] of all the land that can be locked up" by reinfecting the West with endangered wolves, which he calls "cockroaches." Senator Symms warns that wolves "pose a real danger to humans," although 100 percent of the nonfiction literature indicates that they do not. Senator Simpson goes a step further, claiming that wolves *eat* humans. And now Senator Wallop is saying that if the Park Service can't control fires, it obviously can't be trusted to control wolves.

Incineration of Yellowstone

"I think wolf reintroduction has been set back in a major way," John Varley says. "The credibility of the agency has taken such a nosedive that our going out and saying, 'Here's our program, trust us,' isn't going to fly."

As I fished and hiked my way through Yellowstone during the summer and fall of 1988, I kept imagining what the park must have looked like before the first white trappers from Europe, before the last ice sheet from the Arctic, before the first Asians from Siberia. I saw meadows shrink and expand and lodgepole forests—in varying shades of black, brown, and green—sweep and recede. On the hillsides, aspen roots exploded into trees and crashed to shrubs. In the endless plains between the ragged mountains bison grazed, grunted, and wallowed. Elk came and went, lived and died. In the deep glides of the main river, two-pound cutthroat trout rolled and waggled their dorsal fins. Now and then the indigo sky was filled with enormous mushroom clouds.

The day before I returned to the managed East I stopped the car about three miles downstream from where I'd finished. Turning my back to the asphalt and traffic, I looked out over the Hayden Valley. A raven rode an updraft, and bison dotted the yellow plains beyond the winding, silver river. Apart from the missing wolves, all of Yellowstone was still there. Nothing basic had changed. The park had survived all those millennia with scarcely any human help.

Selection from

Fireline: Summer Battles of the West

MICHAEL THOELE

BEISLER FELT IT FIRST. Something still, heavy, ominous. Something speaking to him from that place where experience lives, distilled to intuition. Something filtering to him through a dozen years of chasing big fire across the West. Something left in him from the chaparral of California and the big timber of Oregon and the piney slopes of the Rockies. But something that the diggers and the sawyers, sweating, panting, pushing, yellow shirts sticking to their backs, still didn't feel in the waning hours of this 104-degree day.

They were the Wyoming Hotshots, best damn fire crew in the Forest Service if you cared to ask them, and they'd been at it for days, pounding in line and touching off roaring burnouts on first one eastern Montana fire and then another. It was Thursday now, and they'd stolen maybe twelve hours sleep since Monday. With fire on their flank, they were at it again, shovels and pulaski tools clinking, chainsaws screaming, heads down, elbows pumping.

The dragon seemed complacent today. He crept downhill on their right, close enough that his glow beat back the twilight and his breath cooked the sweat from their faces as they worked the toe of the slope. But his march was slow and his teeth were short, no more than two feet tall as they gnawed through dry grass and the duff blanket of needles beneath the towering ponderosas. Still, it was odd, aggressive behavior for a fire this late in the day.

Bad stuff, maybe, for a rookie crew shanghaied away from painting picnic benches in some national forest. But they were hotshots, this Wyoming bunch—wildfire professionals who ranked up there with the smokejumpers and the best of the West's helicopter rappel crews. They had seen the dragon in worse moods. What was a ground crawler with two-foot flames easing downhill against the wind to them? They were drawing their line in the dirt, stealing the grass and needles and trees that the dragon needed to live, fighting fire with fire by touching off the duff with their long, red fuses, and burning out any sustenance that he might find as he stalked toward their thin trail of bare soil. And behind them were two crack crews of Cheyenne Indians, the seasoned firefighters of Western legend, reinforcing the line, chasing down hot spots.

But in that moment, Beisler's foreboding grew.

Forest fires, like new ships and new babies, are christened. If a fire survives its first day, it gets a name, drawn usually from a geographic feature but occasionally tugged from a creative vein hidden in the psyche of some fire bureaucrat. The great campaign fires of the West have had names as poetic as Sleeping Child and as rude as a Hog. The Wyoming Hotshots had drawn the fire named Brewer, after a spring that burbled a few miles away.

They were a good crew on that June day in 1988, twenty strong and fresh from spring training. In a season that was off to an eerily early start, they could already claim three fires. Rogers, the ramrod of the Wyoming Hotshots, thought of his crews the way high school coaches talk of their teams. This one was younger and a bit less experienced than some he'd had, but strong and smart, and jelling in a way that pleased him. Officially, in the fashion that hotshot seasonal crews are organized in the nation's wildfire agencies, he was the unit's superintendent. Figuratively, he was captain of an elite little infantry platoon, one of the sixty-six outfits that fire bosses scream for each summer when the dragon goes thundering through the forests. Beisler, the foreman, the crew's nominal top sergeant, had chased the dragon through every state in the West.

In the paramilitary world of wildland fire, smokejumpers are the Special Forces, dropping deep behind the lines, risking that long step between airplane door and rocky landing to catch the enemy when he is small, insurgent, and least expecting opposition. And hotshots are the Marines, gung-ho groundpounders charging up the beach against stacked odds. Hotshots, who number only 1,360 in all of America, go where the big fires walk.

From their base in the Wyoming town of Greybull, Rogers and Beisler had crafted this crew around a nucleus of veterans, returnees such as the squad bosses, Graham and Meier, and the sawyers, Mader and Halvorsen. They'd stirred in a batch of recruits, all new to the hotshot business, but most of them bumping up from lower echelons of the wild land fire game. They were a diverse bunch, with three Crow Indians, a Chicago black, and two women in their ranks. They were as old as thirty-six, as young as eighteen. Among them marched athletes, ranch kids, college students, ex-oil-field workers, world-traveled adventurers, locals from Bighorn County, and Easterners from as far away as New Jersey.

Today, the twenty had become nineteen. The fire bosses, sequestered back at camp with their maps and radios, had pulled Rogers off the crew and made him a division superintendent [sic]. He'd turned the crew over to Beisler—they'd done it before—and moved up to oversee a five-mile section of the Brewer fire's north flank, a piece of the battle that included his own crew, the Cheyenne, a pair of off-road pumper engines, and a bulldozer. The shots had seen Rogers occasionally that evening as he came through their sector and heard him talking on the radio with Beisler.

The engines had never caught up with them. And they'd lost the bulldozer around eight o'clock. It had been easy going until then. Rogers had relayed a helicopter pilot's message to Beisler. Ahead of the crew lay a meadow, an open island of an acre or so, surrounded by trees. It ran just a bit below the slow-moving line of fire, opposite a small draw at the bottom of the slope they were working. A gift. With a bit of a detour, Beisler could get the crew onto kinder terrain just above the meadow. Beisler had passed the word to Graham, his squad boss at the front of the crew. They'd bent the line and headed north, moving well, with the sawyers sprinting out ahead and knocking down trees, the dozer peeling a ten-foot swath, the diggers cleaning up behind and firing out, creating a blackened line to stop the approaching flames.

But the 'dozer jockey was a flatlander, not like the ones they'd seen on so many other fires, the sure-handed artists who spurred their diesel steeds into action like tank commanders in warfare. This one was a grader of subdivision lots, a new hire seeing action he hadn't contemplated. Craning over his shoulder at the approaching fire, he'd pulled up short at the top of a modest sixty-foot grade. Too steep, he'd said. Graham, decisive and always a bit impatient, had argued. Nothing to it, he'd said, the regular fire dozer guys do it all the time. But, face pale and hands shaking, the flatlander had spun his iron monster in its tracks and gone clanking back the way he'd come.

There was nothing for it after that but to dig. Digging, after all, is the quintessential work of forest fire. Birds sing, fires burn, hotshots dig. So they'd set off, tools swinging hard, taking out trees to break the forest canopy and cutting fire line, gouging their two-foot trail through the dirt beneath the ponderosas as if digging were an Olympic event. They'd expected to don their helmet headlamps after dark and to punch in maybe two or three miles of line before their shift ended at six the next morning. Killer work. The hardest work there was. Their work. Beisler had trotted off to ribbon a stretch of the new course with bits of plastic tape. His path took him down across the small draw, then up again to the edge of the tree-rimmed meadow. In minutes he was back.

It was then that he felt the strangeness.

The temperature was climbing paradoxically as twilight deepened. It was up maybe fifteen degrees since he'd hiked down the trail. Odd. The uphill wind was dropping, disappearing. The humidity was skittering downward, the air becoming a desiccant that sucked the moisture off his skin. And there was the stillness, the dead calm, the heaviness. The fire still crept at ground level. But up the line, two or three trees torched off in a momentary seventy-foot tongue of flame, as if the dragon had cleared his throat and spit into the sky.

In war stories told by the old hands of Western forest fire, the spooky calm before the monumental blowup is standard fare. The stuff of rustic mythology, the academics used to say, like the business of moss growing only on the north side of trees. But no more. Now the meteorologists and the fire behaviorists know it's so. They can explain how the dragon holds his breath just before he breathes fire across the land in an explosion that comes faster than the fastest runner. They can chart it and graph it, though they can never predict its precise time or place. And they can detail the incidents, tragedies often, where no one read the signals, no one felt.

But Beisler felt it now. He moved to Graham. They shut down the saws, told the diggers to take a break. They listened. Beisler turned and trotted the two hundred yards ahead to the meadow, wondering if it could be a safety zone if things went sour. By the time he returned, Graham, too, had picked up the drop in the wind, the faintest hint of some new vigor in the fire.

A few airborne embers, now without the uphill wind to hold them off, flitted down across the line, dropped into the parched grass on the crew's left, and blossomed instantly into tulips of fire. Graham set the diggers to chasing them. Farther back along the line, toward the Cheyenne, more embers drifted over, more fires erupted. Another tree torched off, then another, momentary Roman candles rising above the ground fire, their resinous needles sizzling like bacon. Spectacular but hardly urgent. The Wyoming crew plunged to the task at hand willingly, chasing down the spots even as more ignited.

Beisler watched for a minute or two, thinking and feeling. Logic battled instinct. Then he turned to Graham: "Get 'em out. Let's get 'em out now. Up to the meadow." In the years that Graham and Beisler had worked together, they had gone toe to toe with fire vastly more threatening. This was not a fire to make a hotshot crew turn tail. But there was a trust between the two of them. Not questioning, Graham began rounding up his spot chasers. The rookies responded quickly. A couple of the sawyers balked for just a moment, reluctant to leave a fray they were certain could be won. Graham moved them out.

The dragon was stirring now. The wind, no longer neutral, blew lightly downhill. Beisler ran back down the line. Below, spot fires were picking up on his right, and up the hill the main fire began to drive down on his left. Graham was leading the crew out of the trees, counting heads. Beisler turned and trotted after them. Behind him, the embers were falling in earnest, like bits of hot, red snow.

The oral history of every Western hotshot crew has a chapter for tales of being chased out. A crew boss makes a decision and the troops retreat to a burned-out black zone, a rock field, a meadow. Like freight cars on a siding, they sit it out and let the fire go highballing past. It is often searing and uncomfortable, so hot that firefighters hide their faces behind hard hats or backpacks. But it always plays well in the retelling: "Fire all around us, three-hundred sixty degrees, and we had our cameras out and were eating lunch." As Graham pushed them toward the draw that separated them from the meadow, the veterans on the crew saw one of those forced respites coming. The meadow would be safe.

But the dragon was growing. More embers were falling. Farther up the ridge in the trees behind them, an insistent roar was building. Kulow, a rookie less than a month out of Greybull High School, picked up his pace as the crew broke from a walk to a jog. He felt the growing urgency but had no perspective in which to place it. This was why he'd joined. It was exciting. It was great.

They broke out of the trees, rushed to the bottom of the draw and hit the upslope on the opposite side. As they reached the meadow, a stand of trees torched off down the line, between them and the Cheyenne. The fire was working harder, growing faster. It had become a crescent pushing toward them, its tips beginning to hook around the meadow. Beisler caught up with them. He and Graham conferred. Their message rippled through the crew. Start preparing shelter sites. Just a precaution.

Across the West, those who head off to do business with wildfire carry a yellow pouch, not much larger than a box of chocolates. It is worn always at the ready, usually at the waist. It seems almost too small to yield what it contains—a tiny, mansized, aluminum foil pup tent, a floorless, frameless, poleless, doorless pop-up shelter that a trained firefighter should be able to deploy in twenty seconds. A bonded inner lining of heat resistant glass fiber lends the foil strength, so it will not tear like a chewing gum wrapper. Even so, the aluminum pup tent's walls are thinner than a firefighter's shirt, and the whole improbable structure weighs less than four pounds.

The Wyoming Hotshots had renewed acquaintances with the shelter only three weeks before. In a ritual of spring training that plays out across the West, the thousands of seasonals who hire on for fire duty practice with old shelters, like toddlers climbing under cardboard boxes. They learn about the corner straps for hands and feet, the narrow flaps that tuck under the tent's perimeter to be held down by elbows and knees. They are told that the shelter could save them from flames as hot as a thousand degrees. They are also told that they do not ever want to prove the point. There is no fun in facing the dragon in his foulest mood with only a handful of tinfoil. And across the years very few firefighters have—some minuscule fraction of one percent.

So, even as they began to clear spots in the meadow, few of the hot-shots expected to pull their aluminum tents. To the most jaded of the veterans the digging was just another Forest Service safety precaution, part of life in an outfit that could sometimes seem more preoccupied with abating risk than with fighting fire. Beisler started back toward the draw, wanting to make a last check on the line. He raised Meier, his sec-ond squad boss, on the radio. Just before the crew had pulled off the line, Meier had dropped back to touch base with the Cheyenne.

Beisler never made it to the draw. From above it, he could see fire surging over the line where the crew had labored moments earlier. The wind clearly had reversed. It was pushing strongly downhill now. Barely a quarter mile away, up behind the line, a thickening column of black smoke climbed into the sky, and fire romped on the crowns of the trees. The dragon, having spent the afternoon preheating and drying the forest canopy above, was coming after it hungrily. And out just a few hundred yards, the crescent of fire was becoming a horseshoe, its two sides driving down to flank the meadow. Meier could not possibly rejoin them. Beisler radioed him to stay with the reservation crews and to fall back. In the meadow, they would be eighteen.

Even before Beisler turned back to the meadow, the pace there quickened. There was an earnestness now to the digging but little progress. Their haven was no grass savannah. It was covered instead with a thick, knee-high, vinelike brush that resisted their tools. Worse, the six sawyers had no hand tools at all; they could only stand and wait. Hamilton, strong and capable from years of work in the oil fields, had cleared only a one-foot square. She found the going almost impossible. She handed off her pulaski to McWilliams, the geology major from Michigan. Kulow stood, watching fire build on the ridge and hearing a new sound, a huffing like a locomotive building speed. Sembach, one of the veterans, heard it too. He shouted at Kulow, "C'mon Kevin, you gotta dig, you gotta dig!" Somewhere in those moments, Graham told them they would deploy shelters. Not all of them believed. It was a possibility too rare. The digging went on.

But it was hopeless work. The strongest among them had hacked out barely two feet. Embers, larger now, fell in the meadow. Momentarily, Graham was gone. Now he was returning, "Up here, up here!" he yelled. "There's a road. It's more open." Nearer to them now, the fire rose in the trees. It was still beyond the closest trees, the thick wall of pine that ringed the edges of the meadow. But its smoke darkened the twilight sky, and in the near distance flames marched across the roof of the forest.

Some of the veterans shed yellow backpacks. They dug out the metal gasoline and oil bottles they each carried to feed the saws, and the flare-like fuses they used to touch off burnouts, and they began flinging them away. Others took the time to dig the flammables off the backs of the rookies still carrying packs. Through it all they walked, stumbled, ran toward the road. Beisler, returning to the meadow as they were moving out, trailed them. It was a few minutes before nine o'clock. Daylight was waning. Barely fifteen minutes had passed since they left the fire line.

The meadow was not much of a meadow and the road that ran along its north edge was not much of a road. A two-track, really, a pair of wheel lines pounded into the dirt by hunters' pickup trucks. But it was brush-free, covered at its shoulders and center with dry grass. The crew arrived in a rush. The wind whipped their yellow shirts and tore away their words. In the rising noise, the ember shower became a storm. Bits of branches and fist-sized ponderosa cones, resinous firebrands that had been swept hundreds of feet into the air and ignited by the fire's updraft, tumbled from the sky.

Graham sensed time getting away. In the crew, he saw disbelief. The never-never moment was at hand, but most of them still wore shelters at their belts. He stepped to the head of the line, the approaching fire over his shoulder and the crew before him. He ripped his shelter from his pouch and flipped it open into the wind. He shook out the last folds and hooked his boots into the foot straps. Then he looked down the line and saw with satisfaction that shelters were coming out.

Beisler reached the road as his crew wrestled their foil tents in the wind, like Kansas farm wives trying to clean off the washline before an approaching tornado. Hamilton had her tent unfolded. She looked fearfully at Beisler. "You can handle it," he yelled. "You'll be okay." As he tucked into his shelter, Antos, the recruit from New Jersey, saw spot fires dancing downward in the meadow and the trees beyond. The horseshoe was closing. They were encircled. The seconds raced. Beisler turned to see Mader, the sawyer, with a shadow of resigned doom on his face. His hand protruded through a huge seam split in his shelter. "No, no, you're okay," Beisler yelled. "Remember the training film. Grab the rip. Tuck it under you."

As he rushed to throw his own shelter down, Beisler stole a glance at the fire. He had watched fire race across grassy hills faster than an antelope could run, and he had seen it thunder up the chaparral canyons of California, eating houses like popcorn. But he was seeing something different now. He looked into a firestorm, a panorama of flame. Down low, sheets of fire danced beyond the trees at the meadow's edge. Farther up the ridge they whipped above the forest and licked at the sky. The smoke column boiled ten thousand feet into the air. The embers and ash blew so fiercely that he lowered his head and squinted his eyes against them. Down the line to the south, a stand of trees was crowned in fire. To the north, like an image in a mirror, a second batch raged. Pillars of fire, to the right and left.

And then, in the second that Beisler watched, the pillars connected and became a wall. As if marinated in gasoline, the trees at meadow's edge, the last barrier between the hotshots and fire, crowned out in an eighth-mile sheet of flame. Like it was driven by a bellows in a forge, the ground fire had simply lifted, vaulting to the canopy above. It matched nothing in Beisler's experience. And it roared and seethed now, a giant red-orange picket fence, with flames spiking 150 feet above the treetops and benign before the wind, stretching toward the meadow. The dragon was at the door.

Beisler was in trouble. Along the line of shelters, elbows and knees poked and bumped behind the foil, hands reached out to pull in flaps and tuck down tight. The fire was close now, and waves of heat rolled over him. Near the spot Beisler had chosen for himself, Bates, the recruit from Colorado, stood alone, gloved hands fumbling with his still-folded shelter. Beisler ripped it away, shook it out in the rising wind and handed it back. "Get in! Get in!" he yelled.

Out of time now, Beisler spun to his spot, shaking out his shelter, falling to the ground. As he went down, pulling the shelter over his shoulders like a cape, a sheet of flame rolled out of the trees and swept horizontally over the meadow. The grass at his feet ignited. He pulled the shelter in around him, hurrying, hurrying. He stole a final look at the meadow and took into the tent with him a vision of surrealist hell. Before a backdrop of orange flame, giant maroon and purple balls of unburned gases rolled toward them. They coursed two feet above the meadow, like an armada of great, malevolent, sinuous, airborne steam-rollers, seeking oxygen so they could explode into flame, while white vapor streamed off their tops like foam off an ocean curler.

And then the fire was on them.

The shelters were arrayed across the road in rows of two and three, packed in so tightly that some of them touched. They were boulders now in a river of flame, and the rapids eddied and curled and broke over each of them differently, with a venomous sort of whimsy. At the head, Graham felt the superheated wind buffet his shelter and push it down against his back. Beneath the edges he saw a thin line of flickering light, like a racing dynamite fuse, as the grass outside his tent erupted and the fire swept over him. On his right, he could hear Beisler struggling, still working to secure the edges of his tent and coping with tiny grass fires inside. Beisler had been caught with gloves off and sleeves rolled up. But he had a plastic water bottle in each hand and, as he secured the edges of his shelter, he used the canteens to eat out fire and to hold down the front corners.

The fire's first wave was the curtain of flame sweeping off the trees, igniting the volatile gases ahead of it. It was a flash flood, a stampede of flame that filled the meadow and swept over the road. It buffeted the tents and lifted their corners. Into most, it drove heavy smoke and into some, fire. Stewart, one of the Crows, was in the tallest grass along the road. He took fire inside the back of his tent and then in the front. He beat the flames out with his legs and hands, taking more searing air beneath the edges of his tent, choking on smoke. He fought the urge to do what he had been taught would be instantly fatal—to stand and run.

McWilliams had fire. Old Horn had fire. Bates had fire. Red Horn had fire, and in his tent he lifted himself to his fingers and toes, and watched little tongues of flame run beneath his body. Kulow saw that the shelter had pinholes, tiny openings that glowed red-orange, just as the training film had promised. The walls of his tent were too hot to touch, and the temperature inside was climbing. But, with an eighteen-year-old's sense of immortality, he was still fascinated and excited. Then the corner of his tent lifted. He took fire and smoke. In the next moments, he thought about dying. And he heard the screaming begin.

It came first from Trummer. The shortest member of the crew, she had struggled with the long stretch between the foot and hand straps of her shelter. Now wind lifted the back of her tent and for the briefest moment a wave of fire washed inside. Even as she screamed she fought the flaps back into place. Beside her, McWilliams cursed in frustration and shouted above the wind, "Don't panic, Lori! Don't run!" She beat flames out with her hands and rolled onto her side to smother a patch that was searing her leg. As Trummer's cries died, they could hear others. Long, tortured, repeated. Sembach. Those closest to the back could hear him screaming, thrashing in his tent, then screaming again.

Among the tents there was talk. Names were called out, and people checked in with each other even as they fought their interior fires and struggled for breath. They could hear McWilliams swearing colorfully at each new scream, voicing for them all the frustration of being able to do nothing for the others. Up front, Beisler and Graham talked over hand-held radios. They had heard the screams, too. They were certain that some had stood and run, entering the race that could not be won. Graham narrated each moment into his radio, not knowing if his transmission was reaching outside the meadow, wondering if his words would be the only record of what happened there. Kulow had heard nothing from the four crew members between his tent and Sembach's, and he counted them for dead.

Some in the crew sensed the briefest of pauses. The flame front from the trees roared past them, into the forest downwind from the meadow. It had been a prelude, an airborne attack that passed so quickly and claimed so much oxygen that it had burned only the lightest fuels around them. Now the dragon would send an army of towering flame marching at ground level through the brush of the meadow. It came with a volcano of sound, as if they were standing in the afterblast of a battalion of jet engines. It was on them with winds that approached sixty miles an hour. The tents filled with smoke, much thicker than before, and new fingers of fire crept under their edges.

They had heard of the noise and the wind that came with big fire. Some had experienced it before, from a distance. But mere humans were not meant to be at its epicenter, with breakers of flame washing over their tinfoil tents. The shelters shook and flattened and flapped and filled with thick smoke. Inside, as the temperatures rose toward two hundred degrees, the hotshots fought fire with water from their canteens and pressed their mouths close to the dirt, cupping their arms around their faces and struggling for breath. In the enveloping noise, each was alone.

In her tent, Hamilton thought over and over, "Some of us are dying." Bates had weathered the first blast of fire, but he was suffocating now, wrestling with the impulse to run. Hearing nothing but the roar, Kulow began to think that he was the only survivor. Alone in his shelter, Antos had a crystalline vision of the faraway New Jersey girl named Donna and wondered if he would make their wedding, just two months off. McWilliams took a shallow, searing breath. He ripped the earth with his fingers, trying to create a hole for his mouth and nose. There was little oxygen in the smoky air he had drawn; he held it perhaps twenty seconds, then let it go and pulled in another breath. Worse, much worse. Now he was frantic, digging the ground with his fingers, and finally with his teeth, as if some reservoir of sweet air could be chewed from the earth beneath him. He could hold the second breath only thirty seconds. Face in the dirt, he let it go and drew a third. He was dizzy now, choking, losing concentration.

And then, in all the tents, the smoke was gone. Some curious passing eddy of the fire drafted it out as quickly as it had come. A few on the crew felt the smallest whiff of cool air as the smoke exited, though the fire still raged around them. At the rear of the formation, Sembach no longer screamed. But they heard his moans, heard him calling out, heard him thrashing in his shelter. Up front, Graham and Beisler still talked. They listened for a while, felt the foil walls cool slightly. Briefly, they raised the edges of their tents and peered out. Still too hot. Beisler waited another minute, then rose to his knees. A fifty-mile-an-hour wind pulled his shelter from his hands and rolled it back. But it was wind without fire, and he called to Graham as he rose to his feet.

Beisler turned, and he was sickened. Twilight had given way to the first edge of night. He noted vaguely that the racing flame front was gone, already out of sight beyond the next ridge. The meadow had become a blackened moonscape, with clouds of ash and smoke whipping across it. On its edges, as far as he could see, the seared skeletons of pines stood, their branches fingering the night without a single needle. Here and there, small fires burned in the gloom, and several of them were very close—burning clumps of yellow. Yellow, the color of fire shirts. For the briefest moment Beisler saw bodies that had fallen where they'd run. The nearest of the fires was on the road and he went to it. It was a backpack, a piece of fire gear discarded in the headlong dash into the shelters. And so, he realized, were the other yellow lumps, because the tents, battered and misshapen, were shining there before him, row on row.

He and Graham went down the line, shaking shelters, softly calling names and hearing answers in smoke-rasped voices, bringing people out into the darkness and the wind. They found Sembach, rolled into his shelter, delirious from pain. He was burned, seriously, and he had inhaled superheated air. He had deployed at the edge of the road. The fire winds had swirled most cruelly around his shelter. The brush and fuel next to it were heavy, and they had burned with extreme heat. For long moments, as he fought his solitary battle, the winds had curled back both ends of the shelter. His legs, arms, and face were burned. But he would live, they would all live.

They would be alone for almost an hour in the dark before help arrived. Beisler and Graham, sensing the shakiness of the moment, spun the crew into action—gathering packs, counting heads, inventorying equipment, digging out first-aid gear and canteens. The medics, Antos and Bates, treated Sembach. They gave him water, swathed his burns in gauze, and talked him through the pain. The first van into the meadow carried him away, starting him toward a Montana hospital two hundred miles distant.

The crew was alone for most of another hour, treating its minor burns, talking, sharing food salvaged from the packs, waiting for transport. They swapped stories. Mader, the sawyer with the huge rip in his shelter, had survived unscathed. McWilliams had risen from the ground to see his silhouette etched in burned grass, like the police outline of a murder victim chalked onto pavement. Their sense of family was heightened. In the spirit of their moment, they posed for a group photograph, facing the retreating fire and mocking it with the universal one-finger salute. The T-shirt committee conducted its first meeting. Though they didn't know it that June night, they had survived the opening round of the fire siege of 1988, the season like no other. The blazes that would burn until November already were up and running in Yellowstone Park. The grapevine would do its work, and in the fire camps that never seemed to close in that endless summer of drought and flame, others would nod knowingly when they saw the shirts that read, "Been to hell and lived to tell. Brewer Fire."

At dawn they walked through medical checkups. Hamilton called her parents in Wyoming. Like so many other young people who wander onto fire crews, she was a second generation firefighter. Decades before, her father had cut line on Western fire. He had supported his daughter's decision to chase the dragon. He listened knowingly to her story. His memories of other fires in other times were keen. So was his fire camp humor. "See," he said, "I told you it wasn't dangerous."

When the doctors and the training counselors were done with them, the Wyoming Hotshots faced a choice. They knew that Sembach would live. And they knew that, most often, crews that have survived an entrapment go home, take a week off, regroup. The choice was theirs. It was no choice at all. They went back to the Brewer Fire.

Selection from

The Control of Nature

JOHN McPHEE

THE SLOPE THEY WERE sampling had an incline of eighty-five percent. They were standing, and walking around, but I preferred—just there—to sit. Needle grass went through my trousers. The heads of needle grass detach from the stalks and have the barbed design of arrows. They were going by the quiver into my butt but I still preferred to sit. It was the better posture for writing notes. The San Gabriels are so steep and so extensively dissected by streams that some watersheds are smaller than a hundred acres. The slopes average sixty-five to seventy percent. In numerous places, they are vertical. The angle of repose—the steepest angle that loose rocks can abide before they start to move, the steepest angle the soil can maintain before it starts to fail—will vary locally according to the mechanics of shape and strength. Many San Gabriel slopes are at the angle of repose or beyond it. The term "oversteepened" is often used to describe them. At the giddy extreme of oversteepening is the angle of maximum slope. Very large sections of the San Gabriels closely approach that angle. In such terrain, there is not much to hold the loose material except the plants that grow there.

Evergreen oaks were fingering up the creases in the mountainsides, pointing toward the ridgeline forests of big-cone Douglas fir, of knob-cone and Coulter pine. The forests had an odd sort of timberline. They went down to it rather than up. Down from the ridges the conifers descended through nine thousand, seven thousand, six thousand feet, stopping roughly at five. The forests abruptly ended—the country below being too dry in summer to sustain tall trees. On down the slopes and all the way to the canyons was a thicket of varied shrubs that changed in character as altitude fell but was everywhere dense enough to stop an army. On its lower levels, it was all green, white, and yellow with buckwheat, burroweed, lotus and sage, deerweed, bindweed, yerba santa. There were wild morning glories, Canterbury bells, tree tobacco, miner's lettuce. The thicket's resistance to trespass, while everywhere formidable, stiffened considerably as it evolved upward. There were intertwining mixtures of manzanita, California lilac, scrub oak, chamise. There was buckthorn. There was mountain mahogany. Generally evergreen, the dark slopes were splashed here and there with dodder, its mustard color deepening to rust. Blossoms of the Spanish bayonet stood up like yellow flames. There were lemonade berries (relatives of poison ivy and poison oak). In canyons, there were alders, big-leaf-maple bushes, pug sycamores, and California bay. Whatever and wherever they were, these plants were prickly, thick and dry, and a good deal tougher than tundra. Those evergreen oaks fingering up the creases in the mountains were known to the Spaniards as chaparros. Riders who worked in the related landscape wore leather overalls open at the back, and called them chaparajos. By extension, this all but impenetrable brush was known as chaparral.

The low stuff, at the buckwheat level, is often called soft chaparral. Up in the tough chamise, closer to the lofty timber, is high chaparral, which is also called hard chaparral. High or low—hard, soft, or mixed—all chaparral had in common an always developing, relentlessly intensifying, vital necessity to burst into flame. In a sense, chaparral consumes fire no less than fire consumes chaparral. Fire nourishes and rejuvenates the plants. There are seeds that fall into the soil, stay there indefinitely, and will not germinate except in the aftermath of fire. There are basal buds that sprout only after fire. Droughts are so long, rains so brief, that dead bits of wood and leaves scarcely decay. Instead, they accumulate, thicken, until the plant community is all but strangling in its own duff. The nutrients in the dead material are being withheld from the soil. When fire comes, it puts the nutrients back in the ground. It clears the terrain for fresh growth. When chaparral has not been burned for thirty years, about half the thicket will be dry dead stuff—twenty-five thousand tons of it in one square mile. The living plants are no less flammable. The chamise, the manzanita—in fact, most chaparral plants—are full of solvent extractives that burn intensely and ignite easily. Their leaves are glossy with oils and resins that seal in moisture during hot dry periods and serve the dual purpose of responding explosively to flame. In the long dry season, and particularly in the fall, air flows southwest toward Los Angeles from the Colorado Plateau and the Basin and Range. Extremely low in moisture, it comes out of the canyon lands and crosses the Mojave Desert. As it drops in altitude, it compresses, becoming even dryer and hotter. It advances in gusts. This is the wind that is sometimes called the foehn. The fire wind. The devil wind. In Los Angeles, it is known as Santa Ana. When chamise and other chaparral plants sense the presence of Santa Ana winds, their level of moisture drops, and they become even more flammable than they were before. The Santa Anas bring what has been described as "instant critical fire weather." Temperatures rise above a hundred degrees. Humidity drops very close to zero. According to Charles Colver, of the United States Forest Service, "moisture evaporates off your eyeballs so fast you have to keep blinking."

Ignitions are for the most part caused by people—through accident or arson. Ten percent are lightning. Where the Santa Anas collide with local mountain winds, they become so erratic that they can scatter a fire in big flying brands for a long distance in any direction. The frequency and the intensity of the forest fires in the Southern California chaparral are the greatest in the United States, with the possible exception of the wildfires of the New Jersey Pine Barrens. The chaparral fires are considerably more potent than the forest fires Wade Wells saw when he was an undergraduate at the University of Idaho or when he worked as a firefighter in the Pacific Northwest. "Fires in the Pacific Northwest are nothing compared with these chaparral fires," he remarked. "Chaparral fires are almost vicious by comparison. They're so intense. Chaparral is one of the most flammable vegetation complexes there are."

It burns as if it were soaked with gasoline. Chaparral plants typically have multiple stems emerging from a single root crown, and this contributes not only to the density of the thickets but, ultimately, to the surface area of combustible material that stands prepared for flame. Hundreds of acres can be burned clean in minutes. In thick black smoke there is wild orange flame, rising through the canyons like explosion crowns. The canyons serve as chimneys, and in minutes whole mountains are aflame, resembling volcanoes, emitting high columns of fire and smoke. The smoke can rise twenty thousand feet. A force of two thousand people may fight the fire, plus dozens of machines, including squadrons in the air. But Santa Ana firestorms are so violent that they are really beyond all effort at control. From the edge of the city upward, sixteen miles of mountain front have burned to the ridgeline in a single day.

So momentous are these conflagrations that they are long remembered by name: the Canyon Inn Fire, August, 1968, nineteen thousand acres above Arby's by Foothill Boulevard, above the world's foremost container nursery, above the chief executive officer of Mackinac Island Fudge; the Village Fire and the Mill Fire, November, 1975, sixty-five thousand acres above Sunland, Tujunga, La Crescenta, La Canada. The Mill Fire, in the words of a foreman at Flood, "burnt the whole front face off."

It is not a great rarity to pick up the *Los Angeles Times* and see a headline like this one, from September 27, 1970:

14 MAJOR FIRES RAGE OUT OF CONTROL
256 HOMES DESTROYED AS FLAMES BURN 180,000 ACRES

In millennia before Los Angeles settled its plain, the chaparral burned every thirty years or so, as the chaparral does now. The burns of prehistory, in their natural mosaic, were smaller than the ones today. With cleared fire lanes, chemical retardants, and other means of suppressing what is not beyond control, people have conserved fuel in large acreages. When the inevitable fires come, they burn hotter, higher, faster than they ever did in a state of unhindered nature. When the fires end, there is nothing much left on the mountainsides but a thin blanket of ash. The burns are vast and bare. On the sheer declivities where the surface soils were held by chaparral, there is no chaparral.

Fine material tumbles downslope and collects in the waterless beds of streams. It forms large and bulky cones there, to some extent filling the canyons. Under green chaparral, the gravitational movement of bits of soil, particles of sand, and other loose debris goes on month after month, year after year, especially in oversteepened environments, where it can represent more than half of all erosion. After a burn, though, it increases exponentially. It may increase twentyfold, fortyfold, even sixtyfold. This steady tumbling descent of unconsolidated mountain crumbs is known as dry ravel. After a burn, so much dry ravel and other debris becomes piled up and ready to go that to live under one of those canyons is (as many have said) to look up the barrel of a gun.

One would imagine that the first rain would set the whole thing off, but it doesn't. The early-winter rains—and sometimes the rains of a whole season—are not enough to make the great bulk move. Actually they add to it.

If you walk in a rainstorm on a freshly burned chaparral slope, you notice as you step on the wet ground that the tracks you are making are prints of dry dust. In the course of a conflagration, chaparral soil, which is not much for soaking up water in the first place, experiences a chemical change and, a little below its surface, becomes waterproof. In a Forest Service building at the foot of the mountains Wade Wells keeps some petri dishes and soil samples in order to demonstrate this phenomenon to passing unbelievers. In one dish he puts unburned chaparral soil. It is golden brown. He drips water on it from an eyedropper. The water beads up, stands there for a while, then collapses and spreads into the soil. Why the water hesitates is not well understood but is a great deal more credible than what happens next. Wells fills a dish with a dark soil from burned chaparral. He fills the eyedropper and empties it onto the soil. The water stands up in one large dome. Five minutes later, the dome is still there. Sparkling, tumescent, mycophane, the big bead of water just stands there indefinitely, on top of the impermeable soil. Further demonstrating how waterproof this burned soil really is, Wells pours half a pound of it, like loose brown sugar, into a beaker of water. The soil instantly forms a homuncular blob—integral, immiscible—suspended in the water.

In the slow progression of normal decay, chaparral litter seems to give up to the soil what have been vaguely described as "waxlike complexes of long-chain aliphatic hydrocarbons." These waxy substances are what make unburned chaparral soil somewhat resistant to water, or "slightly nonwettable," as Wells and his colleagues are wont to describe it. When the wildfires burn, and temperatures at the surface of the ground are six or seven hundred centigrade degrees, the soil is so effective as an insulator that the temperature one centimetre below the surface may not be hot enough to boil water. The heavy waxlike substances vaporize at the surface and recondense in the cooler temperatures below. Acting like oil, they coat soil particles and establish the hydrophobic layer—one to six centimetres down. Above that layer, where the waxlike substances are gone, the veneer of burned soil is "wettable." When Wells drips water on a dishful of that, the water soaks in as if the dish were full of Kleenex. When rain falls on burned and denuded ground, it soaks the very thin upper layer but can penetrate no farther. Hiking boots strike hard enough to break through into the dust, but the rain is repelled and goes down the slope. Of all the assembling factors that eventually send debris flows rumbling down the canyons, none is more detonative than the waterproof soil.

In the first rains after a fire, water quickly saturates the thin permeable layer, and liquefied soil drips downhill like runs of excess paint. These miniature debris flows stripe the mountainsides with miniature streambeds—countless scarlike rills that are soon the predominant characteristic of the burned terrain. As more rain comes, each rill is going to deliver a little more debris to the accumulating load in the canyon below. But, more to the point, each rill—its natural levees framing its impermeable bed—will increase the speed of the surface water. As rain sheds off a mountainside like water off a tin roof, the rill network, as it is called, may actually triple the speed, and therefore greatly enhance the power of the runoff. The transport capacity of the watershed—how much bulk it can move—may increase a thousandfold. The rill network is prepared to deliver water with enough force and volume to mobilize the deposits lying in the canyons below. With the appearance of the rills, almost all prerequisites have now sequentially occurred. The muzzle-loader is charged. For a full-scale flat-out debris flow to burst forth from the mountains, the final requirement is a special-intensity storm.

Some of the most concentrated rainfall in the history of the United States has occurred in the San Gabriel Mountains. The oddity of this is about as intense as the rain. Months—seasons—go by in Los Angeles without a fallen drop. Los Angeles is one of the least-rained-upon places in the Western Hemisphere. The mountains are so dry they hum. Erosion by dry ravel greatly exceeds erosion by water. The celebrated Mediterranean climate of Los Angeles owes itself to aridity. While Seattle is receiving its average rainfall of thirty-nine inches a year, Chicago thirty-three, the District of Columbia thirty-nine, and New York City

Fire as Foe, Fire as Friend

forty-four, Los Angeles does well if it gets fifteen. In one year out of every four over the past century, rainfall in Los Angeles has been under ten inches, and once or twice it was around five. That is pure Gobi. When certain storm systems approach Los Angeles, though—storms that come in on a very long reach from far out in the Pacific—they will pick up huge quantities of water from the ocean and just pump it into the mountains. These are by no means annual events, but when they occur they will stir even hydrologists to bandy the name of Noah. In January, 1969, for example, more rain than New York City sees in a year fell in the San Gabriels in nine days. In January, 1943, twenty-six inches fell in twenty-four hours. In February, 1978, just before the Genofiles' house filled with debris, nearly an inch and a half of rain fell in twenty-five minutes. On April 5, 1926, a rain gauge in the San Gabriels collected one inch in one minute.

The really big events result from two, three, four, five storms in a row coming in off the Pacific. In 1980, there were six storms in nine days. Mystically, unnervingly, the heaviest downpours always occur on the watersheds most recently burned. Why this is so is a question that has not been answered. Meteorologists and hydrologists speculate about ash-particle nuclei and heat reflection, but they don't know. The storm cells are extremely compact, deluging typically about ten miles by ten. One inch of rain on a patch that size is seven million two hundred and thirty-two thousand tons of water. In most years, in most places, a winter rain will actually stabilize a mountainside. The water's surface tension helps to hold the slope together. Where there is antecedent fire, water that would otherwise become a binding force hits the rill network, caroms off the soils' waterproof layer, and rides the steep slopes in cataracts into the nearest canyon. It is now a lubricant, its binding properties repelled, its volume concentrating into great hydraulic power. The vintage years present themselves when at least five days of rain put seven inches on the country and immediately thereafter comes the heaviest rainfall of the series. That is when the flint hits the steel, when the sparks fly into the flashpan. On that day, the debris mobilizes.

Selection from

Fire on the Mountain

JOHN MACLEAN

THE WIND BLEW PAST Rifle, across the Grand Hogback and on toward Storm King Mountain, pushing the cloud cover ahead of it. The sky turned blue as steel. At approximately 3:20 P.M. a wave of wind swept over Canyon Creek Estates and advanced on Storm King and its misshapen ridges, gulches and canyons. It crossed the low ridge beyond Canyon Creek Estates, where Sam Schroeder's engine crew had made the first, aborted attempt to hike to the fire two days earlier, on July 4.

The wind dipped into the western drainage on the far side of the low ridge. It crossed above the western drainage and, disturbed by the terrain, struck the slope of Hell's Gate Ridge in an oscillating wave. Light currents of air fluttered around Don Mackey and the others on the west-flank fire line, protected by oak at the midway point on the slope.

The wind broke over the crest of Hell's Gate Ridge in an erratic pattern, sweeping tossed branches into the East Canyon in one spot but too light to be felt a hundred yards away.

Leaves smoldered, trees torched. Flames crackled along the fire's ragged edges. The wind blew clouds of smoke over the top of Hell's Gate Ridge, creating a thick haze on the lee, East Canyon side.

At 3:23 P.M. Butch Blanco radioed the chief dispatcher, Flint Cheney, at the BLM's Grand Junction District. Blanco noted from his vantage point atop Hell's Gate Ridge that the fire had begun to flare; he told

Cheney he considered the situation "normal" for late afternoon. He told Cheney he needed a few supplies—ten gallons of gasoline for the chain saws and fresh AA-size batteries for the two-way radios. Cheney noted in the log: "Lots of increased fire behavior."

By now Dick Good in 93 Romeo had become a one-man air show. He had hauled people and gear to the ridge, hauled gear away and in between tried to deal with questions from Don Mackey and Dale Longanecker about what the fire looked like from the air. Good was not a trained aerial observer and already had too much to do. Afterward he had no memory of radio exchanges about the look of the fire, though others remembered hearing the questions and his attempted answers. It was only by luck that Good and 93 Romeo remained on the fire, well beyond the half-day commitment made for the helicopter that morning. The Grand Junction dispatch office had called at 3:30 P.M. to check how things were going and, with no fire more urgent in the district, had told Good to stay on.

Good was heading to the mountain with a refilled water bucket, intending to make another drop near Longanecker, when he received a change in orders. The firefighters on top of Hell's Gate Ridge needed a water drop. Michelle Ryerson had radioed Mackey and told him, "It's real windy, and the fire's jumped the line." She had asked who had higher priority, she or Longanecker.

Her fire line was the last line of defense. Mackey told her to take the water drop.

Good altered course and flew toward the ridgetop, a bit more than a quarter mile above Longanecker's position. As the helicopter gained altitude, the west wind caught it and whisked it over the ridgetop like a tumbleweed. Good regained full control in the lee of the ridge and, using the wind as a brake, edged back toward his target. He released the water with a generous allowance for wind drift and watched it burst into a mist. He figured that the drop had been wasted, but firefighters on the ridgetop, with a better view than he below the helicopter, observed half the water hit and knock down flames. In the next minutes that dousing probably kept a group of firefighters from being trapped by flames.

Good radioed Ryerson and, half apologizing, said he would hurry back with a refill. As he flew off, he looked into the bottom of the western drainage. Spots of fire flickered on both sides of the deep V. Good could hear chatter on the radio about "spot fires" and figured that everyone saw the same thing. He flew on without reporting his sighting.

When Good returned, nearly ten minutes later, a thick column of black smoke poured out of the bottom of the gulch. The wind "was howling" at forty-five to fifty miles an hour, and Good again had to fight for control of 93 Romeo. He held the helicopter far to windward of his target on the ridgetop, allowing for maximum drift, and released the water; this time the entire load misted.

Good took another glance into the western drainage. Spot fires had climbed two thirds of the way up the slope opposite Hell's Gate Ridge. Ribbons of scarlet appeared though the churning smoke. The fire had grown beyond anything water could control. Oh, shit, this is really bad, Good said to himself.

There was only one mission left for 93 Romeo: a rescue pickup. Good's first responsibility was to the helicopter crew, Tyler and Browning, working at the helispot, H2, on the top of Hell's Gate Ridge near the jump spot. It would be insane to try to pull people off the mountain while trailing a cable and water bucket below the helicopter, but maybe he could manage it, Good thought, just maybe. First, though, he had to establish radio contact with Tyler and Browning. If nothing else, he then could arrange to pick them up once he jettisoned the cable and bucket.

Again using the wind as a break, Good edged 93 Romeo toward the helispot, H2. The ridgetop was clear of smoke, and he could see many people strung out along it, but could not tell whether they were hotshots, BLM firefighters or Tyler and Browning.

"Rich, Rob. Hey, guys, where are you? Talk to me!" Good called on the radio, once, twice and a third time without a response. Time was running out. He aimed 93 Romeo for the meadow at Canyon Creek Estates, leaving the ridge behind.

Good barely touched down as the ground crew unsnapped the cable and bucket, freeing him for a rescue pickup. Aloft again in seconds, he spun 93 Romeo to face Storm King.

In the few moments it had taken him to jettison the bucket, Hell's Gate Ridge and its human cargo had disappeared behind a thundering column of gray-black smoke. The mushrooming cloud blotted out the top of Hell's Gate Ridge, along with Blanco's firefighters, half the

Fire as Foe, Fire as Friend

Prineville Hot Shots, Tyler and Browning and the west-flank fire line with its smoke jumpers and hotshots.

The sky over the Colorado River remained a brilliant blue with a few lingering clouds, as though it were nothing but a pleasant summer afternoon. Good could fly toward the river, half-circle Hell's Gate Ridge and come to the ridgetop from the opposite direction, from the East Canyon side. It was the only chance left.

Good turned 93 Romeo away from the erupting smoke column. Once over the Colorado River, he turned into the river gorge in the direction of Glenwood Springs. He flew with the wind at his back, past the stubby outcropping of Hell's Gate Point overlooking the river, past Hell's Gate, where Blanco's crew had started from that morning, until he could look back at the East Canyon.

He flew into the smoke haze over the East Canyon and headed for Hell's Gate Ridge.

Good began calling Tyler and Browning but again heard no answer. The two helicopter crewmen must be somewhere along Hell's Gate Ridge—why didn't they respond?

Above him a curtain of black smoke ran across the sky like a squall line, pouring toward him over Hell's Gate Ridge. Its frontal edge had a curling lip.

Good felt wind pressure on 93 Romeo as he ascended parallel to and just below the ridgetop, under the roof of smoke. He used plenty of "cross-control," leaning the craft to counter the effects of the wind. Dirt, sticks and leaves blew through his rotor wash and into the helicopter's open doorway, stinging his face. Even a momentary lull would set 93 Romeo turning cartwheels, but now he had a clear view along the top of the ridge.

Tyler and Browning were nowhere in sight. Instead Good saw a "wide, wide flame front" beginning to rise on the far side of the ridge. In seconds a rescue pickup of anyone would be impossible. "Rich, Rob where are you, guys? Come on!" he called. The radio had become a blare of voices without names shouting orders, questions of orders and reversed orders, but nothing from Tyler or Browning.

Then, as if by magic or theatrical direction, a line of firefighters in anonymous yellow shirts and green pants appeared out of the smoke, running along the ridgetop toward the helispot, H2. They were two hundred yards from H2, then one hundred.

Behind them an enormous wave of flame arose from the western drainage and began to sweep the ridgetop, driving the firefighters before it. It swelled to a height of 50, 100 and then 150 feet. It moved faster than any human could run; everything was happening too fast. The flame wave began to break over the ridgetop, transforming the people into surfers riding the curl of a scarlet-orange wave of fire. One by one they peeled off the ridgetop ahead of the wave, heading into the East Canyon. Good saw small spot fires beginning to burn in the canyon.

The shouts on the radio died out; there were no orders left to give or reverse. Good heard a click as someone keyed a transmitter, and then a scream, a long AAAAHHHH without identifying name or gender. The scream ended, or more accurately, the transmission broke off, and the radio went silent.

Why the hell didn't someone scream five minutes earlier, when there'd been time to do something? Good thought. He let 93 Romeo slip away from the ridge and instantly lost touch with the wind. He flew out of the East Canyon, over the blue band of the Colorado River, and landed in the meadow at Canyon Creek Estates. One of the helicopter's ground crew, Steve Little, rushed up to 93 Romeo. Good sat slumped in his seat.

"They're gone," Good said. "They're all burned over."

In Canyon Creek Estates Allen Bell once again went into his yard and aimed his video camera at Storm King. As the huge smoke column rose in the background, a neighbor hurriedly drove up.

"That's a nice how-do-you-do," the neighbor said, getting out of his auto.

"They've got everything available on the way out here," Bell replied.

"They're evacuating."

"Where, here?"

"They're telling everybody to get out. That's what the firemen are doing. Boy, for just one guy with a shovel on Sunday morning [July 3, the first day the fire was seen]. *Now* they're excited."

"They're not worried about this side of the development, are they?"

Fire as Foe, Fire as Friend

"I think they're going to evacuate the whole thing."

A child joined the conversation. "Not good, is it?" the neighbor said to the child as they watched the billowing smoke.

"There are firemen in there, too," the child replied.

"There sure are," the neighbor said. He drove off to set water sprinklers as a fire buffer around his house.

When the wave of flame swept the top of Hell's Gate Ridge just after 4:00 P.M. on July 6, it could have marked the end for the forty-nine firefighters on Storm King Mountain. It did not; a majority survived. Natural disasters strike down one person and spare another steps away; the fate of individuals depends on anything from blind luck to a good pair of legs to history's repeating itself. Brains, the most valuable commodity in avoiding disaster, become just another item once it strikes.

For most of the four previous days, brains could have prevented what happened next, a fatal race with fire. The BLM could have followed its own directives and put out the blaze in the first days. The firefighters could have acted on their suspicions earlier on July 6 and retreated, though no place was safe after the fire blew up.

Chance took a leading role as events played themselves out, but the fire on Storm King Mountain left time for purposeful action, so character counted, too. For fourteen firefighters the next minutes would be their last and define them forever; for thirty-five who survived, the memory of what they did and what they might have done would remain with them, haunting some, resting more easily with others.

The fire became overwhelming at the most vulnerable time for the firefighters, in late afternoon, when they were dull with fatigue and at their point of maximum dispersal on the mountain. Since much depended on location, the places where people were standing, and since after 4:00 P.M. events moved in a rush, it would be well to survey where everyone was at that moment.

The forty-nine firefighters had broken down into four groups, plus one loosely joined bunch who walked between groups. The most numerous group worked at widening the fire line on top of Hell's Gate Ridge: Butch Blanco and three other BLM fire fighters, Michelle Ryerson and a mixed Forest Service-BLM crew of four, and eleven Prineville Hot Shots, including both Prineville supervisors, Tom Shepard and Bryan Scholz.

Fire on the Mountain

Two helicopter crewmen, Rich Tyler and Rob Browning, formed a separate group at H2, the helicopter landing zone cleared that morning on the ridgetop.

There was the bunch, numbering five, who walked between the ridgetop and the west-flank line for various reasons. Sarah Doehring and Kevin Erickson, the Missoula jumpers sent by Don Mackey to check back along the west-flank line, met up with Sunny Archuleta, the Missoula jumper who had been helping out at H2, as Archuleta started down the west-flank line to rejoin Mackey's crew. They then briefly encountered two men from Blanco's BLM crew, Brad Haugh and Derek Brixey, who had been sent to widen the west-flank line near its junction with the top of Hell's Gate Ridge.

Two other groups were on or near the west-flank line. There were thirteen firefighters in one of these groups, the same number as the unlucky thirteen of Mann Gulch: Mackey, three other smoke jumpers and nine Prineville Hot Shots. They were at the farthest extension of the line, nearly seven hundred yards from the junction with the top of Hell's Gate Ridge, starting back to work after a lunch break.

The last group—nine smoke jumpers, including Dale Longanecker and Tony Petrilli—had eaten lunch on Lunch Spot Ridge, the major spur ridge running off Hell's Gate Ridge, and after eating had walked ahead in the direction of the Double Draws, the eroded gullies beyond the crest of Lunch Spot Ridge.

That was the situation at 4:00 P.M., moments before everything changed.

The nine jumpers who had walked across Lunch Spot Ridge had been transfixed by flames dancing in the crowns of Douglas fir and ponderosa pine trees beyond the Double Draws. All forty-nine firefighters on Storm King Mountain had seen smoke rising from this place during the afternoon, their view partially blocked by Lunch Spot Ridge. Why the smoke column caused no greater concern is a question many asked themselves afterward. A lookout on Hell's Gate Ridge might have been able to give an earlier warning, but not by much. No one was in doubt that fire caused the smoke. At the crucial moment, when the smoke signal became an inferno, there were witnesses aplenty.

Longanecker, the line scout, had walked ahead of Petrilli and the other smoke jumpers, who, from an outcropping on Lunch Spot Ridge, watched as flames surrounded Longanecker on three sides. Longanecker was standing at midslope on the far side of the Double Draws.

The flames flapped and soared around him. Longanecker felt no immediate threat—he planned to retreat toward Lunch Spot Ridge before the fire completely encircled him. But the race to come to that conclusion happened at the moment Dick Good and 93 Romeo swept away from his location to handle the flare-up near Michelle Ryerson's group on the ridgetop. "We have a real bad situation here," Longanecker heard someone say over the radio. Indeed they did.

But even so, Longanecker stood rooted where he was, hypnotized by the flames, and the other jumpers on Lunch Spot Ridge stood spellbound where they were. The spectacle unfolded before their eyes. Flames danced into a sky shimmering with sunlight. Clouds of white smoke rose into an otherwise nearly cloudless sky. A blowy, beautiful summer's day swelled to fullness as the earth joined the heavens, until a movement in the deepest part of the western drainage broke the spell.

A jet of flame shot upward and then another, seeming to spring from nowhere. Piles of dead brush, branches and tree trunks ignited. Living brush, tinder-dry from drought, took fire. Darts of flame transformed into bonfire, which merged into a single, expanding flame front. A booming wind raced up the western drainage and struck the flames, pressing the telltale smoke column nearly flat to the ground.

Muscular strands of scarlet flame appeared through the smoke. The fire drew back to renew itself, taking in oxygen, and the smoke covered the flames; then the fire surged forward, and again ribbons of flame came into view.

As the smoke jumpers swung their eyes in near-unison to the sight, recognition struck home. They had fire below them on a mountain, and no ordinary fire: It was a blowup. There is no agreed scientific definition for a blowup, but it is unmistakable in appearance and overpowering in effect. The Forest Service has a working description of the event: the rapid transition of a fire burning in debris and litter to one involving all available fuel, from the ground to the tops of trees. But this falls short of describing the majesty of the occasion.

A blowup is one of nature's most powerful forces, equivalent to a mighty storm, avalanche or volcanic eruption. It can sweep away in moments everything before it, the works of nature and of humankind, and sometimes humankind itself. It is destructive, but neither good nor evil; it goes where wind and terrain take it.

Blowups happen every fire season across the West when wind, fuel, dryness and terrain come together in the right combination and meet with a spark. The blowup stokes itself by creating its own wind, the heat drawing cooler air by convection. If it happens in a gulch, as is common, the sides of the gulch—in this case the western drainage—act as a chimney and compress its energy. The flaming tempest can send a smoke column to a height of forty thousand feet or more. The blowup may die out once the gulch is burned or move on and reduce thousands of acres to ash. The blowing-up, in any case is over in minutes.

A blowup is as different from the smoldering, four-day-old fire on Storm King as a hurricane is from a summer squall. But it was the sputtering fire in the upper slopes of Hell's Gate Ridge that caused the blowup in the western drainage. Flames, slowly backing down the slope of the ridge, marked a thin, broken trail into the bottom of the drainage. This is what a lookout would have seen, and what the jumpers who walked across Lunch Spot Ridge did see; it was not a terribly threatening sight. The flames advanced one tree or clump of brush at a time, slowly but surely. Flames also made downhill leaps as wind eddies scattered sparks toward the bottom of the V.

The west wind created the eddies when it struck the ridges of Storm King and partially turned back on itself, just as flowing water turns in eddies when it passes rocks or other obstacles. The eddies carried aloft fistfuls of burning duff, that is, decayed leaves, twigs and other matter. Most likely a combination of flames backing down the slope and embers spinning in eddies ignited the initial, small fires in the bottom of the western drainage.

The west wind fanned those fires into a blowup, but to do so it first had to curl around a mountain and become a south wind. The west wind entered and was intensified by the gorge of the Colorado River, a natural wind funnel, in a phenomenon known as a venturi effect, named for the nineteenth-century physicist G.B. Venturi, who discovered that a throatlike, constricted tube will increase the velocity of fluids. Once in the river gorge the surging west wind quickly found an escape valve and turned at a right angle into the mouth of the western drainage, transforming itself into a south wind. It now raced up the narrow V of the drainage, which further compressed and accelerated it.

As the south wind sheared around a turn a half mile up the western drainage, it came upon the spot fires. When the wind struck the flames, they exploded. A thunderous roar rose from the gulch. The transition from a "normal" fire to a blowup took seconds.

Minutes before, the forty-nine firefighters had been ordering gasoline for their saws, taking the fire's photograph and making a game of the similarities to a legendary killer, the Mann Gulch fire. Then disaster took its unmistakable shape, and the firefighters, almost as one, began a race for their lives.

The Fires Next Time

RICK BASS

I T IS A WINDY DAY IN mid-August 1994 here in the wet Yaak Valley, northwest Montana's greenest valley. Almost the whole valley—100 or so of us—is gathered in a little log church that doubles as a community center. We've had bake sales in this little cabin, and we've voted here. Today we are listening to a heavyset Army sergeant, all dressed up in camouflage, explain to us how to try and keep from burning to death.

There is copper-colored smoke filtering through the sunlight all around us, like fog, and it just won't go away. It feels as heavy as the lead apron that you wear during X rays. The last really good fire that came through this valley was in 1910, and it burned from Spokane to Kalispell—3 million acres. The smoke was visible in Chicago.

There's no phone service in most of this valley. We are cut off from news of the outside world—which is usually how we like it. But what we are most interested in today is a weather report, and we get one: high winds, possibly 30 to 40 miles an hour, from the west, with dry lightning—no precipitation. Already the flames are sawing their way up the logged-over slopes of the Mount Henry McIntire country, chewing their way through dead lodgepole pine that the timber companies said they would log but didn't. (Instead they took the big green trees, spruce and larch.)

Closer to home, the flames are also sawing their way up the side of Lost Horse Mountain, leaping from clearcut to clearcut. All the fires are curiously here on the south side of the river—a function of the spectac-

Fire as Foe, Fire as Friend

ular lightning storms that moved down the valley in late July, and again on the 14th and 15th of this month, lighting certain trees in the forest like candles, tongues of lightning flickering and splitting the heavens open with white light, each one searching for the one tree, the one dry dead tree with the itch, the specific itch, to be born again. Over two nights in mid-August, more than 160 fires were reported in the Kootenai National Forest. From that point, it was up to the wind to see if the fires would run (they almost always climb, rather than descend) and bring new life behind them, in their wake and in their ashes—or whether the old order of rot and decay would be preserved, in places, for at least another year.

At night some of us have been driving up to the top of Hensley Face, on the other side of the river—for now, the "safe" side. From the top of Hensley Face we can look down on the valley and see the lights of the fires blinking yellow through the bed of smoke, fires blinking like a thousand flashbulbs, seeming sometimes strangely synchronized as breezes blow across them. It's like a near vision of the underworld—as if we are watching from a cliff, the last cliff, before the final descent.

In the meeting that day the sergeant guy—who had fought fires before, though never in this valley, which is unlike any other (part Pacific Northwest rainforest, part northern Rockies)—talked to us about the Fowler and Turner and Fish Fry fires, all of which were less than a mile from my home and, in his words, really rocking.

They had it down to a science, which was both reassuring and terrifying. They'd measure the humidities in combustible materials—wood—in advance of the fire, and the per-acre volume of fuel. They'd break these measurements down into size categories, too: Was the fuel composed of twigs and branches, or limbs, or, hottest burning of all, entire downed trees? It all mattered.

Evacuation orders and alternate plans were discussed; we took inventory of who wasn't there. If the roads were aflame, we'd all meet in Gail's big meadow along the river and hope helicopters could get through—though I had my doubts about that, as it seemed the smoke would pool in those places. It's the smoke that kills you usually, not the flames. We were instructed, if trapped, to lie down in the river or creek with a wet towel over our face.

The lecture was sometimes drowned out by the sound of choppers and big bombers cruising low over the woods, the helicopters carrying 1,000-gallon buckets of water dipped from the river and lakes, and the bombers roaring right over the ridges and spraying cloacal plumes of water, or smoking trails of fire retardant, onto the flames below. I wondered idly if the retardant was good for the soil—good for the watershed. That wind was coming, the sergeant said, and there was a good chance that the whole place could go, and go quick. We'd know within 24 hours. He wanted us to be ready to leave with less than five minutes' notice, if it came to that.

Some of us had begun leaving already, but most of us stayed. It's an incredible pull—the bond to home, the bond to your own place.

That afternoon I went up to the mercantile to get extra gas, but it was closed. That would be a real bummer, I thought, to be evacuating and run out of gas. Murphy's Law to the nth. A friend was sitting on the porch of the tavern drinking beer and watching the hypnotic sight of a mountain on fire—the mountain right across the river. "If we burn, we burn," he said.

I went up into the woods behind the house, up to the top of Zimmerman Hill, to peer down at the Okaga Lake fire; but I couldn't see anything for all the smoke. My wife was pregnant with our second child that stormy summer, and it occurred to me that this would be an even less opportune time than usual to get myself killed—to do something dumb—so I turned and went back down the hill, down the safe, unburned side. On my way down, I encountered a curious thing: a covey of blue grouse ground-roosting, midslope, with a covey of ruffed grouse. I'd never seen or heard of such a thing, and I wondered if the blue grouse had moved down off their usual roosts on the ridge because they knew the fire was going to come up over the ridge. I wondered if they could feel it coming, like a tingle or an itch, in the rocks beneath their feet, in the forest soil.

Down low, deer were moving around at all times of the day, looking dazed and confused; many of them were standing midstream in the little creek.

I decided to begin moving some things out of the cabin—books, family pictures. I took my old Ford Falcon down to the nearest town, Libby, while the road was still open—before it became crisscrossed with burning timbers and became a hot-air wind tunnel of flame.

Fire as Foe, Fire as Friend

In Libby I was stopped and given a citation because the old Ford had a brake light out. I argued with the officer. Ash floated down on us as we argued. He lives in town, where it's safe. I live in the country.

The fires ran out, as they always do; as they did even in 1910. The weight of their own smoke—the lack of oxygen—put them out, the ennui of their own existence. The firefighters put some of them out, and the rains that came on Labor Day put them out, the rains that always come on Labor Day. I would have liked to see everyone go home then—there were nearly 2,000 National Guardsmen and soldiers from as far away as Alabama, Arkansas, and Louisiana camping in this shy valley, a 20-fold increase in the social and cultural stress on the valley—but I have to say that for a couple of days I was glad they were there.

The whole town, pretty much the whole West, was glad to see them there. The belligerent yellow signs in a few storefront windows that claimed, "This Business Supported by Timber Dollars" were replaced by bumper stickers that read, "This Business Supported by Burning Timber Dollars." Perhaps it's the value-added industry we've been looking for. Instead of just growing big trees and sawing them down and shipping them off, we can set them on fire. We'd get paid twice that way: for putting the fires out and then for cutting them down and shipping them away. Forget all this fairy-tale talk of bookcases, cabinetmaking, toy and furniture factories, finger-joint molding and post-and-beam plants. Firefighting on the public lands dished out close to $1 billion last year—$6 billion in the last decade—even though, as we're beginning to understand intellectually if not yet emotionally, the only final way to fight fire is, as the saying goes, with fire. That which does not rot will burn, one day, and to me it seems to be the same process, simply at a different rate. In the wet forests, the dead trees have a good chance of rotting; in dry forest, or on dry aspects, they have less chance of making it all the way to rot. Everyone agrees that the more fires you put out, the bigger the next ones will be—or the next next, and so on. It's just a matter of biology—of waiting for the right conditions to combine, the right mix of heat and aridity and fuel and wind and ignition.

All over the West, scientists as well as residents are trying to figure out how to apply this most basic truth that has just popped up seemingly out of nowhere: *The forests have to burn.* Suppression only makes the forest lean more toward this truth. Many parts of the Yaak, for instance, are changing from the previous stable, fire-resistant system of predominately larch and cedar–hemlock to a more combustible mix of fir and lodgepole pine. In the past, the thick bark of the older larch trees and the cedar's affinity for swamps have protected those two species. But now the highly flammable fir and lodgepole, without fires to keep them in balance, are encroaching into new territory, displacing slower-growing, more fire-resistant species such as larch and cedar. Stresses on the forest beyond the cumulative stress of total fire suppression include the possibility of insect infestations of forests adjacent to clearcuts; in addition, there are diseased, blister-rusting white pines and weakened firs. All this adds to what's called, ominously and accurately, fuel loading.

In the past three decades of fire suppression in the nearby Lolo National Forest, for example, the volume of wood that has burned annually is about one-tenth of what it used to be. Additionally, most fires in the past burned "cooler," since excess fuel was kept from loading up by the frequency of fires. The cooler fires spared many trees and left behind a diverse mosaic of burned and unburned species and age classes, different for each fire. The forests must have been seething with diversity.

But more of today's fires—and we haven't seen a truly big one yet—are burning hotter.

The timber industry has an answer, of course, and it isn't shy about touting it. All last autumn, ads blared over the radio saying that if industry had been allowed to do more logging, the fires wouldn't have happened.

Never mind that most of the fires in the Kootenai were in logged areas. The industry had it figured: Cut down all the trees before they catch on fire.

Except: It is our past and present logging practices that have helped cause the very problem. Since in most logged-over areas there are not enough big dead trees left behind to rot slowly on site—to live out their cycle of rebirth—the soils on these lands are becoming impoverished at rates so startling that they often cannot even be measured. Sometimes the soil is washing away following the clearcuts, while other times it just sprouts knapweed, a noxious grass-replacing exotic weed that is completely indigestible to big game.

The forest isn't always coming back on its own—not the forest type that the land has fostered naturally. When new species of trees are planted, at great expense, they are often weaker, growing without the shade of a canopy and hence more prone to the stresses of sun and wind. This can result in more deaths, and greater volumes of tree death—"fuel loading"—which can make a stand more susceptible to hot fires. The hot fires then do further damage to the soil, and the ashes from these hot fires often slump into the nearby streams and creeks, causing severe sedimentation.

It's big-time out of balance. We need to back off and try to reestablish order—and, certainly, to keep our hands off the roadless areas, which are the true sources of and models for forest health. But the current Congress, greedy for all the big burned sticks, won't hear of it. It's declared an "emergency." To make sure industry can go in and cut all that wood before any of it returns to the way wood has been for roughly the past 4 billion years, Congress has passed a bill—written by the timber companies—outlawing any environmental restrictions or regulations on "salvage" harvests.

Salvage in theory refers to dead trees, but it is defined in this bill as anything with the potential to burn, which basically covers any tree in the world. Bill Clinton vetoed the bill: it was a rider tacked onto the budget rescissions bill—the first veto of his presidency. The Yaak—and the West—was granted one more year of life.

The aerial photos of postfire forests tell an interesting story. The blackest areas—the fires' origins, in many instances, and places where they burned hottest—radiate from the edges of the big clearcuts and into the weakened, diminished forests. A favorite saying in the timber industry is "Clearcuts don't burn," but they do. The sun at the clearcut-forest interface scorches that area exceedingly, making it unnaturally dry, as do the strong winds that sweep across the clearcut's lunar surfaces. These winds blow down excessive snarls of weakened timber around all edges of the clearcut.

But, says industry, the clearcuts hold their snowpack longer, since they release most of their radiant heat back into the atmosphere each night, without that pesky heat-trapping overstory. And it's true, they do. And then along about the first of June, about the time the streams and rivers have finally started to clear up from normal spring runoff, all the remaining snowmelt (and sediment) goes at once, in slumps and muddy gushes, rather than trickling slowly out of the old cool cedar woods, like a tap being slowly turned on—the way nature, and springtime in the Rockies, are designed to work.

It's 1995. Are we really still debating clearcuts?

I never set out to become a pagan. It just kind of happened. It's as if, rather than my moving toward it, a whole lot of other things receded, leaving me stranded on some peninsula of paganism. More and more, it seemed, everything else around me looked dumb, or dishonest. There seemed to be an incredible wisdom in the woods, so simple that even a child could understand it. The way the old-growth forests create their own stable world and maintain it and its health far better than we could manage either our world or theirs, in terms of health. The thick bark of the oldest trees, and the way they shed their branches almost coyly, almost tempting little grass fires to catch in those brush tangles and limb tangles, keeping the forest cool and clean and nutrient rich.

All those old lichens hanging down from the oldest trees, hard earned, are not just for show. Firefighters tell me that sometimes, if floating sparks land in them, the lichens can flare up like a torch and then extinguish themselves, having used up all the surrounding oxygen available in that quick flush—leaving the old tree almost totally unscathed.

Even the timing of the fire season in the West is a thing of great beauty and great health. The way the fires come, sometimes in July but usually in August, allowing just enough time to download some fuel and recycle some nutrients, but not so much that things get out of hand. In September the rains come, turning the fires to smolder, and in October and November the snows come, extinguishing them. Even the way the larch needles fly through the air in the autumn wind seems to be full of purpose. One morning in October you wake up and there's a quarter- or half-inch mat of beautiful gold needles, and beautiful gold aspen leaves, spread all across the countryside. This golden blanket helps pin down the charred coals and ashes of August, keeps too much of the ash from blowing away or slumping into creeks, and speeds up the soil-making process—as much as that glacial pace can be helped along.

The interconnectedness of things. I'm all for prudent salvage logging, as long as it's not in roadless areas. But when some industry asks to be put above or beyond the law, I get frightened, and angry. It is not the fires of late summer I fear. I respect those—they are nature's way and can no more be controlled than the wind or the rain. They're part of the weather of the West. But going out and clear-cutting forests, or entering roadless areas, under the guise of preventing forest fires is like going into the forest with gallon watering cans during a drought. It's just not going to work. What we're dealing with is too big.

The fire season has taught me a lot, has taught me a new way of looking at the woods. Now when I go for a walk, or climb a forested mountain, I'm very conscious of the mosaic, of the microsites—those spots in the forest that could start a fire, and those that could spread it, and those that would absorb and stop it, too. I look at diversities of vertical structure, and lateral structure, in unlogged country; at species mix. In the Yaak, especially, due to the unique diversity, there are amazing bands of change on any mountain in the valley. You'll move through a forest of old lodgepole and then, 50 or 100 feet higher, into a forest of fire-buffering cedar or cedar–hemlock. Then the slope will flex more sharply, will cross to a southern aspect, and you'll be in a grove of fire-promoting ponderosa pine; and then, at the top of that ridge, fire-resistant old-growth Douglas fir.

I'm learning to look at nature.

Sometimes I think it is the wolves who are helping, aiding and abetting, joining in with the resurrecting fires in the West—or rather, not the wolves but the absence of them. I noticed it just the other day. I was planting some young cedars and had put gated slats and screens around them to keep the deer, elk, and moose from browsing them in winter. I'll keep the enclosures around them until they get tall enough that their branches are above the browse line.

I began planting cedars and aspens a couple of years ago. And it just hit me this spring: the before and after of it. I haven't been seeing any young aspens anywhere in the woods; just big old ones, 30 and 40 and 50 years old—trees born back in the days of predators. I noticed too that in my enclosures the aspen sprouts are doing great, but only in my enclosures. The deer herds are increasing so steadily and dramatically that they're eating all the young aspen and perhaps cedars. The cedars especially help cool the forest, which helps retain moisture—which helps buffer fires.

There are too many deer—or rather, not enough predators. They are perhaps near the edge of stripping the woods bare—changing the composition of the forest, over the past 50 years, in ways as subtle as our ways have been offensive and immense. The ways of rot versus the ways of fire.

It is not just the wolves, of course. It is everything; it is all out of balance.

It was a good snow year, this year. By April we were already watching the sky, like farmers. But the snow and rain mean little. A greenhouse-hot summer followed by a lightning storm, followed by a windy dry day—everything can change, and will change; if not this year, then next. For this reason, and so many others, we need to keep the untouched wilderness cores—the roadless areas—in each national forest. They act as buffers, absorbing and diffusing the spread of huge hot fires throughout the West. They're better at putting out fires, or diluting them, then 10,000 or 100,000 National Guardsmen—better than a billion-dollar-a-year effort. Every forest needs a big wilderness area—a chain of dedicated roadless areas, in perpetuity—come hell or high water, come war or peace, come world's end or world's beginning. Call it a place to run to when things go wrong. When the whole rest of the world goes up in conflagration.

We're just now learning new things in the West. We're always learning new things: things known by people before us, old civilizations, but now forgotten.

We scan the hot western skies in August for signs of approaching storms and try to detect the feel of electricity in the air. Any breeze at all can feel ominous. We are remembering another of nature's rules: Payback is hell.

Pride and Glory of Firefighting Is Hard to Resist

LOUISE WAGENKNECHT

THE SOUTHWEST WINDS brought waves of red smoke streaming into the valley from the fires near Boise and McCall every day last summer. A helicopter would come in overhead, and I'd hear the almost subsonic whump-whump-whump that meant a *big* craft.

The smoke and the morning air and the noise took me back to a mountainside, to a morning years removed, when that most reassuring of sounds hit my ears: large helicopters, flying again, after our long night of cutting fireline into the dark.

The firepack is on my back and the pulaski in my gloved hands. With a scoop of chew tucked into my lower lip, I see the river, 2,000 feet below, and the faint wisps of September fog trailing up the canyon. And cutting through it all, rising like a dragonfly off the helibase pad, Helitack 1, or 2, or 3. Whump-whump-whump. It sounds very, very good.

That's the part of firefighting that makes you just a bit cocky, just a bit proud. You feel stronger and smarter than you really are. Firefighting is a skill, a craft, a yearly dance in which roles are clearly defined and where certainties abound to compensate for the uncertainties of the enemy. It requires specialized, even arcane knowledge, and those who master some particular part of it are professionals.

Pride and Glory of Firefighting Is Hard to Resist

Line boss, sector boss, buying unit, camp leader: Titles that often have nothing to do with our usual jobs are ours on a fire. Actual GS-ratings mean very little: GS-4s order GS-13s around.

I started "going out on a fire" because I needed the money. Bit by bit, my firepack acquired the little comforts that make 48-hour shifts more bearable. I kept a few cans of baked beans, fruit cocktail and juice stashed away in case of inadequate sack lunches. Headlamps furnished by the Forest Service were awkward and unreliable; most of us bought better ones from an industrial catalog with our own money. My pockets were full of hard candy, gum, tobacco, paperbacks (as in any military operation, much of firefighting consists of waiting) and toilet paper.

Firefighting changes your ideas about outdoor recreation. Standing on an 80 percent slope at midnight, listening warily for the ominous creaking noises that mean a giant vegetable is about to kill you, then curling up just before dawn to catch a few winks in a ditch filled with ashes and the odd scorpion, erodes the desire to go camping just for the fun of it.

Once, while mopping up in deep ash in a grove of giant, conk-ridden Douglas-firs, we heard the fearful groaning of a dying tree.

Whirling 360 degrees in panic, we tried to see the assailant. Impossible. The sound was everywhere. With a final seismic thump, the tree fell. It missed everyone, but the concussion raised a blinding ash cloud that reduced visibility to zero. The crew boss shouted, and we groped our way uphill, out of the grove, and into an open area. Shaken, we all sat down.

"Lunch!" said the crew boss. We made it last until our shift was over.

In my experience, it is the common sense of crew bosses that saves lives on a fire, but it takes a strong one to refuse a hazardous order. It was a brave crew boss, for example, who refused to continue night mop-up on a nearly vertical slope with rocks the size of clothes dryers hurtling by in the dark. In the face of Al's assertion that this was dangerous and unnecessary on a 12-acre fire already plastered with retardant, the honchos down at fire camp insisted that we continue.

Al stopped arguing, but led us out of the burned area to the firelines, where we spent the night improving the trenches, out of range of rocks, while Al lied his head off on the radio.

It took a tough crew boss to categorically refuse to have our crew flown to the top of a 100-acre fire burning in heavy fuels so we could dig line downhill toward the fire.

"No," said Rick to the line boss. "We're not going to do that. We're going to start digging *here*, at the bottom, and you will have *two* crews coming up behind us, and you will have a spotter across the canyon to keep us informed, and you will get some engines down here and start pumping out of the river and putting a hose lay up behind us."

Through a long night of chain-saw work in dense, jackstrawed trees, while squirrelly winds fanned the flames and 80-foot firs crowned out above us, ours was the only line that held. If we had been up on top cutting line downhill, would we have died for the line boss's error in judgment?

Working downhill toward a fire has been a factor in many fire fatalities over the year, yet it continues to be done on uncontained fires, as happened on the fatal fire in Colorado this summer [1994].

I stopped going on fires after the Great California Cookout of '87. I saw the plantations that we had thinned so carefully only a couple of years before go up like A-bombs as the slash ignited, torching so thoroughly that not even stumps remained.

I saw fire fronts come to a dead halt as they hit an area of old growth that had experienced an underburn a few years before. I came off the fires in October with a raging ear infection, bronchitis that swiftly became pneumonia, and the realization that firefighting, like combat, is for 20-year-olds who still believe they're immortal.

Yet, when the chopper came in that morning last summer, just for that moment, I missed the dirt and the smoke and the camaraderie of the fireline. I suddenly mourned the fact that the fire stories I have to tell are the only ones I will ever have.

When I work on fires now, it's in an air-conditioned building, and although I know I've done my bit and don't need to suck any more smoke to prove my self, the smoky winds can still send adrenaline into my blood.

Danger Is the Drug

As the Forest Service struggles—perhaps more than any other wildland agency—to change its attitude toward fire and reject the put-'em-all-out-now shibboleth that has landed us in this fix, Chief Jack Ward

Pride and Glory of Firefighting Is Hard to Resist

Thomas may find an unexpected barrier to true fire management: It's this love of the rush that belongs to firefighting, all the more powerful because no one talks about it.

Any threat to the status accruing to blackened, sleep-deprived, hard-hatted, snoose-dipping smoke warriors will be resisted; any suggestion that those who make a career of firefighting do so because they *enjoy* it will be rejected as somehow immoral.

Ending the war games will be unpalatable to many. But the game will end.

The beginning of the end came last summer when the Payette National Forest in Idaho announced that an all-out effort to extinguish the Blackwell and Corral Complexes would cost $42 million and stand only a 15 percent chance of succeeding before winter did it for free. With that, the government admitted it can no longer afford to indulge career fire managers in their hobby of battling an element which should never have been allowed to become an enemy in the first place.

It is time for the fire gods to admit that they love battle for its own sake, and for what it has brought them in the way of pride, and power, and glory. It is time for them to recognize this, and get over it, and get another life.

Those who have died deserve that from us, at least.

Firefinder

ALIANOR TRUE

I T'S LATE AUGUST, temperatures are cooling down, and yellow tints the quaking aspen. It's my second to last day on the fire crew, and I've been assigned to tower duty. Nine hours, spent in solitude in a 6 by 6-foot enclosure, 180 feet off the ground. Crowded, with a folding army cot, a wooden chair on chipped glass insulators, and a centered pedestal. Streaked window-panes comprise the upper half of the four metal walls, giving me views of the park, the forest. It is cool today, and cloudless skies lift away above the forest, just like the past two days. No recent lightning or storms; no sleeping fires are likely to creep up on us today. I scan the canopy through binoculars. To the north, the Kaibab National Forest stretches away, shaded ridgelines concealing chains of connected meadows. To the west, the park: Kanabownits, the Basin, Crystal Ridge, and to the south-west, Swamp Ridge and Fire Point. Though shadows and distance conceal the details, I don't need the topographic map to know where these places are and how to get there.

I know Greg didn't have to send me up here today. I know he's doing me a favor, giving me a chance to reflect on what we both know has been an amazing season. Thinking of the winter flurry of phone calls and job applications that had me landed at the North Rim of the Grand Canyon. My first time out West, living in near isolation on a high, forested plateau in the middle of the Arizona desert. My first year in wildfire, a green college girl from back East, years younger than the rest of the crew. And this summer has seen the worst drought in over forty years. The biggest wild-fire in Kaibab Forest history, the 53,000-acre Bridger Knoll Complex.The thrill of watching the canyon fall away beneath the helicopter, the thud of heavy blades all around. And the pulling tension between crew members, the monotony of fire camp food.

I sit up here, occasionally pacing the cramped space around the centered chest-high pedestal, on which sits a prized firefinder. The Osborne Firefinder, a tool that determines the bearing and angle of a fire from a lookout tower. The brass ring sits atop the pedestal, placed over and coordinated with a topo map, vertical sight and front sight opposite each other. The flat ring rotates over the map. Find and center the smoke in the horsehair of the front sight while looking through the vertical sight, check for bearings and direction, and you've found yourself a fire. A simple tool, outdated by modern technology, where tour planes report the smokes, and dispatch finds the fires with GPS. But when wind and rain keep planes grounded, when GPS is paralyzed, firefinders are indispensable. In a 180-foot tower made of steel, even compasses won't work, their needles confused by the metal's own magnetic field.

This has been an extreme season. With less then 12 percent of the annual snowfall, and a bone-dry spring, the plateaus of northern Arizona began the season in a dry deficit. Situated between 8,000 and 9,000 feet, this area is not usually a center of wildland fire activity. Modest fires, maybe up to ten acres, but mostly less than one, are the norm. Nothing a small fire crew can't handle. But this year has been spent almost entirely in Level IV, at a "very high" fire danger. And crews from all over the West have been rotated through the Southwest. Every year there is a hot spot, and extra crews from areas of low danger are sent there to supplement the regular fire crews. It was Yellowstone in '88, Idaho in '94. In 1996, it's the Southwest, and I've worked with hotshot crews from California, from Idaho, engine crews from Montana and Wyoming. The highest level, V, "extreme," is where our parched conditions really place us, but the overhead at fire management won't acknowledge this reality. They don't want to have to work the 12-hour days, 21-day shifts. I can't say I do either, even if I do get paid by the hour.

This summer has been a collection of atypical occurrences: "Now, we wouldn't usually do this." "In a normal year...." "When we get some rain, when we go down to Level III, it'll all be different." Chris and Steve, returning for their second season, tell me that the North Rim is usually a mecca for wildflower enthusiasts, but all I see this year are a few wilted Indian paintbrush lining the sides of the roads. And Kristy and Ann of the prescribed crew work weeks upon weeks doing prep work, thinning the drop zones of prescribed burns, too dry to actually burn the plots. We have had more fires than usual this year, though smaller than the models predicted. They serve to punctuate the growing list of maintenance and upkeep jobs on the office clipboard. "Make two new benches for the lodge walkway," "Replace steps at Kanabownits tower," "Brush the E-4 road." Amid the daily toil of brushing trails, felling hazard trees, and refilling distant water tanks, I have seen some good fire. And it is due to these routine tasks, in addition to actually fighting wildfire, that I have become acquainted and familiar with the North Rim.

It is today, on fire watch, checking and rechecking the landscape, that I realize the familiarity I have gained over these three months. The recognition of ridges and ravines, the different trees and their forms, the weather, constant and assertive. I have begun to feel this strange land. This place was so foreign just yesterday, and while I will not pretend to have mastered this landscape, I can admit to a thorough introduction. Now the evergreens have become white fir with flat, flexible needles, Engelmann spruce with sharp, four-sided ones. Subalpine fir with smooth, pale gray trunks, blue spruce with hanging cones and rough-textured branches. I am reassured by the inland winds that prevail from the southwest and the constant canyon winds at the rim, upslope during the day and downslope, rushing into the deep shadows, at night. I can approximate my elevation from recognizing that ponderosa pine dominate the upper 7,000s, while fir, spruce, and quaking aspen prefer the 8,000- to 9,000-foot range. Driving down the winding road that leads to the surrounding desert, I see pinyon and juniper, known to us as "p-j," crowd the roadsides from 5,000 to 6,000 feet. I have even met the elusive Kaibab squirrel, with its white tail and tufted ears: Over 60 percent of them die every year because they don't store food for the long snow-packed winter.

I remember exploring the North Rim under the guise of work. An endless task of brushing the W-I road runs through the Basin, an enormous collection of meadows dotted with wooded hillocks and criss-crossed with gopher burrows. It is the way to Crystal Ridge, and to Point

Firefinder

Sublime, made famous by Edward Abbey. Eventually it gives way to the W-4, a route to Kanabownits, to the Big Springs dip site, to Swamp Ridge and Fire Point. It is this last area, far to the west, that has seen the most fire activity this season. It is as if a lightning rod has been centered there, directing the storms to release their fury on this distant area, concentrating the smoke reports and fires, leaving the whole eastern region of the park virtually flame free. King Arthur's Court has seen the most action. A wide stone-framed amphitheater whose isolated monuments grace fanciful names. Elaine's Castle, Lancelot Point, even the Holy Grail, a narrow stack of rocks piled impossibly high, no way to reach the top.

I cannot see King Arthur's Court from here. In fact, no one can see that collection of monuments except from a rare helicopter flight or a long hike from a little used dirt road. And it is now, in reviewing the landscape and the season, that it occurs to me that our knowledge is so limited by access. A simple fact, that we can only know what we experience. I think of the tourists who drive for days to spend five minutes gasping over the canyon. And the contrast of our fire crews, hiking in to a remote fire, off road and trail. Knowing that in their isolation no other human eyes have seen those distant places for a hundred years or more. I think of what I personally know about, the secret meadow that appeared behind the ridge blackened by the South Fork fire. The bobcat that sprinted across the road as I struggled with the gears on the chase truck. The hidden hollowness of aging aspen, which rot from the inside out. And the way they can pinch down your saw, freed only by a long afternoon of pulling and prying, ropes and wedges.

I would not have seen or experienced any of this, this new and thrilling landscape, without my privileged access. Tourists hardly ever make it off the three paved roads on the North Rim, and only a handful of others travel off the dirt roads at all. My place on the fire crew has given me an amazing opportunity; the uniqueness of my experience surprises me at every turn, burning itself into my memory. And I revel, realizing that my intimate familiarity with the North Rim has been explicitly shaped and carved by my access to it. It may be a simple thought, that one's awareness of a situation is correlated to experience. That is, after all, how one learns. But this summer, I have exceeded this basic tenet. I realize that I view the North Rim, the Grand Canyon, even the surrounding Arizona desert, as if I were peering through a firefinder: looking for bearings and distinct landscape features, following the weather's tracks across the sky. For it is the nature of my access to the landscape, that of firefighting, that has shaped my consciousness. What I learn, and why it is important, how it is connected to other bits of information, have all been determined by the fact that I am a firefighter. And because I learned this landscape, the North Rim, as it relates to fire, I can never see it in a vague way, just seeing the stark scenery, the contrast of plateau against desert, of canyon and rim. I'll never casually notice trees; they will always be specific to their kind, their fire resistance. Just as the clouds will indicate the type of front moving through, and tell me from what direction I can expect the winds, and when they'll change, pulling the fire with them.

The firefinder accompanies me on every walk and every workday. I examine a side gully that drains into the mammoth canyon, and I see a quick fire run. Fire could whip through here, fed by updraft winds and the flashy quick-burning fuels of scrub oak and locust. I glance upward, noticing the vertical buildup of cumulus clouds over the South Rim. The potential lightning storms, and then the fires, they may bring as they move northward. I march through the woods, hiking into a fire, and I listen for the telling crackle of pine needles and small twigs beneath my boots, a sure sign of low fuel moisture. I know that white fir reestablish themselves quickly following a fire. We call them "regen," short for regeneration. I see a jumbled weave of fallen logs, vines, and prickly black locust, and I know that the choking forest needs to burn. That the remaining dominant trees are suffering with all the competition around their feet. I call standing dead trees "snags." I know they are dangerous. I measure brief hours of needed rain against its effect on 10-hour and 100-hour fuel moisture. I unconsciously scan for evidence of past fires in catfaces, or firescars, on the older ponderosa. I carry this firefinder with me everywhere. It is in my eyes and ears; it has wedged itself into my memory.

I think of the fires I have seen this summer, how they have guided me through tangled forests and wrinkled topography until I recognize each ravine and ridge, each shrub and tree. These pieces form a puzzle, an interlocking collection of facts and objects that I use to make sense of the North Rim. For I can examine the pieces, their qualities and characteristics, and predict how they fit together to solve the problem, to fight the fire. I remember that Scott insisted we haul in two chainsaws for the Thunder Spring fire because he knew that area, between Swamp Ridge and Fire Point, was a jumbled mass of jackstrawed timber, huge matchsticks that would slow our progress and hamper an escape. Finding the Imperial fire, smoking on a distant ridge tip, we were armed with triangulated bearings from the helicopter, the roadside departure point, the fire tower. But we actually found the fire with our knowledge of the terrain; we hiked in through the Bright Angel Creek drainage until the fourth ridge tilted up to the south. We have all learned the daily weather pattern. The morning inversion that clouds the inner canyon, the haze that burns away by noon, and the bright, blue skies that lead to afternoon buildup and evening lightning storms.

All of us took special care with the Lancelot II fire, perched on the edge of Lancelot Point, and subject to the furious canyon winds. Still, a near-miss, as over thirty firefighters had to be evacuated when the fire made a midafternoon run, crashing up the slope, consuming a half mile in ten minutes. We returned later to find abandoned firepacks and rations melted, charred. I use the skies, the lay of the land, even the type of tree, to guide me to a fire, and through a fire. Those details can dictate how to find a wildfire, how to fight it, how to survive it. My access to this land has given me the awareness and ability to understand it, to predict it, to live and feel it.

I wonder about those before us and what relationship they shared with this land. Theo, who constantly points out the fragments of Indian pottery around our firelines, tells us stories of those people. Anasazi ruins and cliff dwellers' caves appear in our binoculars; ancient fragments of black and white pottery and arrowheads surface in our shovels. We fly high over the Havasupai Reservation, nestled within the canyon walls. Still thriving, a patchy green beneath our helicopter. More recent, a crooked shack, once used by Teddy Roosevelt's hunting expeditions, sits astride Muav Saddle, bridging Swamp Ridge and Powell Plateau. Theodore Roosevelt, credited as the founder of the park system, shot more of the now-absent mountain lions than any other man in canyon history. And now the mule deer population has exploded, no predators left to curb their growth.

Did these people realize the value of fire? The rejuvenating force it possesses? The way it lets a forest breath anew, black and ash only temporary? I've heard tales about how Indians used to set their forests on fire, to clear the underbrush, to flush out the game. And I know that fire is natural. It is as much a part of the ecosystem of a forest as the seed of a maple or the fungus on a rotting log. Temperate forests evolved under the pressure of fire; the trees and soil depend on its life-giving properties. I also know it is my job to extinguish fire. And that it is the modern tradition of firefighting that gives rise to unhealthy forests, choking on the shrubs and seedlings that would have been eliminated in a forest fire. This is why the fires get worse, and burn hotter, every year. It is because there is more fuel accumulating every year. It is never burned when nature intends. This is the conflict I live with: fighting fire in a forest that needs to burn. And quietly hoping for a place with the prescribed fire crew next year, the program that reintroduces fire into a natural landscape in a controlled manner, a job that eases my conscience.

After three months here, learning and living, fire now serves as my reference point. I drive the main highway, scanning the woods to the south. I was told to pick up our abandoned tools at "mile two," but I know it's closer to the orange flagging that led us to the Fawn Spring fire. A tourist asks me why ponderosa pine are so special, aren't they famous for something? All I can think to reply is that they are fire resistant—their hardened sap-rich bark shields against excessive heat—and fire dependent—the cones will only release seeds when they reach a certain temperature well above 400 degrees, possible only in a scorching forest fire. I explain the topo map to a visiting friend. "This is Rainbow Plateau. We had a two-acre fire there." "This is the Dragon. It gets hammered by lightning all the time." "See this drainage? It leads to the Kanabownits area, and the Big Springs fire was right on this ridge." "This is called the Elephant Bogs road. It's closed, but we can still hike on it to get to fires."

I have found that wildland firefighting lends a significance to natural details, to Nature, in a way we have forgotten. It is a way I never knew. How to read the weather to predict and plan, to be aware of one season's shortfalls and next season's gains. No spring rain, so fewer mosquitos, but more yellow jackets. Little snowfall last winter, so less wildflowers and more wildfire this summer. There is a way to be more alert, to notice what Nature is telling you. It is a heightened perception, looking for causation and reason behind and within the landscape. Farmers and hunters of my grandfather's generation know what I mean. My parents and brother do not. This intimate sensing of the land is not possible from behind a car window, or even a short hike. It is in the daily, regular interaction with the land. Letting the dusty soil creep beneath your fingernails, the morning dew coat your boots. The sunburn on your face, the smell of cactus flowers in monsoon season. This is the way to read Nature, to understand the stories she has to tell us. Be aware, and make sense of the world around you.

Today, viewing and reviewing the North Rim, scanning and rescanning the eye-level canopy, I think of how differently I relate to other landscapes, distant terrains. I can look at the skies of upstate New York every day and never see the signs of coming storms or of atmospheric disturbance that I see in Arizona. I can hike the Appalachian Trail in Pennsylvania and have no idea how fast or slow the yellow birch and striped maple would burn. I can hear rain on the roof in Atlanta and wonder what shoes I will wear, not how moist the fuels will be at the end of the day. I did not learn those landscapes as a firefighter; I cannot see them as they relate to fire. Our knowledge is so encased in our experience, and access so greatly shapes our experiences. I cannot help but wonder how happenstance it all is. How the tiny turns in our lives can so greatly affect how and what we know. Why we think the way we do, how we relate to a situation. And how the choices that lead us down certain paths can shape us as people.

I know I view the North Rim as it relates to fire. I also know that my actions, my character have been shaped by my firefighting experience. I can make decisions and act on them quickly; I work well under pressure. I can orient myself and survive in almost any situation; I work well on a team. And the land and the fires that I have manipulated and controlled have also molded me physically. Just as I dig line, cutting a swath through the groundcover baring mineral soil, the land has subtly influenced and sculpted me. It is in the calluses on my hands, the blisters on my heels, my hardened biceps. My tanned forearms and blonding hair. Ours is a persuasive, give-and-take relationship. Handing off influence, impressing upon and compelling each other's form.

In reflecting on this, I think how everyone could tell a similar story. How they had a job, or an encounter, that influenced the way they thought about, or acted in, a situation. My story has this element in common with everyone else's. The backbreaking nature of firefighting, the solitude of the desert plateaus, the isolation of the North Rim. It is no coincidence that I crave hard work, being alone, and sparse company. Like this, we have all been shaped by our own experiences; we have all learned to internalize what we are taught. It is within this incorporation of knowledge and incidents that we grow and learn. We must combine new acts with old ones, constantly juggling information and purpose, in order to apply what we learn. And it is this assimilation that teaches us how to look at, and understand, the world. We are what we come from, and where we have been.

My season is coming to a close. I leave in two days, only halfway through the fire season, to return to college, one last year awaiting me. I realize that this summer has been a privilege, a unique chance to see the canyon, the North Rim, and Arizona as a firefighter, looking through a firefinder to explain and understand a remarkable natural wonder. As one of the fire crew, I have enjoyed access to the North Rim as few have. I know this land because I have lived it, I have cared for it, and, like the time I had to nestle beneath the branches of a white fir for warmth, a brief rest from cold nighttime fireline patrol, it cares for me. I have learned to read this landscape, perceiving the canyon and the rims in an intense and intimate way, just as a blind woman runs her fingers over a page, feeling and sensing her way to a better understanding.

As I prepare to leave the tower, I take one last look in every direction. I will not see these views, these vistas, again until next June, when I return to the North Rim. I take one last peek through the firefinder, horsehairs centered over the southeast, where although I cannot see the rim from here, I know the canyon opens wide. Shades of brown in every direction but up, swifts darting beneath and through the late afternoon thermals. Hawks and raven the only contrast to the deepening sky. My day is over, and I must leave the firefinder in the tower, a motionless brass ring, to guide other people's eyes, other people's lives. As the slivered moon rises in the east, I think one last time about the direction my life is taking, and how I will never be able to look at this land, or my life, without seeing them as they relate to fire. My own firefinder now rests beneath my skin, buried in my heart and mind. Content, I make my way down the steps to the truck, to the half-hour drive that will take me home.

First Burn

GRETCHEN DAWN YOST

I T'S SOMETHING THAT I had always known: that I would find myself here, one day, face-to-face with a wildland fire. The shrouds of myths surrounding forest fires—the gap in my own perception—stripped away, exposing the bare, burning ground beneath my feet. We aren't working the underside of a crown fire, nor are we saving Bambi from the ravaging flames. Instead, our "fighting" is more of a communion between the fire, the land, and ourselves.

I live and work in the woods of the Bridger–Teton National Forest in western Wyoming. A humble cabin bordering the forest is where I call home and in the summer season I work as a wilderness ranger in the Wind River Range. The tail end of La Niña whipped the West with a dry winter, spring, and now summer. Our district has been on a "red flag alert" all season, but two days of intense lightning storms that shook my house and sent even the chickadees to cover made a good enough reason to pull all the backcountry rangers and trail crew workers from our regular jobs, assigning us to fire standby. For three days we milled around the Pinedale Ranger District office doing odd jobs while we waited. Waited for smoldering lightning strikes to signal us with their smoke.

My cabin is just outside of Bondurant—one of the notoriously small "blinker" Wyoming towns—and about an hour's drive from Pinedale. So when I got the call that Saturday morning from the fire supervisor: "You don't need to drive to town today; we're coming to you," a rush of excitement and nervousness hit me at once: *my backyard is on fire.*

Fire as Foe, Fire as Friend

The smoke had been spotted a couple of hours earlier that morning, near Monument Ridge. *Monument Ridge?* I think about how I had hiked up there just a few weeks ago, traipsing through the endless fields of mule's ears with their big, green, perfectly shaped leaves and bright yellow sunflowers. I recall how it was a cow moose that sent me off the trail and into the mule's ears as I coaxed and skirted my way around her. And the two deer grazing near the ecotone of open space and stands of aspen, their milk-chocolate coats soaked warm with sunshine. My destination was, ironically enough, an abandoned fire lookout. I saw no other humans that day but only their sign as I approached the lookout: mountain bike tracks, the cattle belonging to local ranchers bellowing in the background, candy wrappers, crushed aluminum cans. The ranger in me usually carries away such items, but I remember leaving one behind that afternoon. It was an old, flattened, rusted-out tin can with a hole in the middle where a wildflower had sprung up. I figured earth and time had already captured that artifact, so I quietly smiled at the subtle reclamation and continued on up the hill.

But today I won't be hiking to Monument Ridge. I am at the bottom, at Hoback Guard Station, waiting—with my hard-hat strapped snug to my chin—for the helicopter to deliver me to the fire. My first helicopter ride and I find myself at an eagle's altitude over Bondurant, over the meandering Hoback River, through the Cliff Creek Canyon, then down south again, paralleling Monument Ridge. From the air I notice something not evident from the ground: the landscape is already getting spots and splatters of the colors of fall: the mule's ears blooms are gone and their leaves are drying yellow, brown, orange, and red. The pilot flies in a circle around the fire so we can size it up; get an idea of what we are dealing with. The fire is small, working its way slowly up a draw wooded with lodgepole pine, Englemann spruce, subalpine and Douglas fir. I am in the air for only a few short minutes before my feet land upon the familiar earth again, about a quarter of a mile from the fire. We strap on our "line gear" and prepare to walk toward the smoke as the "initial attack" crew. All accounted for, we total five. Three of us have never seen a wildfire before.

At the "helispot" I gaze, mouth open and chin dropped, as plumes of smoke silently rise to meet the still air. Excitement and uncertainty battle in my quivering knees as we bushwhack toward the fire, playing follow-the-leader. Our supervisor gives us little instruction except to work slowly; it will be a long day. That said he leaves us under the care of a young man, the only other person who has been on a fire before.

We are to build a sixteen-inch trail—fire line—at the bottom of the fire then follow it along the side flanks. I work hurriedly at first, digging in the green earth, wondering if I am doing things correctly, worried that I will accidentally pull a burning coal to the "green" side of the line, thus starting a new fire. But soon another helicopter load of firefighters arrives and eight smoke jumpers fall from the sky. With the more experienced firefighters there to guide us, I begin to realize that we needn't rush, that we are not "racing" the fire and we certainly won't "beat" it. And for the first time, I stand up, lean on my shovel, and let the fire capture me and enter my being.

I close my eyes and am taken back to the western Oregon of my youth: the pops and crackles of the fire sounding like heavy drops of Pacific Coast rain—gathering on roofs and tree limbs, spattering on car tops and pavement. It's an irregular sound, the mixture of light rain and thick, collected globules. Every few minutes or so, an entire pine goes up in flames—*whoosh*—and even the seasoned firefighters gaze in admiration at the wall of red. Again, I close my eyes. The pines on fire encompass the power, beauty, and force of an ocean wave—and although I stand in an inferno, the sound alone sprays my hot body with a light ocean mist. The fire creeps along the underbrush and downfall, drying out the live trees shortly before the flames engulf a pine, taking the needles first—the smell of burnt hair—and later the branches: waves of flame, sounds of the sea.

Ash floats down onto my arms like fat, feathery snowflakes as we continue to work. The smoky haze paints the sun a brilliant, glowing orange—filtering through the blackened trees onto the burning soil of white ash and coal. My stepdad refers to wildland fire as "beauty and the beast" but at times I wonder: where is the beast I'm fighting? My coworkers talk of the bleakness, of war, of the apocalypse. Maybe it's the airplanes and helicopters buzzing overhead. For me, I'm taken by that blood-red, primeval sun to a place where sandhill cranes become pterodactyls.

My wake-up call is a fixed-winged plane dropping a stream of bright, red "retardant" overhead. Maybe the war analogy isn't forgotten after all. After a moment of delay the retardant falls, giving us a baptism of a kind, spattering our hardhats and nomex uniforms with a brown rain. I turn and ask the man next to me: what *is* fire retardant? He says it is just mud: a combination of water, mud, and fertilizer. "Is it carcinogenic?" "Well, I'd wash your hands before you eat," he answers. I feel like a small critter getting sprayed with human toxins: insignificant and forgotten.

The helicopters scoop buckets of water from a small, nearby lake dumping them on the fire. We run from the cloudbursts of cold water meeting hot ash, like running from aerial bombs. They have names, the choppers, like "Three Hotel Pop" and "Four Six November." They lower to the ground—their movement always reminding me of dragonflies—bringing us water, food, and other supplies. Lifting off the earth again, they leave a whirl of the dried leaves of mule's ears flying gently, as though carried by a swift autumn breeze—this breeze from the blades giving our hot, hungry bodies a cool-down while we squint to keep the ash out of our eyes.

As the day grows older we find ourselves farther and farther up the steep hill. I look in all directions and see familiar faces: Hoback and Ramshorn Peaks to the west, Antionette and Corner Peaks to the east. To the south I see the foothills around Noble Basin where my cabin rests. Also to the east, but much closer, I see the Monument Ridge Lookout. Places I've been, landscapes I know, encounters with moose and other critters etched in my memory like scars on my skin.

At the top of the hill our fire, the Marshall Fire, meets a stand of moist aspens and fizzles out. I begin to wonder if our work made any difference or if we were simply seduced by Flame and Beauty to follow them and learn their rhythm. This day's primal sun starts to sink into a long horizon stretched pink with the mountains of the Wyoming and Hoback ranges. I sit, watching, and as the air cools, the stump that still burns behind me—a mammoth campfire—warms the goose bumps on my sweat-soaked skin.

Soon after the sun disappears and leaves only thin wisps of orange smoke clouds, we hike back down the hill to our helispot, where we will camp. Exhausted, bodies blackened with soot and ash, we scatter our bright yellow sleeping bags in the sagebrush, under the stars. But tonight, the hillside burns brighter than the night sky, with occasional pines torching throughout the night: those twinkling, fiery stars lulling me to sleep with a disoriented sense of up and down.

The next morning we return to a fire that is officially "contained" and no longer red with flame. We work slowly, quietly, poking and prodding at smoke spots in what they call "dry mop." We have no water. Our glory days are over. There is another—bigger—fire closer to structures, people, and civilization. It gets first priority. We have no more helicopters, no more water to fill our "piss pump" backpacks. No more food. The work is hot, dry, and quiet with just the harsh sound of our metal tools—shovels and picks—scraping coal and rock.

Inside the burn, I'm reminded of the geyser basins in Yellowstone: earth barren of vegetation, small hot spots sending smoke and steam a few feet into the air. The only form of life inside the burn is a mean-looking, winged insect about the size of my pinky finger. They are black and orange, striped like a wasp, with long, orange antennas and a robust "stinger" on their rear end. They fly all around the warm, burnt logs then land and inject their ovipositor "stinger" into the log for a minute or so, performing an undulating, love-making dance. I ask one of the seasoned firefighters about these insects: what are they and what are they doing here? "They inject eggs into the burned logs," he tells me. "And if you aren't careful, they'll inject eggs into your arm or leg and it'll get infected." Do you know what they're called? "Stump-fuckers," he says, matter-of-factly.

My interest in these insects, however, only grows. They appear to belong to the Horntail family, but are they fire-dependent? Why is it that I've spent so much time in these mountains but have never seen one until I get on fresh burn, where I see hundreds? Are they a native species? Are they harmful?

For two days we work on mop-up with the sole company of "stump-fuckers" landing on our pant legs. We continue to work putting out "smokes"—a frustrating job. It seems as soon as I put out a smoke and move on to the next, I turn around only to see the spot I had just worked on smoking stronger than ever. Then the fire will burn underground, following tree roots, and more smokes pop up in a previously "cold" area.

By the third day of mop-up, a Steller's jay joins us on the perimeter of the fire, squawking and screaming, imitating a hawk. He keeps us company and feeds us eyecandy with his beautiful blue plumage and deep-blue mohawk. As the ground cools, the stump-fuckers slowly disappear back into the same mystery from which they came and small clouds of gnats move in, hovering over warm spots in the earth. Most of the smokes are out and we now "cold trail" for hot spots, which involves running a bare hand through the soft ash until you feel warm heat or retract your hand away in sudden pain. The gnats are a blessing at this stage—a visual clue to hot spots we otherwise would burn our fingers to find.

The fourth day of mop-up on a fire less than 20 acres and exhaustion gives way to mild insanity. But the beauty of resilient life recapturing a seemingly inhospitable landscape carries me through the days. The mornings are crisp, clear, and free of smoke. I am awakened by the gurgles of sandhill cranes and the smell of sage. This afternoon, clouds are rolling in and I can smell rain. One of my coworkers points out deer tracks in the ash, down the middle of the burn. It is one of those quiet surprises—like the mother red-tailed hawk nesting on a building above Central Park. And I think to myself that eternity lingers brilliantly, here—in the silent tracks of a deer—across fresh, white ash... Beginning to wonder how long it will take for the land to recover after a small burn like this, I imagine the lodgepole pines coming in first and I make plans to come back.

The Shape of Things to Come

KEITH EASTHOUSE

THE DENSE GREEN FOREST that served as a scenic backdrop to Los Alamos is charred and blackened now, the once living trees transmogrified into scorched poles, the tangle of deadwood and brush that made up the cluttered understory reduced to a thick carpet of ash. It's a skeleton forest, a disfigured landscape, a visible manifestation of death looming above the place that gave the world Fat Man and Little Boy. That Los Alamos, of all places, should be hit by a firestorm is just one of a string of ironies generated by the Cerro Grande blaze, which burned 43,000 acres of northern New Mexico's Jemez Mountains in May, forced 20,000 people to evacuate, did $1 billion in damage and took more than four weeks to extinguish.

Consider these twists: A deliberately set fire that if successful would have reduced the fire hazard to Los Alamos led to the destruction of more than 200 residences—and grew into the most destructive blaze in state history. The federal agency, the National Park Service, that had done the most to thin out the dangerously overgrown forest near Los Alamos started the chain of events that led to the disaster. Scientists at Los Alamos National Laboratory, so confident of their ability to control nuclear fire, were forced to flee in panic along with everyone else in the face of something as elemental as a forest fire. Although widely reported as a controlled burn run amok, the actual flames that got out of control in Los Alamos sprang from a risky backfire set by firefighters.

Fire as Foe, Fire as Friend

But perhaps the most profound irony of all, and one with frightening implications for the unnaturally thick forests of the American West, is this: In trying for the past 100 years to remove flames from the landscape through aggressive fire suppression efforts, federal fire managers have created infernos. "We haven't got rid of fire. We've merely changed the way fire interacts with the forest," said James Agee, a fire ecologist with the University of Washington. Added Thomas Swetnam, director of the Laboratory of Tree-Ring Research at the University of Arizona, "There were frequent fires up to 1900 and then no fires for 100 years and now one fire comes through and the forest is toast." Toast is a good word for the seared forest behind Los Alamos. Over an eight-square-mile swath of canyons and ridges, virtually every tree has been killed. It looks like a bomb went off—with the exception that the trees are standing, not flattened. The fire burned so hot that air temperatures are estimated to have reached as high as 2,000 degrees Fahrenheit. In places the soil was vitrified, or turned to glass. When topsoil is cooked to that degree, it is sterilized: all the microorganisms that would normally help a forest recover from a fire have been killed. A forest burned to this extent is especially prone to a phenomenon called sheet erosion, where entire hillsides are washed away by rain. It is widely expected that when New Mexico's annual monsoon season kicks in around the Fourth of July, there will be massive erosion in burned areas—and massive flooding through the numerous fingerlike canyons that cross the town of Los Alamos and the weapons laboratory and feed into the Rio Grande.

There have been numerous media reports about the fact that the lab has used those canyons as dumping grounds for decades—and that significant amounts of radioactive and chemical contaminants will almost certainly be carried this summer into the fabled waterway that is New Mexico's lifeblood and that provides irrigation and drinking water to the bulk of the state's population. Less attention has been paid to what extensive flooding and erosion might do to the burned forest west and north of Los Alamos in the Jemez range.

According to Swetnam, even if large amounts of topsoil are not washed away, it will in all likelihood take 100 to 200 years, and perhaps even longer, for the forest to come back—at least in the 14,500 acres that burned hottest. That's how fragile the ecosystem is in the arid Southwest, where even healthy forest soils are unusually thin, requiring millennia to become established. If soil in the Cerro Grande burn area does wash off massively, "it might take thousands of years for these areas to come back as forest," Swetnam said.

Anyone who finds that hard to believe should visit an almost-16,000-acre area immediately southwest of the laboratory that was burned in 1977. The La Mesa fire, as it was known, was only a third the size of the Cerro Grande blaze, and it did nowhere near the property damage. But like Cerro Grande, it was an out-of-control crown fire and it burned just as hot. The evidence for lasting damage can be seen today in the bleak, sparsely vegetated landscape that has replaced what before the fire was a thick, green forest. In the jargon of fire ecologists, an area that has been robbed of its tree cover is known as a "hole." "There are still giant holes in La Mesa. And there's no sign of anything coming back," Swetnam said.

Reseeding efforts, which are already under way in the Cerro Grande burn area, could make a difference. But the La Mesa burn area was also reseeded—repeatedly—and it produced modest results, at best. Reseeding often doesn't succeed in the Southwest because for the first few years after a blaze, the seeds, like the soil, get carried away by the torrential summer rains that hit the region after the spring fire season.

The implications of fires like La Mesa and Cerro Grande are profound. If a forest doesn't come back after a fire, then it isn't merely the landscape that has been changed, it's the whole web of plant and animal life that took thousands, maybe millions, of years to evolve in that location. "You're talking about converting a forest to a grassland or a shrubland," Swetnam said. "If the kind of fires we're getting today are not historical, if there's no evidence they have occurred in recent centuries or millennia, then you're changing ecosystems. That's what's beginning to happen out there."

It's because of the unnatural intensity of the Cerro Grande fire that one can make what would otherwise seem an absurd assertion: The blaze did more damage than the series of fires that scorched about 750,000 acres of Yellowstone National Park in the long, hot summer of 1988. More lasting damage, that is. Although significant portions of the acreage burned by Cerro Grande are not likely to recover quickly—and perhaps not at all—the land burned at Yellowstone twelve years ago has for the most part bounced back.

Fire as Foe, Fire as Friend

The forests torched by the Yellowstone fires were primarily made up of dense, almost impenetrable stands of lodgepole pine—and in lodgepole pine forests, crown fires are a normal part of the ecosystem. A sign that lodgepole evolved with crown fires is that the trees don't drop many of their cones to the ground. Instead, the cones remain in the canopy—for decades in some cases—waiting for a crown fire to come along. When one does, the cones open up in response to the heat and, within days, seeds start to fall out. After a crown fire strikes lodgepole, the burned forest floor is carpeted with the seeds, and before long, lodgepole saplings have taken root.

A ponderosa pine forest is completely different. There, cones typically release their seeds upon reaching maturity. That strategy works well when the only fires that burned through were low-intensity ground fires. While those fires did to some extent destroy the seeds that were scattered on the ground, they didn't destroy the source of the seeds—the trees themselves. But when a crown fire roars through a ponderosa forest—as happened in the Cerro Grande blaze—the seeds and the trees are killed, leaving no way for a new generation to establish itself. The forest is erased.

Though fire suppression—the legacy of Smokey Bear—is rightly blamed for the overstocked forests of the West, there is another, often overlooked factor that has also knocked nature out of balance: livestock grazing. In northern New Mexico, as in many other western areas 100 to 120 years ago, hordes of cattle and sheep brought by the railroads fanned out over the landscape. From roughly 1880 to 1920, wholly unregulated grazing by livestock denuded large areas. In places like eastern Oregon and Nevada, lush grasslands were replaced by sagebrush and fire-tolerant species such as cheatgrass. In northern New Mexico, the disappearance of grass meant that there was no way for ground fires to travel into ponderosa forests. Without fire to clear out the understory, virtually every ponderosa sapling that got established grew into a tree. As the twentieth century progressed, and as fire managers with agencies like the park service and the Forest Service stamped out every fire that popped up, these forests grew thicker and thicker. The densest stands, the ones packed with small, stunted, nutrient-starved trees, came to be called doghair thickets. In some areas of the Jemez Mountains, there are as many as 2,000 ponderosa pines per acre, compared to 25 to 80 trees per acre when fire was a frequent visitor to the landscape. "The basic story is that everything has gotten woodier," said Craig Allen, a fire ecologist with the U.S. Geological Survey and a leading Southwest fire expert. "Meadows are filling in with trees, and forests that were once more open have become thicker and denser."

While the timber industry often makes the claim that logging reduces the fire hazard, others say logging has exacerbated the situation by leaving behind flammable slash piles and by removing the biggest trees. Such trees have the greatest commercial value, but they are also the most resistant to fire. Logging aside, no one disputes this: The forests of the West, particularly the ponderosa forests, which pose the greatest wildfire threat because of their inherent dryness, have lost their natural fireproofing. They have become explosive on a scale no one has seen before. "There's a potential for 100,000-acre crown fires," Allen said.

What's to be done? That question has taken on added urgency in the wake of the Cerro Grande fire—particularly for western communities that are just as much at risk from a forest fire as Los Alamos was. Santa Fe, forty miles southeast of Los Alamos, is one such place, as is Flagstaff, Arizona, located amid the largest ponderosa forest on the planet. Other towns that are standing directly in harm's way include Missoula, Montana, which has seen its population swell with former city dwellers in recent years, and two Oregon communities, Bend, which has built into the extensive ponderosa forests on the east side of the Cascade Range, and Ashland, which like Santa Fe draws its drinking water from a municipally protected watershed that has become overgrown with trees.

To reduce the danger, the Forest Service—acting at the height of the ferocious 2000 fire season—proposed a $12 billion, 15-year project aimed at thinning the 40 million acres in the West deemed most at risk from catastrophic fire. As for prescribed burning, a moratorium on the practice imposed by Interior Secretary Bruce Babbitt immediately after the Cerro Grande blaze got out of control had been partially lifted by early summer. Although the park service, which ignited the prescribed burn at Bandelier National Monument that eventually blew into Los Alamos, remained under the ban, all other federal agencies were allowed to resume prescribed burns.

The fact remains, however, that the Cerro Grande fire has given prescribed burning a bad name—and has all but guaranteed that rural area

Fire as Foe, Fire as Friend

residents will be more prone to protest whenever a prescribed burn is planned near their communities. Conservative western senators such as Idaho's Larry Craig and New Mexico's Pete Domenici have added fuel to the fire, so to speak, by questioning whether prescribed burning should continue at all in the wake of the Cerro Grande fire. Timber industry representatives, sensing an opportunity, have claimed that the fire is proof that burning is too risky and that increased logging is the best way to reduce the fire hazard.

Largely lost in the media frenzy over the Los Alamos disaster is the fact that prescribed burning has been carried out with remarkably few accidents. Since it began setting prescribed burns in the late 1960s, the National Park Service, for example, has set 3,746 burns covering almost 900,000 acres. The agency lost control of only 38—just 1 percent—of those burns. And only one other prescribed burn besides Cerro Grande has wreaked substantial property damage in recent years, a 1999 fire that burned twenty-three homes in a remote part of Northern California.

Still, anytime a fire is ignited, it is by definition a risky situation—a 16,000-acre prescribed burn conducted by the Santa Fe National Forest in 1993, for example, blew up unexpectedly one day and killed a fire-fighter. Such tragedies are likely to happen again. It is, of course, also possible that another Los Alamos could happen in the future. To what extent will people be willing to accept such mishaps?

Only time will tell. But the virtually unanimous consensus of fire scientists is that prescribed burning must not be abandoned. "Particularly with the drier forests of the West, fire is just too important," said Agee of the University of Washington. "It's essential to nutrient cycling, to creating good wildlife habitat, to maintaining the stability of the whole system."

"The worst thing to do would be to stop burning altogether," he continued. "Somehow, we have to increase the scale [of burning] and at the same time be more precise and cautious in its application." Even Wallace Covington, director of the Ecological Restoration Institute at Northern Arizona University in Flagstaff and a strong advocate of thinning, has said that the forests must also be burned—provided the burning follows extensive thinning to reduce the chances of a crown fire. "You need both [thinning and burning]," Covington said.

Agee said one possible approach would be to thin in areas that are close to towns and cities and to burn in areas that are more remote. And it is important, Agee said, to tailor a treatment to the needs of each site. "What you basically want to do with thinning and burning is mimic natural processes," and those processes can vary even within a single mountain range, he said. Swetnam from the University of Arizona said the Jemez Mountains, where the Cerro Grande fire burned, provides an example of such variation. While the midelevation ponderosa forests in the range did not evolve with crown fires, forests higher up in those mountains did. No one is suggesting, however, that fire managers should start setting crown fires. The truth of the matter—however humbling it might be to accept—is that crown fires are impossible to control. What experts like Swetnam and Agee are saying, though, is that the federal fire managers directing burning and thinning efforts need to know their region in detail—or else they might have another Los Alamos on their hands. In Swetnam's mind, a lack of such knowledge was at the root of the Cerro Grande disaster.

It is not widely known—primarily because the media largely missed the story—that it was a backfire set by firefighters, not a prescribed burn, that swept into Los Alamos. Three of the investigators who took part in the government investigation of the blaze told the media in late May that the prescribed fire that the park service set in a relatively high-elevation, moist area would have died out on its own had it been left to burn. They said the decision to treat the fire as a wildfire that needed to be extinguished—rather than merely a prescribed burn in need of guidance and monitoring—was a key error. That decision led fire managers in the field to undertake a risky maneuver, the ignition of a backfire in a much drier, lower-elevation area. The intent was to tie together two fire lines. But the result was that fire, carried by high winds, escaped into a nearby, thickly forested canyon. The rest is history.

"Once the prescribed fire was declared a wildfire, additional fire [was] introduced that ultimately produced the source of spotting and escape when high winds developed," the investigators wrote in the report. That a backfire was the immediate cause of the blaze led some observers to attack the basic conclusion of the government's investigation that the Cerro Grande blaze was essentially a prescribed fire run amok. "It wasn't the planned prescribed fire, but the unplanned, reactive emergency fire-suppression backfire that blew out of the project area," said Tim Ingalsbee of the Western Fire Ecology Center in Eugene, Oregon.

To Swetnam, however, the critical error lay not in how the prescribed fire and the subsequent firefighting efforts were conducted, but in the decision to ignite the prescribed fire in the first place. The prescribed burn may very well have burned itself out if left alone, but that doesn't change the fact that it took place in a very small, relatively moist area surrounded by a sea of tinder-dry, overstocked forest, Swetnam said. Neither does it change the fact that the burn was conducted following an abnormally dry winter and in the midst of a Southwest-wide drought that began in 1996.

"What was lacking was a recognition of what was going on in terms of larger time scales and larger landscape scales," Swetnam said. "The fact of the matter is that there was a very high hazard for a bad fire year this year, and that understanding just didn't filter down to the managers of a small national monument who were planning a burn." That message might have gotten through had anyone from the monument attended a conference for fire officials that was held in Tucson in February. The main topic of the meeting was the unusual fire hazard facing the Southwest in 2000. Swetnam said that although regional park service officials were there, no one from Bandelier who was involved in the Cerro Grande burn was present.

Swetnam mentioned something else that places the blame even more squarely on the shoulders of Bandelier fire officials. The Santa Fe National Forest, which borders Bandelier on three sides, issued a ban on prescribed burning roughly a week before the Cerro Grande burn was ignited. "They did the right thing," Swetnam said. In a larger sense, though, Bandelier officials aren't really to blame. They were, after all, trying to deal with a mess that had been a long time in the making. "Mistakes weren't just made on May 4 [the day the prescribed burn was ignited]," Swetnam said. "They began a century ago. And they extend all the way up to the people in Los Alamos who built their houses up against that forest."

Sources

The text selections in this book were drawn from the following sources. I am grateful to the publishers and authors indicated for permission to reprint copyrighted material.

Part I: Big Country, Big Fires

Mooney, James. The First Fire. From *Myths of the Cherokee*. Copyright © 1900. Reprinted in 1995. New York: Dover Publications.

Merriam, C. Hart. How Tol'-le-loo Got the Fire for the Mountain People. From *The Dawn of the World: Myths and Tales of the Miwok Indians of California*. Copyright © 1910. Reprinted in 1993. Lincoln, Nebraska: University of Nebraska Press.

Lewis, Meriwether. From *The Journals of the Expedition under the Command of Captains Lewis and Clark*. Edited by Nicholas Biddle. First printed in 1814 by Heritage Press, New York.

Irving, Washington. The Alarm Camp. From *A Tour on the Prairies*. Copyright © 1835. London: John Murray.

Thoreau, Henry David. The Allegash and East Branch. From *The Maine Woods*. Edited by Ellery Channing. Copyright © 1864. Reprinted in 1906 by Houghton Mifflin, New York.

Muir, John. From *John of the Mountains* by Linnie Marsh Wolfe. Copyright © 1938 by Wanda Muir Hanna. Published in 1938 by Houghton Mifflin, New York. Copyright © renewed in 1966 by John Muir Hanna and Ralph Eugene Wolfe.

Muir, John. From *My First Summer in the Sierra*. Copyright © 1911 by John Muir. Reprinted in 1972. Dunwoody, Georgia: Norman S. Berg.

Twain, Mark. From *Roughing It*. Copyright © 1872. American Publishing Company, Hartford.

Pyne, Stephen J. *The Big Blowup*. Copyright © 2000 by Stephen J. Pyne. Reprinted with permission of the author.

Part II: Of Fire and the Landscape

Leopold, Aldo. Grass, Brush, Timber and Fire in Southeast Arizona. From *The Journal of Forestry*, October 1924.

Sources

Maclean, Norman. From *Young Men and Fire.* Copyright © 1992. Reprinted by permission of the University of Chicago Press.

Millar, Margaret. After the Fire. From *The Birds and the Beasts Were There.* Copyright © 1967 by Margaret Millar, renewed 1995 by The Margaret Millar Charitable Remainder Unitrust u/a I/12/82. Reprinted by permission of Harold Ober Associates Incorporated.

Caras, Roger. Reprinted from *Panther!* by Roger A. Caras by permission of the University of Nebraska Press. Copyright © 1969 by Roger A. Caras.

Abbey, Edward. Fire Lookout: Numa Ridge. From *The Journey Home.* Copyright © 1977 by Edward Abbey. New York: E.P. Dutton. Reprinted by permission of Clarke Abbey.

Engle, Ed. Fire. From *Seasonal.* Copyright © 1981 by Ed Engle. Reprinted by permission of the author.

Part III: Fire as Foe, Fire as Friend

Williams, Ted. Incineration of Yellowstone. From *Audubon,* volume 91, number 1 (1989). Reprinted by permission of the author.

Thoele, Michael. From *Fireline: Summer Battles of the West.* Copyright © 1995. Reprinted by permission of Fulcrom Publishing, Inc., Golden, Colorado, USA. All rights reserved.

McPhee, John. From *The Control of Nature.* Copyright © 1989 by John McPhee. Reprinted by permission of Farrar, Strauss, and Giroux, New York. Canadian permission granted by MacFarlane, Walter and Ross, Toronto.

Maclean, John. From *Fire on the Mountain.* Copyright © 1999. Reprinted by permission of Harper Collins Publishers, New York. United Kingdom permission granted by Writer's House, Inc., New York.

Bass, Rick. The Fires Next Time. From *Audubon,* volume 7, number 5 (1995). Reprinted by permission of the author.

Wagenknecht, Louise. Pride and Glory of Firefighting Is Hard to Resist. From *American Nature Writing: 1996.* Copyright © 1995 by Louise Wagenknecht. Reprinted by permission of the author.

True, Alianor. Firefinder. From *American Nature Writing: 1998.* Copyright © 1997 by Alianor True. Reprinted by permission of the author.

Yost, Gretchen Dawn. First Burn. From *American Nature Writing: 2001.* Copyright © 2001 by Gretchen Dawn Yost. Reprinted by permission of the author.

Easthouse, Keith. The Shape of Things to Come. From *Forest Magazine,* volume 2, issue 4 (2000). Reprinted by permission of the author.

Contributors

Cherokee territory once stretched across the southeast United States, from Kentucky, Tennessee, western North Carolina, northern Alabama, and into Georgia and western South Carolina. In the 1830s, the U.S. Government removed a majority of the tribe and relocated them to Oklahoma, where a large portion of the tribe remains today. The included myth was collected in the early twentieth century.

Miwok tribes were actually composed of three distinct groups in central California. The Coast Miwok inhabited the San Francisco Bay Area and north, stretching into modern-day Marin County. The foothills and mountains of the Northern Sierra were the territory of the Interior Miwok, and the southern Sierra range, including Yosemite, was the homeland of the Southern Sierra Miwok tribe.

Edward Abbey, author of many works including *Desert Solitaire* and *The Monkey Wrench Gang,* brought his tales of adventure and environmentalism in the American Southwest to life with his unique and pointed writing. Much of his work is based on his experience working for the U.S. National Park Service in Utah, Arizona, and Montana.

Roger Caras served as the eighteenth president of the American Society for the Prevention of Cruelty to Animals from 1992 to 1999. He has also served as ABC's special correspondent for animals and the environment for seventeen years. He has authored over sixty books on pets and wildlife, and thousands of articles for a wide range of popular publications. He lives on a farm in Maryland.

Keith Easthouse was the environmental and science reporter for the *Santa Fe New Mexican* from 1991 to 1998. Before that, he was a staff writer for a weekly newspaper, the *Santa Fe Reporter,* from 1987 to 1990.

Contributors

Currently, he is associate editor of *Forest Magazine*, an environmental issues publication based in Eugene, Oregon. His writing has appeared in publications such as *Outside Magazine, High Country News, Wild Bird,* and the *Bulletin of Atomic Scientists.*

Ed Engle was a seasonal employee in the U.S. Forest Service for 13 years. He served on a number of fire crews during that time, and fought fire in Colorado, California, Oregon, and Idaho. His favorite "time on the line" was chasing down lightning strike smokes with a couple of other firefighters. Engle is currently a full-time flyfishing writer, guide, and instructor. He lives in Colorado.

Thomas Evans has worked in wildland fire for 23 years in the eastern Sierra Nevada of California and throughout Alaska. He has worked on fire assignments as a firefighter and dispatcher in Idaho, Utah, Colorado, New Mexico, California, Montana, Georgia, and Nevada. In 1998, Evans began his current job as a logistics coordinator at the Northwest Coordination Center in Portland, Oregon. The cover photograph was taken on the Dune Lakes Fire, southwest of Nenanna, Alaska, on May 26, 1981, as the fire flared up on the right flank. This 235,000-acre fire was eventually controlled, but only after building 12 miles of line in front of the fire, and then lighting an 11,000-acre backfire.

Washington Irving, born in New York City in 1783, was a considerable contributor to early American literature. His most well known works were *The Legend of Sleepy Hollow* and *Rip Van Winkle,* but he was a prolific writer of many other books and stories. Irving's actual tour of the prairies took place in the early 1830s when he was the secretary of the commission to determine the new location of the Cherokee tribes.

Aldo Leopold was born in Iowa in 1887. After graduating from the Yale School of Forestry, he went on to a career with the U.S. Forest Service, and continued with academic research and teaching at the University of Wisconsin. Leopold is widely acknowledged as a father of the modern conservation movement and was respected internationally for his work as a forester and a scientist.

Contributors

Meriwether Lewis, secretary to President Jefferson and a captain in his army, kept meticulous notes and journals of the famed Lewis and Clark expedition of 1804–1805. The western journey crossed the continent from Mississippi to the Oregon–Washington coast, exploring, mapping, collecting, and recording everything from botanical and zoological information, to geographical and cultural features. Following the expedition, a young magazine editor assisted in editing the journals and publishing them in their present form.

John N. Maclean, author and journalist, was for 30 years a reporter, writer, and editor for the *Chicago Tribune,* most of that time as a Washington correspondent. He resigned from the *Tribune* to write *Fire on the Mountain,* a book about the fire on Storm King Mountain in Colorado in 1994 that killed fourteen firefighters. It became a national best seller and won the Mountains and Plains Booksellers Award for best nonfiction of 1999. Maclean, who divides his time between Montana and Washington, D.C., is at work on other writing projects.

Norman F. Maclean is best known as the author of *A River Runs Through It,* an autobiographical tale of family tragedy that has captured the affections of generations of readers. His second book, *Young Men and Fire,* describes the early days of the now famous smokejumpers and a fatal forest fire in which they were involved in Montana, Maclean's boyhood home. Maclean taught English at the University of Chicago for more than 40 years before he retired and penned his books. He died in 1990 at the age of 87.

John McPhee, author of over twenty books, won the Pulitzer Prize for *Annals of the Former World* in 1999. He was born in Princeton, New Jersey, and educated at Princeton University and Cambridge University. His works include *Encounters with the Archdruid* and *The Curve of Binding Energy,* which were both nominated for National Book Awards in the category of science.

Margaret Millar was most well known in her day as a suspense writer. She was born in Ontario, Canada, but made her home for many years in

Contributors

California. She was also an avid environmentalist and penned the non-fiction work, *The Birds and the Beasts Were There,* in 1967, which included her observations of a local wildfire near her home in Santa Barbara, California.

John Muir, whose family emigrated from Scotland in 1849, traveled to California less than 20 years later at the age of 30. Muir's field journals captured detailed descriptions of the wild California of the late nineteenth century, and were often the basis for his published work. In 1889, he began conservation efforts to preserve the grand peaks and forests of the Sierra Nevada. His efforts led to the establishment of Yosemite, Sequoia, and General Grant National Parks, and led to the creation of the Sierra Club, one of America's oldest environmental organizations.

Stephen Pyne began his career as a pyromantic with fifteen seasons on the fire crew at the North Rim of the Grand Canyon, then segued into the scholarly study of fire, which he has extended through ten books, including the globe-spanning suite, Cycle of Fire. An internationally respected fire historian, he is currently a professor at Arizona State University. He confesses to having started and stopped a fire on every continent.

Michael Thoele, a writer and adjunct faculty member of the University of Oregon's School of Journalism, traveled more than 35,000 miles throughout the West to research his account of modern wildland firefighting, *Fireline: Summer Battles of the West.* Thoele lives in the Coast Range Mountains in Oregon.

Henry David Thoreau, one of the great poet-naturalists to emerge from Concord, Massachusetts, was born in 1817. Allegash and East Branch was the last of the three essays that composed *The Maine Woods,* which was edited and published after Thoreau's death from tuberculosis in 1862. The journey he wrote about was made in 1857 with his friend Edward Hoar, and an Indian guide, Joe Polis.

Mark Twain was still known as Samuel Clemens when he traveled west in 1861. *Roughing It,* written as a series of sketches, recalls his experiences in Nevada and California. It was published upon his return to New York in 1872, and was written only after he had renounced a career as a newspaperman.

Contributors

Louise Wagenknecht was born and raised in Idaho, where she has worked as a seasonal firefighter for the Forest Service and Bureau of Land Management for 20 years. She and her husband maintain a small sheep ranch in Idaho. She has a bachelor's degree in English literature and writes periodically on topics of interest—such as firefighting and logging—for *High Country News*. She is working on a book about the environmental and economic upheavals that have transformed the Pacific Northwest in her lifetime.

Ted Williams was presented with the Conservation Achievement Award by the National Wildlife Federation in April 1997 at its annual convention in Tucson. In March 1999 he received the Federal Wildlife Officers Association Award for his conservation writing. In addition to freelancing for national magazines, he contributes regular feature-length conservation columns to *Audubon* and *Fly Rod & Reel* where he serves as editor-at-large and conservation editor, respectively. For his reporting on the Yellowstone fires, the American Society of Magazine Editors voted *Audubon* one of five finalists in the National Magazine Awards. Williams lives in Grafton, Massachusetts.

Gretchen Dawn Yost is a wilderness ranger in the Wind River Range of the Bridger–Teton National Forest. She is a 1998 graduate of the University of Oregon and has since been living in a cabin outside of Bondurant, Wyoming.

Acknowledgments

I am thankful to all the people who have contributed to the production of this book. I would like to thank my editors at Island Press, Barbara Dean and Barbara Youngblood, for their adept and skillful guidance. My utmost gratitude to John Murray for his encouragement and advice, and to Rick Laven for his thorough review of the fire ecology information. For assistance finding Native American writing, I would like to thank Winona LaDuke, Lyle Carlisle, Bill Downs, Joann Reynolds, and Professor Kenneth Lincoln of UCLA. I am grateful to Dave Aftandilian for his help in providing sources for the Native American myths. Thanks go to Rachel Ray for typing the manuscript, and to Tom Evans, who furnished the striking cover photograph. Thanks also to Kevin MacLean for his personal and practical support throughout the process.

Index

Index

Index

Index

Index

Index

Index

Index

Index

Index

Index

Index

Index

Index

Index

About the Editor

Alianor True holds an undergraduate degree in science and technology studies from Cornell University in Ithaca, New York, and a graduate degree in science education from the University of Michigan, Ann Arbor. In recent years she has worked as a professional wildland firefighter for Grand Canyon National Park, Big Cypress National Preserve in South Florida, Sequoia National Park, and the Bureau of Land Management in Nevada. Her essay, Firefinder, which relates her experiences as a firefighter on the North Rim of the Grand Canyon, was featured as the lead selection in *American Nature Writing: 1998* (Sierra Club Books), and her essay *Chorus* appears in *American Nature Writing: 2000* (Oregon State University Press), in a special edition celebrating the essays of women environmental writers. She is originally from Douglasville, Georgia.